Magnet Theatre

Magnet Theatre
Three Decades of Making Space

Edited by Megan Lewis and Anton Krueger

intellect Bristol, UK / Chicago, USA

UNISA university of south africa PRESS
University of South Africa Press Pretoria

First published in the UK in 2016 by
Intellect, The Mill, Parnall Road, Fishponds, Bristol, BS16 3JG, UK

First published in the USA in 2016 by
Intellect, The University of Chicago Press, 1427 E. 60th Street,
Chicago, IL 60637, USA

First published in South Africa in 2016 by
the University of South Africa Press, PO Box 392, Unisa,
Muckleneuk, Pretoria, 0003, South Africa

A catalogue record for this book is available from the British Library.

Copy-editor: Michael Eckhardt
Cover designer: Stephanie Sarlos
Cover image: Garth Stead
Production Manager: Tim Mitchell
Typesetting: John Teehan

Intellect:
Print ISBN: 978-1-78320-537-0
ePUB ISBN: 978-1-78320-539-4
ePDF ISBN: 978-1-78320-538-7

Unisa Press:
Print ISBN: 978-1-86888-835-1

Prior to acceptance of this publication by Unisa Press, this work was subjected to a double-blind peer review process mediated through the copublishers.

With the support of the National Lottery Distribution Trust Fund

NATIONAL LOTTERIES COMMISSION
a member of the dti group

Contents

PART TWO – Collaboration: Making Space for Empbodied Practice

PART THREE – Community: Making Space for Cultural Interventions

Chapter 1

Plotting the Magnetic Field: Origins and Trajectories

Megan Lewis and Anton Krueger

Cape Town-based Magnet Theatre functions as a nationally recognized theatre institution; not only in terms of its aesthetic originality and excellence, but also because of the company's investments into cultural development and training. Over the course of almost three decades, the company has been 'making space' in South Africa: for creativity, innovation and embodied work, as well as for collaboration, community and cultural dialogue. Since Magnet Theatre's first productions – *Cheap Flights* (1987) and *The Show's Not Over 'Til the Fat Lady Sings* (1991–93) – the company has gained an international reputation for its original repertoire of performance events that emphasize the primacy of the human body. From its inception in Johannesburg in 1987 to the establishment of its own theatre space in Cape Town in 2011, Magnet Theatre has been dedicated to what it sees as its role of exploring sociopolitical issues through personal, unconventional and highly physical theatrical expressions that energize audiences by shifting bodies, feelings and ideas (magnettheatre.co.za). Furthermore, the company is committed to training young artists, and to cultivating theatre in under-represented communities. To this end, Magnet has also played a vital role in cultural interventions within the broader South African community; guided by a spirit of theatrical research, artists who have worked with Magnet have remained deeply committed to social development. Their interventions into multiple communities have reached tens of thousands of people.

To understand the impact and particularity of Magnet's work, we'd like to plot the magnetic field – the trajectories of their influence and influences – by framing the sociopolitical and historical context within which Magnet has functioned over the past three decades. Next, we briefly summarize the various sections and chapters of this book. We then trace the company's origins in terms of co-artistic directors Mark Fleishman and Jennie Reznek's personal and professional journey since their meeting in 1987, situating Magnet within the broader South African theatrical landscape before mapping how this unique and innovative company resonates within discourses and practices of physical theatre, devised work, workshop theatre and performance as research (PaR).

Our primary resources for the explorations of the company have been personal interviews with Magnet members and key collaborators.[1] Extracts from these conversations are woven between more analytical, academic analyses of Magnet's work to form the multi-voiced substance of this project. As editors, we have curated many different voices in this collection to tell Magnet's story, engaging in a dialogue with internal and external perspectives: between reflections by performers and artists involved with Magnet, and scholarly articles responding to Magnet's many productions since 1987. In the spirit of Magnet's 'acts of storying, sounding, moving, feeling and relating' (Fleishman 2009: 126), we have curated a variety of voices so that Magnet's multi-textured nature is represented, pairing established scholars alongside more junior ones, and professional academics alongside fieldworkers and facilitators. We have deliberately ended this collection with the voices of two of Magnet's young graduates, giving the voice of the next generation of South African theatre-makers the proverbial last word.

Historical Context

Over the span of Magnet's existence as a company, South Africa has undergone an historic transition. In 2014, South Africa celebrated its 20th year as a democracy, having made the momentous political transition from the racially segregated apartheid regime in 1994. Since Nelson Mandela's election as the country's first black president, the young democracy has wrestled with what it means to be a truly multicultural society. Theatre artists have been at the forefront of this cultural transition, offering creative interventions that probe, question and (re-)imagine cultural identities as they tackle the viscous endeavours of memory and history in the postcolony (Mbembe 2011).

Apartheid came into being with the National Party's election to power in 1949, which solidified Afrikaner hegemony. Afrikaners (settlers of predominantly Dutch and French Huguenot descent) and Anglo-South Africans (settlers of predominantly British ancestry) had been battling for control of South Africa since the colonial era. South Africa's diverse indigenous populations had themselves been disputing control of contested territories, and, upon the arrival of the Europeans, they were relegated to second-class status. Imagined within the racial hierarchies of the state as a totalized mass, black and brown indigenous peoples were afforded few, if any, rights under apartheid law, while white citizens reaped the benefits of the country's imbalanced system of privilege. Apartheid hierarchized individuals along racial lines while its laws regulated bodies and behaviour: segregating public spaces, schools and workplaces; instituting a system of regulations that determined where an individual was permitted to live, work or travel based on their racial classification; and forbidding cross-racial contact from the boardroom to the bedroom.

When Magnet was formed in 1987, the country was at the height of an extended state of emergency. The African National Congress (ANC) was a banned organization whose aim had been declared as wanting 'to make the townships within South Africa ungovernable.' The state responded with an increasingly militarized clamp down. In 1990, Prime Minister P. W. Botha's successor, F. W. de Klerk, lifted the state of emergency, unbanning the ANC and other organizations. He released Nelson Mandela from his life sentence in prison and began the process of a negotiated transfer of power. Between 1990 and 1994, the legal apparatus of apartheid was gradually abolished, and with Mandela's election to the presidency, South Africa emerged into democracy.

The Aims and Structure of this Collection

This collection documents Magnet Theatre's work and ethos through a thick curation of scholarly investigation, first-hand interviews and visual material. Providing a deep analysis by means of a visual and verbal archive of past productions, the essays and interviews collected here reflect on the impact of almost 30 years of creative and cultural labours by a unique theatre company during a shifting and contested time in South African history. Our goal has been to provide an archive of performance practices easily accessible to the lay reader, as well as critical theory that would be of interest to theatre scholars. Furthermore, in using Magnet as an example, the book hopes to address questions of how theatre can serve as a vital site of cultural production, reflection and practice. While all of Magnet's works are listed in the 'Production History' section, not all of them are analysed in the same detail. Rather, seminal productions such as *Medea* (1994–96), *Cargo* (2007), *Inxeba Lomphilisi – The Wound of a Healer* (2010–14), *Die Vreemdeling* [The Stranger] (2010) and *Every Year, Every Day, I Am Walking* (2006–present) have been selected as the focus of the essays in this collection, since these works represent decisive turning points in Magnet's trajectory, and serve as prime examples of the integration of praxis and theory, which is at the heart of the company's methodology.

Interwoven between the scholarly chapters are the voices of Magnet 'insiders:' performer Faniswa Yisa; director Mandla Mbothwe; former Jazzart collaborator Jay Pather; fieldworker Zwelakhe Khuse; writer Frances Marek; administrator Margie Pankhurst; designers Craig Leo and Illka Louw; musician Neo Muyanga; and former students – Magnet's next generation of theatre-makers and artists – including Nolovuyo Sam and Thando Doni. These reflections collectively paint a portrait of Magnet's style, approach, ethos and larger impact on South African culture through each interviewee's personal perceptions. Individually, they narrate the multiple stories of Magnet's many collaborators.

The critical sections of the collection have been organized into three scholarly rubrics: 'Concepts: Making Space for Ideas;' 'Collaboration: Making Space for Embodied Practice;' and 'Community: Making Space for Cultural Interventions.'

In Part One – 'Concepts: Making Space for Ideas' – Mark Fleishman, Miki Flockemann and Anton Krueger investigate how a profound complexity of thought – exercised intellectually as well as physically – permeates all of Magnet's work. Beyond Magnet's primary objective of creating a repertoire of original African productions lies a less obvious objective: to engage with a spirit of theatrical research.

In 'Making Space for Ideas: The Knowledge Work of Magnet Theatre,' Magnet's co-artistic director Mark Fleishman chronicles and elucidates how the work of Magnet Theatre links practice with the production of knowledge, both with respect to the *content* of individual productions and projects, as well as the *methodologies and processes* developed through its theatrical work. Fleishman reflects on two research foci around which productions and projects have been created and pursued over Magnet's history: remembering in the postcolony and migration.

Since 2001, Magnet artists have explored the possibility that particular practices of dramaturgy and performance might be one way of intervening in the problematic process of remembering in South Africa. Over a period of eight years, Magnet created a series of performance projects that engaged with key 'sites of memory' (Fleishman 2013) in and around the city of Cape Town in attempts to put back together (to 're-member') the fractured social body: Robben Island (a place of banishment and incarceration); District Six (an evacuated apartheid-era working-class city district); The Bleek and Lloyd collection of /Xam records (an ethnographic archive at the University of Cape Town); and the archive of slavery at the Cape (a dispersed collection of trial records, household inventories, legal and bureaucratic documents and physical sites). The productions created from these 'sensitive sites' (Roth & Salas 2001: 3) include: *53 Degrees* (2002–03); *Onnest'bo* (2002–06); *Rain in a Dead Man's Footprints* (2004–05); and *Cargo* (Fleishman 2013). In making each of these works, Magnet faced two fundamental and interconnected problems related to the themes of time and silence: how to 'find an appropriate image in the present for something that has past' and how to make the archive 'speak in unspeakable ways' (Fleishman 2011: 12).

Since 2006, the company's second focus – migration – has yielded four separate performance interventions, framed around three simultaneously conceptual and actual routes (Cape to Cairo, the N2 and the N7): *Every Year, Every Day, I Am Walking*; *ingcwaba lendoda lise cankwe ndlela* [the grave of the man lies next to the road] (2009); *Inxeba Lomphilisi – The Wound of a Healer*; and *Die Vreemdeling*. These works were simultaneously theatrical and pedagogical, involving public performances as well as cultural interventions as part of outreach programmes, including educational workshops around the pressing issues of xenophobia and migration. Fleishman discusses his particular performance-led dramaturgy and also explores how making theatre can become a means of scholarly enquiry.

In her chapter, '"Being There": The Evolution of Performance Aesthetics from *Medea* (1994–96) to *The Magnet Theatre "Migration" Plays* (2012),' Miki Flockemann, drawing on Geertz's notion of the practice of 'thick description' to read cultural events, examines Magnet's performance aesthetic that encourages spectators to get close to a sense of 'being there.' Flockemann explores the evolution of Magnet's performance modality in relation to the landmark production of *Medea*, which coincided with the first democratic election in 1994. This collaborative production with Jazzart Dance Theatre is read in relation to in-house productions of the 'migration' plays: *Every Year, Every Day, I Am Walking* and *Inxeba Lomphilisi – The Wound of a Healer*. *Every Year, Every Day, I Am Walking* indirectly anticipated the xenophobic eruptions of 2008, and subsequent productions have continued to generate fresh unsettlements of recognition and 'being there.' As a companion piece, *Inxeba Lomphilisi* offered an insider perspective on the legacies of internal migration, and has taken the evolution of thick theatre aesthetics to another level as Flockemann examines how these innovative performance modalities unlock audience responses at the moment of performance. In this way, Magnet makes space for spectators to feel they can almost grasp the inscrutable otherness of the experience being performed.

In his chapter, 'The Implacable Grandeur of the Stranger: Ruminations on Fear and Familiarity in Magnet Theatre's *Die Vreemdeling*,' Anton Krueger considers ways in which South Africa could be described as a nation of strangers, marginalized minorities awkwardly pasted together. Krueger explores how Magnet Theatre's approach to intercultural work sidesteps the potential bigotry of ethnicism, as well as the compromise of homogeneity. Following Fleishman's goal of 'reassembling the social' (Latour 2005) and expanding what is considered as the collective, Krueger argues that Magnet's 'creative explorations have inculcated a growing awareness of cultural inclusivity while avoiding demands for conformity' (p. 130). Drawing on works by Zygmunt Bauman, Georg Simmel and Julia Kristeva, Krueger considers seemingly paradoxical notions of inclusivity and unfamiliarity as explored in a number of Magnet Theatre productions. Part of Magnet's longevity attests to their successful navigation of cross-cultural work, which guards against any easy assimilation or the forced enculturation of difference. The problematics of cultural exchange and a suspicion of reactive syncretism inform all of these continuing investigations.

In this first section, the deep conceptual investigative work of Magnet Theatre is explored in detail, with an emphasis on ways in which their theorization has been led by performance-based processes and practices. In Part Two – 'Collaboration: Making Space for Embodied Practice' – Jennie Reznek, Yvette Hutchison and Megan Lewis examine how Magnet's underlying philosophy and spirit of physicality – inspired by Jacques Lecoq's claim that '*tout bouge*' ['everything moves'] – functions in Magnet's staged performances, rehearsal rooms and classrooms, as well as within the larger South African cultural landscape.

In her chapter, co-artistic director and Magnet's featured performer, Jennie Reznek, articulates the particular pedagogy and approach to the training of the body that Magnet Theatre has been developing over the past 29 years. Reznek argues that Magnet has been responding, pendulum-like, to a 'culture of violence' that has persisted in South Africa from the period of colonialism, through the apartheid era, and up to the present historical moment. Reznek analyses the impact of violence on the body by focusing on three of its consequences – stillness, erasure, and rupture – before exploring how Magnet's teaching of the body in physical theatre counters all three of these with a focus on the moving, articulate, individuated body capable of transformation. She discusses how such an approach is useful to the act of theatre-making (at the level of an individual performer) as well as in a larger society (in the sense of the larger cultural context of a democracy coming to fruition).

Yvette Hutchison then traces Mark Fleishman's search for what she calls 'a dramaturgy of displacement' (Fleishman 2011). For Hutchison (p. 209), this is 'about *making* rather than *telling*; about embodiment, where the dramaturgy must find ways of including silence and absence; of telling stories without co-opting the narratives of people who cannot or will not participate themselves.' Through a close reading of *Medea*, *Rain in a Dead Man's Footprints*, and *Every Year, Every Day, I Am Walking*, she explores how

Jennie Reznek exercises her aerial skills in *The Show's Not Over 'Til the Fat Lady Sings* (1991).
Photo credit: © Ruphin Coudyzer FPPSA. (ruphincoudyzer.com)

Magnet Theatre productions trouble narrative, while at the same time negotiating the place of narrative in the work.

One of the narratives that Magnet has explored is the oft-hidden history of slavery and human trafficking at the Cape Colony, and in her chapter, Megan Lewis explores how Magnet has worked through the silences, shattered fragments and incoherent ghosts of the slave archive to re-member the past in post-1994 South Africa. She examines how *Cargo*, a powerful dance-theatre collaboration between Magnet and Jazzart Dance Theatre, made manifest the hybridity of contemporary Africans as they migrate and move through contested spaces, seeking new modes of being in the future while simultaneously engaging – through live bodies in motion – with the troubled past. Lewis analyses this groundbreaking performance piece, mapping how bodies in motion negotiate and enact power, navigate racializing and sexualizing discourses, and generate a powerful language of their own that can reach diverse audiences and catalyse the body politic.

In Part Three of this collection – 'Community: Making Space for Cultural Interventions' – we turn our attention to Magnet's important community-based projects, particularly in Khayelitsha and Clanwilliam. Scholars Gay Morris and Elliot Leffler and fieldworker Lavona de Bruyn delve into the potentials and pitfalls of this work. Some of the chapters in this section – particularly those of de Bruyn and Leffler – change gear from the analytical methodology of the previous chapters. De Bruyn and Leffler were both fieldworkers with Magnet's Clanwilliam project, and in this sense their enquiries are rooted more strongly in first-hand experience and autoethnography. The tonal shift in this section from scholarly critique to reportage highlights the multiple crossovers between Magnet's work in academia and its interventions in communities.

Gay Morris opens this section with her hands-on, critical insights into Magnet's recent performance projects in Khayelitsha – Cape Town's newest, largest and poorest black township. Fuelled by director Mandla Mbothwe's vision to support and develop theatre in the townships, Magnet collaborated through Xhosa-speaking fieldworkers with a selection of local theatre groups, offering regular workshops, think tanks and mentoring to the groups who annually gather each November for the Magnet Theatre Community Groups Intervention (CGI) Showcase. Based on her extensive field research between 2006 and 2008, Morris explores how the character of the township colours all aspects of Magnet's interventions there. Morris also argues that a crucial feature of the showcase festival is that it demonstrates how, in spite of the most rudimentary facilities for theatrical performance, the local playing culture lubricates and 'eventifies' the occasion (cited in Hauptfleisch 2004) and how eventification becomes, in a sense, the community's form of publication.

In her chapter, Lavona de Bruyn discusses her personal experience of working with Magnet Theatre from 2007 until 2012, when she helped them to develop applied theatre activities in the Cederberg region of the Western Cape. Tracing her own journey towards political and theatrical consciousness, she explores two projects as case studies of Magnet's methodology: *Jingle Dreams* (2007) and *Vastrap Van Jan Dissel Tot Tra Tra* [Stand Firm from Jan Dissel to Tra Tra] (2011). De Bruyn explores the impact of Magnet on her role as an applied theatre practitioner (as catalyst, facilitator and interventionist) and the development of the Community Networking Creative Arts Group (ComNet). She argues that the inclusivity of the community in an exploration of their communal past is one of Magnet's most vital interventions in Clanwilliam. Her voice in this collection offers a practitioner's perspective on the important community work that Magnet is doing in this region.

Then, Eliott Leffler rounds out this section with his ethnographic account and critical investigation of ComNet, a community-based ensemble, primarily made up of teenagers, which was under the direction of Lavona de Bruyn. Leffler worked with the ensemble from June to July 2010, and his chapter investigates ComNet's 2010 efforts to nurture cross-cultural relationships in the small rural community of Clanwilliam. Leffler integrates personal insights and observations with a theoretical interrogation of dialogue (Paolo Freire), play (Johan Huizinga, Stuart Brown and Jean Piaget), and *communitas* (Victor Turner) to question how Magnet's theatre-making in post-apartheid South Africa can nurture a spirit of play that engenders not just *communitas*, but also dialogue. Drawing from key moments in ComNet's process, he illustrates the ways that black and white participants play together in the theatre-making process, and traces the evolution of play into *communitas* – a heightened state of enchanted human interaction in which social hierarchies appear to fade away. This state allows cross-cultural relationships to develop, but, Leffler argues, it may impede critical dialogue, which necessitates a sober accounting of well-entrenched power dynamics. As mentioned, De Bruyn and Leffler's chapters bring together experiential engagement with critical enquiry.

Magnetic Attractions

We now turn our attention to Magnet's history, tracing the company's origins in terms of the remarkable couple who have sustained it: Mark Fleishman and Jennie Reznek. Drawing on an in-depth interview with the pair in July 2013, we briefly chart their personal and professional journey since their meeting in 1987. In this way, we hope to narrate the history of Magnet's formation, and to map how this talented, visionary team have sustained a robust company within the fledgling democracy. Frances Marek, Magnet's project manager (2009-2011) and a former student of the couple, describes the partnership between Mark Fleishman and Jennie Reznek as the key to the success of Magnet as a company. She explains how 'Mark takes the long view, he always has a sense of the whole, he is always pulling back and looking at something from a distance and going: "Okay, what have we got, what do we need?"' Complementing Fleishman's macrocosmic perspective is 'Jennie, who just goes to this deep, microscopic level of embodied detail and gets right under the very skin of things when she works.' According to Marek:

Fleishman and Reznek in *The Show's Not Over 'Til the Fat Lady Sings* (1991).
Photo credit: © Ruphin Coudyzer FPPSA. (ruphincoudyzer.com)

> They make an incredible partnership. Both of them are concerned with the details and the whole, but they have found a way to work that allows each of them to focus on the thing that they love best and do best and know that they are always supported by the other.
>
> (Marek 2013)

It all started in 1987, when Jennie Reznek returned from two years of training with Jacques Lecoq in Paris, after having graduated from the University of Cape Town (UCT) with a BA in Speech and Drama. She had already begun to establish herself as an outstanding physical performer when she met Mark, a theatre-maker in his final year of the UCT Performance Programme. At the time, he was remounting a theatre piece after a successful run at the Grahamstown Festival, and he was looking for actors who could work physically. Jennie was urged to audition for Mark by Jazzart Dance Theatre artistic director, Alfred Hinkel, and their professional relationship emerged from their personal chemistry. Long-time collaborator Jay Pather (2013) describes the couple as 'a match made in heaven,' saying that '[t]hey really do compliment each other. They're on the same path.' The couple moved to Johannesburg after Mark auditioned for and was accepted as an actor into the permanent ensemble of PACT (Performing Arts Council of Transvaal), and they shared a house with Handspring Puppet Company founders, Basil Jones and Adrian Kohler.

'I'd learnt to be an interpretive actor at UCT,' says Reznek, 'and I had never been given an indication when I was a student that there might be anything beyond that' (Reznek & Fleishman 2013). But her experience with Lecoq changed her outlook:

> I feel that Lecoq gave me the creative gift of myself. It was quite a validating thing. And it's completely instrumental in terms of why the teaching is such a big part of Magnet, because I feel that [Lecoq] affirmed me in such a significant way that allowed me to be a creative agent in my life. To make your own work is very empowering.
>
> (Reznek & Fleishman 2013)

The first production, which launched the company, was *Cheap Flights*, about a woman trapped in a one-room flat who is frightened by the escalating violence around her and dreams of escape in flights of fantasy. Roz Monat directed Jennie in the piece, and they rehearsed in Jones and Kohler's studio on Magnet Street in Kensington, a suburb of Johannesburg. While Fleishman was not an active collaborator (claiming that all he did was drive the car to the Grahamstown Festival), Reznek describes how Mark watched the rehearsal process:

> I always had a sense that there was something he understood about what we were doing, and something that was interesting to him about the way that we were working, and the kind of physicality and body at the heart of the work. I was very aware – also because we were partners – of his gaze on that first particular process .
>
> (Reznek & Fleishman 2013)

Reznek describes *Cheap Flights* as 'the first of its kind – a quite powerful female voice in response to violence in South Africa in the eighties.' The piece successfully explored a dark topic using an exuberant humour and intense physicality. It immediately found an audience. 'If I'd done Cheap Flights and only me and Roz and Mark found it funny,' says Reznek, 'then it would have ended there, but people responded.' Thus, *Cheap Flights* was the genesis of Magnet Theatre. Mark recounts how the company was formed:

> When [Jennie and Roz] were filling in the form for the Grahamstown Festival Fringe, they had to write down the name of a company. They didn't have a name, so they

> looked out the window and they saw the name of the street – Magnet Street. That's how the company became Magnet Theatre. That's where it started. It wasn't me. I was there, but I wasn't really part of it at that point, I was just driving the car.
>
> (Reznek & Fleishman 2013)

For the next few years, Mark worked closely with Barney Simon, both as an actor and as a theatre-maker, and helped with the establishment of the Laboratory at the Market Theatre: 'This was a formative period for me and informed a lot of my work in what became Magnet' (Fleishman 2013). During this time, the young couple worked as freelance actors, directors and choreographers on various projects, before going to work and train with The Dream Circus, a small and short-lived, non-animal circus based in Cape Town, which had been started by an ex-UCT classmate of Jennie's. Mark, however, soon left the circus to pursue his master's degree at UCT, where he also started teaching. Jennie stayed on, learning trapeze and other aerial skills, until the circus closed at the end of the 1980s. Wanting to apply her circus training to theatre, Jennie set about creating a new show inspired by an image she had conjured of a fat woman (Belinda) driven by voracious hunger and hidden desires, who dreams of flying. Mark became 'the outside eye to that process' and the couple collaborated on their first work together: *The Show's Not Over 'Til the Fat Lady Sings*. They self-produced the piece first at Hiddingh Hall on the University of Cape Town campus and then, about a year later, in the Dock Road Theatre, David and Renaye Kramer's space on the waterfront in Greenpoint, Cape Town. Fearing no one would attend their show, Mark explained his surprise when he looked out the window of Hiddingh Hall and said, 'Jennie, there are people coming!' He adds:

> And there was a decent turnout, and they seemed to love it. And then there was another decent turnout the next night. And we were just collecting money in a box – and it suddenly felt like this theatre thing is easy! We were so excited, because it was really our own product.
>
> (Reznek & Fleishman 2013)

The Show's Not Over 'Til the Fat Lady Sings was a solid success. After its Cape Town run, Fleishman and Reznek were invited by Barney Simon to produce a late night version of the show in The Laager, a small, 150-seat venue at The Market Theatre in Johannesburg. From there, they returned to Dock Road, and as Mark says, 'it just kind of ran and ran.' 'It was just the two of us, we had no dependants,' recalls Reznek. 'It was an incredibly empowering thing to have such a direct relationship with what one made oneself and being able to survive. Talk about owning the means of production!' (Reznek & Fleishman 2013).

The couple were energized by their independence and unique form of theatrical storytelling. Compared to the existing theatrical landscape, Reznek says 'it felt like we were putting out something that was new; in terms of the physicality of the work, and the way that we were working with energy' (Reznek & Fleishman 2013). Since then, South

African theatre has developed many accomplished physical styles and practitioners, many of whom also trained with Lecoq, including Ellis Pearson, William Kentridge, Grethe Fox, Lara Bye, Sylvaine Strike and James Cunningham.[2] In the contemporary theatrical landscape, says Reznek, 'there are a lot of people working with puppets and image and now, in a way, we're one of many trying to push boundaries in similar kinds of ways. [Yet] at the beginning, I had the feeling, that what we were doing was not stuff that I was seeing around me' (Reznek & Fleishman 2013).

Then, in 1991, concerned about the state of the country, and driven by the threat of Mark's conscription into the army,[3] Fleishman and Reznek left South Africa for Europe. Equipped with a handful of leads from Barney Simon, enough money to last three months and a place to stay with Jennie's sister, the couple hustled cold calls to anyone willing to give them a space in which to present *Fat Lady*. 'It was that sort of immigrant mentality,' Reznek remembers, 'We had nothing to lose, so we just tried anything.' Reznek worked long hours to market the show from her 'office,' which she describes as 'a little red telephone booth on the corner opposite Brighton beach, right on the road' (Reznek & Fleishman 2013). Finally they were able to get three bookings in a row: Brighton Comedy Festival, the Glasgow Mayfest (where they were given the slot from a cancelled show from The Market) and the Manchester Greenroom.[4] These successful engagements led to an invitation to Hong Kong before they returned to Europe. The couple then faced the decision of whether to stay in Europe or whether to return to South Africa. Ultimately, Mark says that:

> It was coming to 1994, and the whole situation in South Africa was changing. We came back to South Africa very much with the idea that we wanted to keep Magnet going as a company, because we'd seen the model for similar companies in the UK and around Europe.
>
> (Reznek & Fleishman 2013)

Medea Puts Magnet on the Map

Despite having worked as arts administrator of The Market Lab (under Barney Simon) and as an actor (at PACT), above all Fleishman wanted to be a director. He recounts the story of the moment when his life-long desire became consciously articulated:

> [It was on] a particular night in Paris in about 1992 or 1993 when we went for dinner to this teacher of Jennie's from Lecoq called Sandra [Mladenovitch]. So we were sitting there and it was one of many times I sat in Paris not understanding anything. She's chatting with everybody [in French] and I'm like a fly on the wall and this lady comes up to me and says: 'So, you're a theatre director. What are you directing?' And I thought, that's quite a challenging question; because I'm not really directing anything. So I said the first thing that came into my head, which was *Medea*, because I'd seen

> [Andre Serban's] *Medea* at the Edinburgh Festival. I'd thought it was interesting and I'd wondered how it could be done in South Africa. So I said *Medea* and she said 'Apollonius of Rhodes.' I didn't know what that meant. When I went back to London I found Apollonius of Rhodes and the story of Jason and Medea in prose. That was how *Medea* started.
>
> (Reznek & Fleishman 2013)

On his return to South Africa in 1993, Fleishman began work on his landmark production of *Medea*, the first in a series of many collaborations with Alfred Hinkel and Jazzart Dance Theatre. '[Alfred had] just taken his dance company, Jazzart, into CAPAB [Cape Performing Arts Board – a government-funded organization] at that time, so they had a bit of money; and that money was able to pay for Bo Petersen and Kurt Wustmann and Jay Pather[5] to perform in *Medea*,' recalls Fleishman (Reznek & Fleishman 2013).

Medea was a watershed production. It was Magnet's first big show: it introduced their unique performance style as an eclectic mixture of different cultural voices with expressive physical work and a deep political undercurrent that spoke to the politics of a South Africa emerging into a democracy still reeling from the apartheid past. It also established Fleishman as an 'instinctive' director with 'a really strong sense of investigation' who was able to 'activate' his ensemble (Pather 2013). For Fleishman, *Medea* was important for two reasons: the inclusion in the piece of a mixture of different cultures, and a dramaturgical approach that was complex and multiple, rather than singular.[6] *Medea* included many languages spoken in South Africa: Tamil, Tsotsitaal, Kaapse Taal, Zulu, Latin, English, Afrikaans and Xhosa. It also included a broad movement vocabulary – a combination of contemporary dance with European, Indian and African influences, such as *kathakali* dance alongside African gumboot dancing and other African traditional dance styles. 'There were various languages that were confusing meaning in a way, making meaning more complex,' says Fleishman. Reznek says of Magnet's particular approach:

> Different voices, different sounds – it's still the thing that excites me now in the rehearsal room. When I hear stuff from one context, or one language or one kind of training bumping up against something else, a different thing. [...] When there's an opportunity in the theatre space for very different, diverse kinds of languages, training, thoughts, to come in together. I find that really very exciting.
>
> (Reznek & Fleishman 2013)

In addition to foregrounding the multiple voices of the new democracy, *Medea* also involved the deconstruction and rewriting of a classic Greek text; a practice that is now common, but which, in 1994, according to Fleishman, 'was quite obviously fascinating for South African audiences.' *Medea* was picked up by UCT classics scholar Maggie Mezzabotta, who circulated a brief video of the production, which in turn gave Magnet's work greater visibility.[7] Fleishman says, 'suddenly it wasn't just in the drama sphere that it had an impact [...] [there was also interest from] academic Classics Departments' (Reznek & Fleishman 2013).

Medea was not only a landmark production for Magnet in terms of style and content, but for Fleishman, 'many of the core relationships that helped to sustain the company were established through that production,' including partnerships with Alfred Hinkel of Jazzart, as well as designer Craig Leo.[8] Jazzart's access to funding meant that they could extend the scope of their productions: 'linking to Jazzart allowed us to do something that we couldn't do on our own' (Reznek & Fleishman 2013). *Medea* formally established Magnet Theatre as a physical theatre company. Fleishman is careful to distinguish what this means for Magnet:

> As a physical theatre company [Magnet] traverses two interpretations of what physical theatre is. There's the dance interpretation or what could be called 'dance theatre.' That's the DV8[9] and First Physical Theatre[10] interpretation of what physical theatre is. Then there's the Lecoq[11]/Andrew Buckland[12] style – a more theatrical physical theatre. So the influences from Jennie's training comes out in shows like *53 Degrees*, *Fat Lady*, *'I Do' x 22*. Those are all from the theatrical, Lecoq side. And then there's the dance stuff we did with Jazzart. So there were both those things happening, simultaneously.
>
> (Reznek & Fleishman 2013)

Since *Medea*, Magnet Theatre has mounted over 25 successful productions, which are detailed in the 'Production History' chapter following this introduction. Many of these productions have toured nationally and internationally, where they have been well-received by audiences and highly regarded by critics. Around the turn of the new millennium, the company expanded its reach into the communities around Cape Town, adding community engagement and applied theatre work to its repertoire of high calibre productions. The recipe for its success over almost three decades resides in the company's distinct style and method of working.

The Magnet Method

Magnet emerged in the late 1980s as a physical theatre company with a commitment to social justice. South African theatre has a long history of political activism and resistance, which saw its heyday during the apartheid era, and which gave rise to a particular brand of theatrical practice known as 'workshop theatre.' The workshop method was often used in the creation of protest, township and workers' theatre. As a devised form of politicized performance, this approach to theatre-making evolved alongside the Black Consciousness Movement (BCM) and the anti-apartheid struggle of the 1970s and 1980s. Workshop theatre was pioneered in several important sites across the country, such as

Workshop '71 and Phoenix Players in the Transvaal (present-day Gauteng), and The Serpent Players and The Space in the Cape. It espoused what Wakashe (1986: 41) calls 'a revolutionary tone full of sharp criticisms of the government's policies.' Fleishman calls workshop theatre 'an oppositional form' that resisted and countered existing practices of apartheid era, text-based, western theatre[13] with a communally-devised, oral and overtly political approach. Particularly after the Soweto uprising of 1976, workshop theatre 'emerged as the dominant form of play production amongst people opposed to the system of apartheid' (Fleishman 1990: 99).

The workshop approach is a devising process with several recurring characteristics. It is a communally-created endeavour rather than the work of a single playwright, director or auteur. Although workshop theatre also emerged in Britain (for example, with the theatre of Joan Littlewood, who was a formative influence on Barney Simon), in South Africa it became an overtly political, urban form of cultural expression with 'a particular performance style, generic to the South African townships, which is non-naturalistic, physical, musical and larger than life' (Fleishman 1990: 89). This style is generated and structured like tradition oral forms: 'the expression of thought [...] tends to be heavily rhythmic, to occur in balanced patterns, to be repetitious and to employ communal formulas' (1990: 92). It is concerned with the collective subject, 'more [...] with life than with literature,' and it 'displays an ironic comic vision' which for Fleishman 'is both regenerative in the face of the essential tragedy of the South African situation, and transformative in its ability to estrange power structures through grotesque parody' (1990: 89).

Magnet's work is distinctly influenced by the workshop approach. Fleishman (1990: 100) says that 'workshop plays are not written, they are made'[14] by a community of collaborators who debate differing viewpoints and act out various scenarios as they create the piece together. Despite the uniqueness of each group of collaborators, project or moment in time, common to the workshop practice is a three-phased 'rhapsodizing' (1990: 100) process that involves observation/research, improvisation and selection/shaping. Prompted by exploratory tasks in the first phase, the company members may observe everyday life, and draw on personal experience or research by reading, interviewing or visiting key sites. The second phase, which Fleishman (1990: 102) describes as being 'communal and participatory,' is a process of watching and responding: actors play within a skeletal structure for improvisation, drawing on their observations to create material while a director watches and records. In the final phase, the generated materials are selected or rejected, and stitched together to create the piece to be performed (1990: 101). Jay Pather describes how at this point:

> [T]he democratic work process gets cut off, and becomes a full-on professionally led work; one that needs to have someone at the helm who is aware of all that is going on, not just the fragment. Someone with whom the buck stops.
>
> (Pather 2013)

Workshopping is thus a democratic, playful and responsive form wherein the director facilitates and shapes a piece from work generated by the company. Its aims are not solely the creation of a polished product for the stage; the process also instils a sense of pride and dignity, self-confidence and solidarity in its participants (Fleishman 1990: 111), which extends beyond the theatrical production. For Fleishman, writing at the outset of the democratic process:

> [W]orkshop theatre [is] a form based on the principles of democracy. [It is] a form available to all the people irrespective of education or level of literacy, a form which include[s] all people irrespective of race, [and] exists in an homologous correspondence with [the] new structure of feeling. It is the form which has made theatre in South Africa truly of the people.
>
> (Fleishman 1990: 110)

Workshop theatre's emphasis on process also means that written texts of such performances (when they exist) are considered after-effects of a process, rather than its starting point. This form of theatre devising is what Diana Taylor might call a repertoire practice, rather than an archival one. For writer-director Frances Marek (2013), Magnet values the process of making work, not just the final performance: 'Their focus is always on the process of creating theatre. [...] Both in terms of their dedication to creating new, original work and also more practically to their emphasis on how that work is brought to life.'

Mark Fleishman claims that Magnet's theatrical lineage was inspired by 'the collective creative process of workshopping,' as well as by Barney Simon and The Market Theatre's ethos of doing work that matters to the larger culture. He describes how he and his contemporaries at The Market, like Lara Foot and Clare Stopford, believed passionately that 'theatre is something to be taken seriously; theatre is something to work at with rigour. It's not about making money and it's not about simply being playful for the sake of being playful [...] there is a value system that should pertain' (Reznek & Fleishman 2013). Fleishman also cites the belief, drawn from his Market days, that 'white people who had benefited from the apartheid system had an obligation to make a contribution, to give something back,' as foundational to him as a theatre-maker and artist. He explains:

> It's what Alain Badiou calls 'the work that still needs to be done' [Badiou 2001]. There's also this Kabbalistic notion of *Tikkun Olam* – 'the repairing of the world.' The world is in constant need of repair and the work we do is doing what still needs to be done.
>
> (Reznek & Fleishman 2013)

Space for the Body

Jennie's particular contribution to this work of repairing the world is the moving body, which is central to the workshopping approach Magnet practices: 'I think that there is something profound that links the body and its ability to move to the notion of freedom' (Reznek & Fleishman 2013). She cites a 'fundamentally political notion of change and the ability to change' as the source of her work:

> In a way what you're trying to say to an audience is that if [the actor's] human body [onstage] can transform into different images, different characters, different places, then anything is possible. Then any status quo can shift, and any fixed state can break open and become something else.
>
> (Reznek & Fleishman 2013)

For Reznek, the moving body – a moveable, fluid and free entity – is the ultimate challenge to any hegemonic system: 'The body that moves is a body that's not confined, that's not defined by somebody else from the outside.' She claims that:

> [My] obsession with the body was very much fired up in response to what was happening in the eighties in South Africa, in terms of the levels of oppression and certain immobilities that were being imposed on the body, in terms of where people could move and who people could engage with.[15] It's about saying to an audience – we are fundamentally free and we can transform and we can change. So I think that continues for me in terms of the way that we work with people. When we bring an individual person into the space as a collaborator, we're working with their bodies in the space and their own histories are embedded in their bodies. We're working with them as subjects, as opposed to them as objects. In terms of ethics, this involves relating to human beings as other subjectivities.
>
> (Reznek & Fleishman 2013)

For Fleishman, Magnet's ethos also draws from Hannah Arendt's notion of '"space[s] of appearance" [Arendt 1959] where people appear to themselves as subjects,' as well as Slavoj Žižek's notion of 'radical subjectivities, or subjectification, the way that you become a subject to yourself' (Žižek 2004). For Fleishman, such a coming into oneself is one of the many benefits collaborators gain from workshopping. Over time, a sense of pride and dignity in being able to tell one's story and be witnessed by others emerges, as the solidarity of the group gradually builds and the unity of the collaborators extends into the larger sociopolitical field. Collaborators find a space in which to enact hidden histories, vicariously act out suppressed desires and debate differing points of view (Fleishman 1990: 111). As a theatre-maker, Fleishman sees himself more as a writer than as a director:

> When I go into a room full of other people's stories, as a director [...] I'm not writing with my own words necessarily, I'm writing with other people's stories or what other people contribute to the process. I'm able to shape that more and more as time's gone by; the skill has been about learning how to shape the material that's in the room in a dramaturgical kind of way.
>
> (Reznek & Fleishman 2013)

By dramaturgy, Fleishman means a 'part pedagogical, part facilitatory, and part authorial' practice of weaving (Barba 1985) multiple elements through 'a process – a process of being undecided, always in emergence. It is a refusal of and resistance to closure – to accepting conventional notions and norms of what theatre or performance might be' (Fleishman 2012: 8).

Magnet has remained committed to devising work in a democratic way, working through the body to defy the separation and violent legacies of South Africa's racial and social hierarchies. This approach, and the work it has produced, has offered provocations and challenges to the predominantly western knowledge systems and power structures of South African culture and art-making. Resisting the over-reliance and privileging of the written word, singular authorship and emphasis on pristine theatrical products over process, Magnet's embodied work 'constitute[s] alternative ways of knowing that are non-representational, experimental and potentially political' (Fleishman 2009: 125–6). And over time, Fleishman (2012) has negotiated ways of keeping 'the best elements of workshop theatre' while searching for:

> [...] a new way of doing it that felt more honest in that I accepted that I was functioning in an authorial role and made this transparent to all the collaborators, and that helped to shape work that was created, collaboratively with many bodies in space rather than with words on a page, into more structured and coherent forms using a variety of materials.
>
> (Fleishman 2012)

Thus, Magnet's artists use a devising approach to their theatre-making, collaborating to create an original work, rather than interpreting an existing literary script.[16] Composer and Magnet trustee Neo Muyanga (2013) says, 'Magnet is a devising company, so the script comes to life as different exercises are shaped by [Mark] the director.' Specifically, Mark sets out what Reznek calls 'improvisatory tasks around particular themes' for the collaborators, who then go off and respond to the task with their physical, vocal or musical instruments, as well as their creativity and intellects. They then bring back their responses – choreography, movement, images, text, music – into the rehearsal room. These tasks at times involve responding to research or source material, creating scenarios or improvising around a theme or idea. Muyanga describes how, as a composer, he thrives within this dynamic. Describing the process of working with Jazzart on *Cargo*, he explains that while the choreographers and actors were playing and working on the floor:

> I'd be taking notes of what rhythms they were using, I'd also find themes they were investigating and find a matching equivalent in music [...] then I would go away and write something and bring it back [...]. Then we fix it, edit some things out and new things are written. It takes months before we know what we've got.
>
> (Muyanga 2013)

Space for Play

Central to Magnet's devising process is a deep and abiding spirit of play. According to Fleishman, 'At the heart of Lecoq's work is the concept of *le jeu*, this notion of play [...] the view that fundamentally theatre should also have a heart of joy, in some kind of way. Even if the territory is dark' (Reznek & Fleishman 2013); without *le jeu* or play, he suggests, 'it sticks. The gears don't change, the clutch isn't working. It becomes a deadly

Fleishman and Reznek in the Magnet space.
Photo credit: © Mark Wessels. No images may be used for print or electronic purposes without consent from the copyright holder.

thing if it's too dark' (2013). Fleishman (2009: 124) has written on the importance of experimental play during the process of creation: 'the trial and error method of feeling one's way toward a goal, open to the possibility of bumping into new discoveries along the way, the creation of imaginary or potential spaces within which to engage with specific questions.' These spaces, he explains, are not predetermined, nor does he begin projects with a preconceived notion of what he wants to communicate or address; rather, his process is one of exploration and discovery:

> I don't say to myself: 'I think it's important that we give a message about X and, therefore, let's go and make a play about it.' It's much more about a tantalising thing that's in front of you at the time. I've always treated the theatre as a creative medium to make things in the world. You know, Jacques Rancière [2004: 39] speaks of 'ways of doing and making' as part of his 'distribution of the sensible' [2000: 13] and that's what I feel I'm engaged with – the process of doing and making. [...] We used to say right in the beginning that we didn't know what theatre was. And that each time we made a project we wanted to reinvent the theatre and re-explore and re-find what the theatre actually is.
>
> (Reznek & Fleishman 2013)

Costume designer Illka Louw (2013) says of Fleishman's playful work ethic: 'He has a very clear vision; but he also has a very clear way of playing and letting other people play, and knowing how to access that.'

The Guiding Spirit of Research

Within this playful and exploratory practice, Magnet's work is informed by research, as Fleishman articulates very deftly in his chapter in this collection. Partially driven by Mark's role as an academic at UCT, Magnet has an intimate relationship with research:

> As an academic there was an imperative to produce work involved with research, so a whole series of history plays began to emerge... *53 Degrees*, *Onnest'bo*, *Rain in a Dead Man's Footprints* and *Cargo*. Four plays that set the tone for the kind of way that we work in terms of a more thematic kind of process, working on the theme of performing history or staging the archive.
>
> (Reznek & Fleishman 2013)

Fleishman has written eloquently of his commitment, as both a scholar and a practitioner, to performance as research (PaR). For him, 'performance' is both a noun (a product) and a verb (a process or a practice), as well as an epistemology; a way of knowing that challenges traditional binaries of body-mind dualism, the separation of theory and practice, and the valuing of the archive of fixed representation over the repertoire of sensation (Fleishman 2009: 117–19). Fleishman (2009: 122) advocates for a type of performance that is 'active, immediate, on the move, embodied, sensual, fluid, interactional and affectively engaged.' Magnet's work strives to challenge the textual, political and dramatic hegemonies of South Africa over the past three decades, and works towards a 'strategy for agency in the face of disempowering circumstances' (2009: 125).

The spirit of research that guides the company means that Magnet takes time to devise and create works, rather than working under a pressured timeline or to aim solely for box office profits. Frances Marek says she:

> […] found it incredibly freeing and very satisfying to work for a company who were not in it for commercial gain. The focus when we created or discussed new work was never on what would sell tickets, but rather on what those involved were interested in investigating and how we wanted to put that on stage. I have a huge respect for that ethos.
>
> (Marek 2013)

Fleishman adds that they never really relied on the box office: 'I think one of the reasons that we made the company, and certainly one of the reasons why I went into a full-time job at the university, was to create the conditions that we wanted to work under' (Reznek & Fleishman 2013).

Magnet benefits from Mark and Jennie's own research and also informs it. As an academic, Fleishman (2013) explains that 'you are doing this all day every day – working with students, thinking about work, talking about work, conceptualizing, theorising – you can't help but do that to your own creative work.'

'It isn't always "academic" research though,' adds Reznek. For her, the process of making theatre pieces is about a particular kind of engagement with the world:

> It's an opportunity to have a conversation. To say 'research driven' also means, for me, an opportunity to define a territory and live in that territory and really understand the richness of whatever area it is you're working with. *53 Degrees* was for me the first time that I really discovered the South African archive in terms of looking at photographs and at the history of Robben Island. And it was such a rich personal experience going into that territory, into that time and imagining.
>
> (Reznek & Fleishman 2013)

This type of personal investment in the work is vital to Jennie:

> I think I've managed to find metaphors in the archives that in a way connect with my own internal landscape. [For example,] *Every Year, Every Day, I Am Walking* is a public story about refugees and yet it also completely intersected with a much more private

> narrative of my own, about loss and recovery, packing up my childhood house, and the loss of both of my parents. So the work, for me, has always been about landing on these stories, histories, metaphors, finding an external social and political landscape that kind of cuts down into my own story.
>
> (Reznek & Fleishman 2013)

Space for Images

With their emphasis on bodywork, Magnet has a recognizable style of powerful imagistic theatre based on a 'combination of image and social conscience' (Pather 2013). They are known for creating arresting images in their productions, which have emerged from their archaeological research processes. Fleishman describes the work as driven by a principle he borrows from Leibniz: 'compossibility' (Jones 2009); that is, the bringing into existence of 'fleshes alongside texts alongside images, sight alongside hearing and touching and feeling and moving' (Fleishman 2012: 30). Designer Craig Leo says that what he finds exciting about Magnet's work:

> [...] is that they aren't afraid to work with the language appropriate to the subject matter, including the language of the body. So there are a lot of different languages going on; but the images are so strong that often the piece we are working with doesn't rely solely on the text. The meaning is so beautifully incorporated into the image that I'm compelled, that I'm drawn to it. [...] I think one can be a lot more open to interpretation when working with images...I think that the image, certainly in this country, often speaks so much louder than words [...]. Because we have eleven official languages and people communicate very differently from person to person, I think that images can be useful. Also, they can have different meanings for different people. I mean, what you see is not the same as what I see, because of our unique histories and our individual pasts, and so we add meaning to a picture or an image. As soon as you bring a string of text in, it begins to lock the meaning down somewhat.
>
> (Leo 2013)

Thus, for Magnet, performance involves multiple creative registers, including embodied 'acts of storying, sounding, moving, feeling and relating' (Fleishman 2009: 126).[17] Magnet's multi-textured style is also highly fluid, evolving over time and always open to explorations, re-explorations, and what Fleishman (2012: 33) calls (after Bergson) 'creative evolution,' which he sees as a process of continual invention and reinvention of strings or series of forms. Because of their openness to, and embracing of, process and evolution, it is no wonder that Magnet has weathered the past three decades so effectively, and that they continue to change and shift to meet the changing demands of the arts and political landscapes of South Africa.

Expanding the Collective

Drawing on Bruno Latour (2005), one of Magnet's central goals in the new millennium has been to expand the collective. Committed to 'looking for who and what is outside the collective and finding ways of bringing them in,' Fleishman says that:

> People have been left out. So in the history plays we've done, there are stories which haven't surfaced, or which have been hidden in the archive. We want to bring them to the fore, onto the stage, into the public sphere.
>
> (Reznek & Fleishman 2013)

One of many spaces in which Magnet works. *Onnest'bo* performed in a local school (2002).
Photo credit: © Mark Wessels.

Over their history as a company, Magnet has embarked on several different projects in under-represented areas – such as the townships of Khayelitsha and Dunoon, or the community in Clanwilliam – which several of our contributors address in this volume and which we will discuss further momentarily.

Another strand of inquiry for Magnet in this new century has been that of migration. Mark explains a concern and interest in:

> [...] people who come into the country but are then excluded on the basis of not belonging to the nation, being foreigners. With shows like *Every Year, Every Day, I Am Walking, Die Vreemdeling, Voices Made Night*, we try to bring those stories to the fore. Rancière speaks about the distribution of the sensible, the way the world or society is cut up into different sections, which determine who is allowed to participate and who is allowed to speak and make and do in different contexts. So certain people are allowed to do this, but other people are not. And I think the politics now is about how we expand the collective of people who can participate in what we call theatre-making. How can we bring other stories into play? How can we bring other languages in? How can we change the demographics of the thing?
>
> (Reznek & Fleishman 2013)

One of the ways in which Magnet has expanded the collective is linguistic.[18] They have created several new works which have brought languages other than English onto the South African stage: Xhosa productions like *ingcwaba lendoda lise cankwe ndlela* [the grave of the man lies next to the road] and *Inxeba Lomphilisi – The Wound of a Healer*; *Die Vreemdeling* [The Stranger], which was in Afrikaans; and *Every Year, Every Day, I Am Walking*, which is in French and English. For actress Faniswa Yisa (2013), Magnet's use of the 'universal language of the body' and their inclusion of 'non-mainstream languages' like Xhosa – the ability to 'use my mother tongue,' as she puts it – are what excites her most about working with Magnet. These two signature features of Magnet make their work 'accessible to a wide range of people' (Yisa 2013). She believes that Magnet's commitment to 'tel[ling] stories about other people who don't have the opportunity of telling their stories for themselves' is their most vital contribution to South African culture. But she is quick to clarify that:

> [...] if you're going to take it on yourself to tell the story of someone else, it's very important that you find the source, as opposed to making assumptions about them. What I like about working with Magnet is that they'll say: 'we want to know what you have to tell us.' When they're dealing with other people's stories Mark and Jennie don't say: 'this is how I see you.'
>
> (Yisa 2013)

Musician and composer Neo Muyanga especially values Magnet's linguistic interventions. In post-1994 South Africa, he says:

> Language is still one of the biggest barriers to communication, and the fact that Magnet are invested in making language interventions is, I think, quite activist. Very few companies in the country have been brave enough, since the new dispensation, to make work that is in Afrikaans and in Xhosa, in the way that Magnet does. They've disrupted the view of the South African lexicon. I think, actually, we're offered a different picture in a work like *Die Vreemdeling*. My Afrikaans is not great, but I could understand it, and I think anybody can understand it, because the presentation is of Afrikaans as a subversive language, not Afrikaans as a dominant, traditional language.
>
> (Muyanga 2013)

In addition to linguistic inclusivity, Fleishman claims 'we need to effect structural change in the way that theatre is practiced' (Reznek & Fleishman 2013). This was the impetus for Magnet's work in Clanwilliam, a small town with a population of under 8000, situated in the Cederberg Mountains, about 200 kilometres from Cape Town. In 2001, Magnet Theatre was invited by Professor Pippa Skotnes of the Michaelis School of Fine Art to bring performance elements to the Clanwilliam Arts Project. In the years since then, Magnet has taken over leadership of the project, which now involves an annual week-long intervention and lantern festival community performance, as well as ongoing outreach projects, which have given rise to ComNet and the farm schools project. Their goal in Clanwilliam has been to provide theatre training to the local population so that they could own the means of their own productions. 'It allows somebody to say – you can be part of this, and you can say the things you want to say, and you can make it yourself,' reflects Mark (Reznek & Fleishman 2013). These efforts are about bringing people into the collective who historically have not participated, or who have not been able to participate. They are included in the creation of a work, making them part of the Magnet community, encouraged to create something new – to author their own stories.

In addition to the site-specific work and the community work in Clanwilliam, Magnet instituted the Community Groups Intervention (CGI) in Khayelitsha, which ran from 2001 to 2008.[19] Magnet worked with several drama groups a year, impacting about 250 young people, running monthly skills workshops, organizing theatre visits, providing career guidance and producing a community showcase at the end of each year. Following seven years of successful township projects, Reznek, Fleishman and Mandla Mbothwe started the Full Time Training and Job Creation Program in 2008, a two-year immersive training programme for under-served students that aimed to bridge the divide between the community and the university, and to effect structural changes in a theatre industry that has historically been white-dominated.[20] Their intention is to empower and train talented young South Africans for work in creative fields. Mark and Jennie see their contribution to South African theatre and culture as living on in the hands of these young theatre-makers. Mark says, 'the legacy of Magnet won't be in someone taking over and trying to keep going what Jennie and I have built. The legacy will be – as the Lecoq legacy is and I would suggest Barney's legacy and Mavis'[21] legacy are – that all the people who have been influenced by Magnet go on to do their own thing' (Reznek & Fleishman 2013). This is already very clearly happening; for instance, director Mandla Mbothwe is now creative manager at Artscape, and has developed a strong *oeuvre* of work and his own unique style; performer Faniswa Yisa has made her own work independently; and the young director Thando Doni is making exciting new work that has garnered him a nomination for the Fleur du Cap Award for Best New Director.

Neo Muyanga confirms the impact of Magnet's work on the trainees in their programme:

> I've seen how it has changed the way they feel, in terms of their own self-confidence and their skills and the way they relate to the world. I've also seen Magnet do that from an academic point of view, at the university. I've engaged with lots of students from UCT who've been trained either with Magnet or with Jennie and Mark. [...] [They have managed to enhance] the capacity of that individual to imagine themselves in a different way, based on the work that has been done. Some of the people I've engaged with are in Clanwilliam [...] I got the sense that a lot of the people in the programme felt it was a very special moment, that we were part of a very special discovery. I think it changed Clanwilliam in a certain way, and it changed the way Clanwilliam understands the place of art in the public sphere.
>
> (Muyanga 2013)

The Magnet Family

Every Magnet collaborator we interviewed for this book expressed how people consistently felt empowered by working within Magnet. For Jay Pather (2013), 'When we were doing *Medea*, we really did have a sense of being part of a very close group. It's very much like a family.' Designer Craig Leo adds:

> With Magnet it's more than just work, it's a kind of – I want to say the word 'family.' Maybe that sounds sentimental, but they really do care deeply about the people they work with. They cultivate that kind of relationship with you, so it's not just that you come in to do the job and go. You really get a sense that they care not only about the product, but about the people. In this industry it's [often] always about an end product that appears on the stage and it gets done, but for me it's about relationships that you build. Without that element to my career, I wouldn't do this. Magnet has really generated and cultivated that quality.
>
> (Leo 2013)

And Nolovuyo Sam, who trained in Magnet's Community Groups Intervention (CGI) programme, then was one of the first trainees to go on to study at UCT, and is now an educator in her own right, says that:

> Magnet Theatre will always have a special place in my heart. The minute you are part of them, you feel like a member of a family, like you belong. They care, and they treat people with respect and love. To them, you are not just an employee or just their student, but you are someone special. They give their equal undivided attention to each and every one who works with them and I don't know how they manage to do that. Everyone is treated fairly. You would swear we are all living under one roof with our parents and siblings, it's like a family. There's a 'do unto others what you wish to be done unto you' type of vibe. Yes, there are strict measures and boundaries not to be crossed (like in any other family), but it's all done in an amazingly fun way.
>
> (Sam 2013)

Writer-director Frances Marek adds that Magnet's idea of community extends beyond their company into the larger social field:

> There is something about the way they work and the way they are as people that makes you feel very involved. And you feel very strongly that you're not just involved in Magnet, but you're serving South African theatre and theatre generally [...] it was a very strong sense I always had, that we were conscious of and working towards something greater and more far-reaching than just this one show for the company.
>
> (Marek 2013)

Reznek asserts that Barney Simon's philosophy that 'the only dignity you have is in your work' has always informed Magnet's approach:

> Our work happens to be with people, engaging with people. Yes, we do care about the people we work with. We make the work from the people who are in it. I love the people that I work with and I want to work with people I love.
>
> (Reznek & Fleishman 2013)

Costume designer Illka Louw (2013) also says that Magnet has 'a deep investment in people' and 'a true interest and commitment to communities. Their commitment to South Africa is very strong.' Neo Muyanga (2013) describes Magnet as an 'activist theatre company' because it 'does work that is relevant to society.' For Muyanga, Magnet's deep explorations of questions of identity and history in a country like South Africa, with its legacies of oppression and conflict

> [...] mean that they're constantly at the tension point where we are as a country. They do have a political platform, without explicitly going out there to make political theatre. It becomes political theatre because it deals with race relations and the idea of identity politics in the country.
>
> (Muyanga 2013)

He avows that Magnet is concerned with changing

> [...] the way we imagine what is possible, despite the fact that we don't have it with us today, to start looking at yourself and to start looking at our history and finding a new suggestion of what can be. Imagination changes the world, and I believe in changing the world. I believe that every time one steps on stage one should commit to changing the world.
>
> (Muyanga 2013)

And finally, Fleishman articulates the ethos of collaboration and connection that has guided Magnet over its lifetime as a company:

> I do believe that Magnet is in a sense a model for a particular way of being in South Africa, in which people can learn to be together as opposed to separate, which is what apartheid was all about. So what is important for me is the possibility that people of different ages, and people of different classes, and people of different races can be together in the space making stuff together, and feel heard and empowered in the process as people. And that ultimately is more important for me. That is the project beyond the making of art. If in the process interesting artworks happen to emerge – great; but we try every day to make this community of people work, which is ultimately what we do in this country or what we should be doing in this country.
>
> (Reznek & Fleishman 2013)

Over the past three decades, Magnet Theatre has developed critically acclaimed work that interrogates South Africa's complex and contested history through archival explorations and performative excavations of relevant contemporary issues. This collection of essays and interviews celebrates an innovative company that operates beyond buildings, migrating fluidly into empty spaces they find while creating rich potential out of liminal zones. Renowned arts critic Adrienne Sichel says that Magnet Theatre has 'magnetized audiences, critics and academics with their very singular way of transforming everyday happenings – the ordinary and the extraordinary – into a visual, physical and aural vernacular which tends to defy regular journalistic analysis and critical description' (2012). We hope to approach this vernacular by providing an in-depth study of Magnet's history, practice and philosophy, serving as a culturally-specific case study of South African culture in transition, as well as a global reminder of the ethics and practice of making theatre in contested, complex social spaces. As the company increasingly extend their international reach, our hope is that this collection will serve also to introduce what Sichel calls 'the Magnet brand of magical realism and tactile mysticism' (2012) to an ever-widening audience.

Acknowledgements

This collection is the fruit of our collaborative labour over many years, across time zones, and in consultation with many voices. We would like to thank Tim Mitchell at Intellect Books; Hetta Pieterse and Sharon Boshoff from Unisa; Michael Eckhardt, our copy editor; as well as the generosity of all the interviewees and scholars who contributed to this collection. We would also like to thank the National Lottery Distribution Trust Fund (NLDTF) of South Africa for funding provided towards this publication; our photographers for their exquisite images and especially to Mark Wessels for curating the Clanwilliam photo essay; and Rhodes University and the University of Massachusetts Amherst for their institutional support. Megan would like to thank her partner, Michael Schurter, and Anton would like to thank his wife, Louise. We offer our most special thanks to Mark and Jennie for having supported this project over many years and through many different incarnations.

Megan Lewis (Amherst, Massachusetts)
Anton Krueger (Grahamstown, Eastern Cape)
2015

References

Arendt, H. (1959), *The Human Condition*, New York: Doubleday.

Badiou, A. (2001), *Ethics: An Essay on the Understanding of Evil* (trans. P. Hallward), London and New York: Verso. First published 1993.

Balme, C. (1996), 'The Performance Aesthetics of Township Theatre: Frames and Codes,' in Geoffrey V. Davis and Anne Fuchs (eds), *Theatre and Change in South Africa*, Netherlands: Overseas Publishers Association, pp. 65–84.

Barba, E. (1985), 'The Nature of Dramaturgy: Describing Actions at Work,' *New Theatre Quarterly*, 1: 1, pp. 75–78.

Bergson, H. (1944), *Creative Evolution* (trans. Arthur Mitchell), New York: Random House.

Coplan, D. B. (1985), *In Township Tonight! South Africa's Black City Music and Theatre*, New York: Longman Group.

Davis, G. V. and Fuchs, A. (eds) (1996), *Theatre and Change in South Africa*, Netherlands: Overseas Publishers Association.

Doni, T. (2013), personal interview with A. Krueger, 10 June.

Fleishman, M. (1990), 'Workshop Theatre's Oppositional Form,' *South African Theatre Journal*, 4: 1, pp. 88–118.

——— (2009), 'Knowing Performance: Performance as Knowledge Paradigm for Africa,' *South African Theatre Journal*, 23, pp. 116–136.

——— (2011), '*Cargo*: Staging Slavery at the Cape,' *Contemporary Theatre Review*, 21: 1, pp. 8–19.

——— (2012), 'A Genealogy of Playwrighting in South Africa,' in *GIPCA Directors and Directing: Playwrights Symposium*, 24–26 August, University of Cape Town.

——— (2013), 'Lapsing Into Democracy: The State of Theatre in the Transitional State,' 30 January, Amherst College, University of Massachusetts.

Hauptfleisch, T. (2004), 'Eventification: Utilising the Theatrical System to Frame the Event,' in V. A. Cremona et al. (eds), *Theatrical Events: Borders, Dynamics, Frames*, Amsterdam and New York: Rodopi, pp. 279–302.

Huizinga, J. (1949), *Homo Ludens: A Study of the Play-Element in Culture*, London, Boston and Henley: Routledge and Kegan Paul.

Jones, S. (2009) 'The Courage of Complementarity: Practice-as-Research as a Paradigm Shift in Performance Studies,' in L. Allegue et al. (eds), *Practice-as-Research: In Performance and Screen*, Basingstoke: Palgrave Macmillan, pp. 18–32.

Khuse, Z. (2013), personal interview with A. Krueger, 11 June.

Larlham, P. (1991), 'Theatre in Transition: The Cultural Struggle in South Africa,' *TDR*, 35: 1, pp. 200–11.

Latour, B. (2005), *Reassembling the Social: An Introduction to Actor Network Theory*, Oxford: Oxford University Press.

Leo, C. (2013), personal interview with A. Krueger, 11 June.

Louw, I. (2013), personal interview with A. Krueger, October.

Magnet Theatre (2015), www.magnetheatre.co.za. Accessed 24 April 2015.

Marek, F. (2013), e-mail interview with A. Krueger, 22 June–18 July.

Mbembe, A. (2001), *On the Postcolony*, Berkeley: University of California Press.

Mbothwe, M. (2013), personal interview with A. Krueger, 9 June.

Muyanga, N. (2013), personal interview with A. Krueger, 12 June.

Pankhurst, M. (2013), personal interview with A. Krueger, 7 June.

Pather, J. (2013), personal interview with A. Krueger, 7 June.

Peterson, B. (1990), 'Apartheid and the Political Imagination in Black South African Theatre,' *Journal of Southern African Studies*, 16: 2 (Special Issue: Performance and Popular Culture), pp. 229–45.

Rancière, J. (2004), *The Politics of Aesthetics* (trans. Gabriel Rockhill), London: Continuum. First published 2000.

Reznek, J. and Fleishman, M. (2013), personal interview with A. Krueger, 13 June.

Roth, M. S. and Salas, C. G. (eds) (2001), *Disturbing Remains: Memory, History and Crisis in the Twentieth Century*, Los Angeles: The Getty Research Institute.

Sam, N. (2013), e-mail interview with A. Krueger, 23 June–16 August.

Sichel, A. (2010), 'Grappling with South African Physical Theatre,' *South African Theatre Journal*, 24: 1, pp. 41–50.

——— (2012) 'Magnet Theatre 25th Anniversary address at the launch of *The Magnet Theatre 'Migration' Plays*,' [unpublished], May, Cape Town, Magnet Theatre.

Taylor, D. (2003), *The Archive and the Repertoire: Performing Cultural Memory in the Americas*, Chicago: Duke University Press.

Wakashe, T. P. (1986), '"Pula": An Example of Black Protest Theatre in South Africa,' *TDR*, 30: 4, pp. 36–47.

Yisa, F. (2013), personal interview with A. Krueger, 12 June.

Žižek, S. (2004), 'Afterword: The Lesson of Rancière,' in J. Rancière, *The Politics of Aesthetics*, London: Continuum, pp. 69–79.

Notes

1. Anton Krueger conducted personal interviews with many Magnet collaborators in 2013 in preparation for this book; they included Jennie Reznek and Mark Fleishman, Jay Pather, Neo Muyanga, Faniswa Yisa, Mandla Mbothwe, Thando Doni, Illka Louw and Craig Leo, Frances Marek, Margie Pankhurst, Zwelakhe Khuse and Nolovuyo Sam. All quotations in this introduction are from these unpublished interviews.
2. Ellis Pearson is a performer and director specializing in 'grass roots' physical theatre. A graduate of the École Jacques Lecoq, he has performed at major festivals all over the world. William Kentridge is an internationally acclaimed artist and theatre director whose animated films have won worldwide acclaim. He has worked with Junction Avenue Theatre Company and Handspring Puppet Company. His most recent works include operas for the Metropolitan Opera in New York. Grethe Fox is a South African actress working in film, television and theatre. Lara Bye is an award-winning South African theatre director. Sylvaine Strike is a South African theatre director who won the coveted Young Artist of the Year award in 2006. James Cunningham is a South African performer and director best known for his comedy roles.
3. The conscription of all white males into the South African Defence Force (SADF) was compulsory from 1967-94, during which time military service varied from between nine months to two years. Towards the end of the 1980s, South Africa was engaged in a low-intensity border conflict with Angola (which formed the border of South West Africa, later Namibia, which had been colonized by South Africa). At the time, the SADF was also involved in numerous confrontations in black townships with factions of the African National Congress, Inkatha and other underground liberation movements.

4. They also performed at the Glastonbury Festival, the Melkweg in Amsterdam, the Battersea Arts Centre and the Old Bull in London, and the Edinburgh Festival, before being invited to Hong Kong. The Hong Kong invitation came to them while in Edinburgh.
5. See interview with Jay Pather ('Full Gamut of an Ideal Company').
6. See Flockemann ('Being There') for a more detailed analysis of *Medea*.
7. Mezzabotta circulated the video through her network of classics scholars. Their particular interest was in the way the classical narrative of *Medea* was reimagined in a contemporary African context.
8. See interview with Craig Leo ('Ideas Dying to be Born').
9. DV8, a London-based dance theatre company established in 1986 and run since then by Lloyd Newson, describes its work as 'taking risks, aesthetically and physically [...] breaking down the barriers between dance and theatre and, above all, communicating ideas and feelings clearly and unpretentiously. It is determined to be radical yet accessible' (https://www.dv8.co.uk/).
10. First Physical Theatre Company was founded in Grahamstown in 1993 by Professor Gary Gordon of the Rhodes University Drama Department. For more on First Physical and Gary Gordon, see Adrienne Sichel and Juanita Finestone-Praeg, both published in a 2010 Special Issue on Movement and Physical Theatre in *South African Theatre Journal* (SATJ).
11. Jacques Lecoq, who founded the École International du Théàtre Jacques Lecoq in Paris in 1956, espoused several principles in his training of actors for physical performance, or his Theatre of Gesture, including physical control, timing, the actor as creator, and thinking with/through the body (www.ecole-jacqueslecoq.com).
12. Andrew Buckland is an accomplished physical performer who, since 1981, has employed 'a dynamic and exciting combination of visual comedy, sophisticated political satire, clowning, physical theatre, mime and an explosive performance style' (andrewbuckland.wordpress.com).
13. Wakashe (1986: 45) says that 'In South Africa, the "West" in theatre terms most often means mainstream, bourgeois, naturalistic or Broadway-type musicals and dramas that are rejected by practitioners of protest/workshop theatre.'
14. Fleishman's essay 'Workshop Theatre as Oppositional Form' (1990) emphasizes the relevance of the workshop approach to devised productions emerging specifically from the early post-apartheid period. Since then, his views on play-making have been further developed and become more nuanced. In his more recent essay, for instance, 'A Geneology of Playwriting in South Africa' (2013), he works through the dynamics of devising in greater depth.
15. The apartheid system was founded on a series of laws which designated where members of certain racial groups (classified by the government) were permitted to live and work. It also segregated the population in terms of economic activity, education and sexual relations.

16. With only a few exceptions (Melville's *Moby Dick* [1993], Mia Couto's *Voices Made Night* [2000–14] and Max Frisch's *The Fire Raisers* [2004]), all of Magnet's productions have been devised creations. Both *Moby Dick* and *Voices* were adaptations of existing texts, although they did not use the text as a pre-determining script in the same way that working on a traditional play text might. Only *The Fire Raisers* used an existing play in anything like a conventional manner (see Fleishman ['Making Space for Ideas,' p. 75, note 2]).
17. See Fleishman ('Making Space for Ideas') for a deeper analysis of Magnet's image work.
18. The Constitution of South Africa guarantees parity to 11 linguistic groups (listed here in order of number of mother tongue speakers, from least to most): Ndebele, Venda, Swati, Ttsonga, Sotho, Setswana, Northern Sotho (Sesotho sa Leboa), English, Afrikaans, Xhosa and Zulu (http://www.gov.za/documents/constitution/chapter-1-founding-provisions, accessed 24 April 2015). Most South Africans are multilingual, i.e. able to speak more than one language. White English- and Afrikaans-speaking people tend not to have much ability in black African languages, but are fairly fluent in each other's language. Most South Africans speak English, which is ubiquitous in official, commercial and public life.
19. Another community engagement endeavour, The Culture Gangs Project, was started in 2010 and is ongoing in various townships around Cape Town.
20. According to Magnet's internal tracking as of January 2015, of the 15 first-time university attendees that have gained entrance to UCT with Magnet's support, eight have graduated and six are still currently in the system. 82 per cent of the remaining graduated trainees from the Full Time Training and Job Creation Program have either found employment in the professional theatre industry or are engaged in creating their own work.
21. Mavis Taylor (1924–97) was an actress, designer, director and an enormously influential teacher. She taught at the UCT Drama Department for many years, and was a formative influence on both Mark Fleishman and Jennie Reznek.

Production History

1987 *Cheap Flights*

Jennie Reznek's one-woman show that sparked the creation of Magnet Theatre. A woman is alone, trapped in a one-room flat, dreaming of escape in flights of fantasy. Directed by Roz Monat.

Reznek in *Cheap Flights* (1987). Photo credit: © Ruphin Coudyzer FPPSA. (ruphincoudyzer.com).

1991–93 *The Show's Not Over 'Til the Fat Lady Sings*
Reznek and Fleishman's first collaboration: a one-woman piece about a hungry woman weighted to the earth by her voracious appetite and her demons, who still dreams of flying. Starring Jennie Reznek as Belinda. Directed by Mark Fleishman.

1993 *Moby Dick*
An imaginative theatrical take on Melville's classic novel, melding its grand and gothic language with a rich physical imagery, and introducing an Everywoman character, who waits and hopes at home. The production featured Nicholas Ashby, Jamie Bartlett, Leslie Fong and Anna-Mart van der

Nicholas Ashby as Ishmael in *Moby Dick* (1993).
Photo credit: © Ruphin Coudyzer FPPSA. (ruphincoudyzer.com)

Leslie Fong as Queequeg in *Moby Dick* (1993).
Photo credit: © Ruphin Coudyzer FPPSA.
(ruphincoudyzer.com)

Merwe. It was adapted and directed by Mark Fleishman, with movement direction by Jennie Reznek, set design by Nadya Cohen, and masks and heads created by Adrian Kohler of the Handspring Puppet Company.

1994–96 *Medea*

Magnet's landmark production and first collaboration with Jazzart Dance Theatre. The story of two cultures incomprehensible to each other, Fleishman's *Medea* was a physical and linguistic adaptation of the Greek myth into Tamil, Tsotsitaal, Kaapse Taal, Zulu, Latin, English, Afrikaans and Xhosa. Performed by Bo Peterson, Kurt Wustmann, Jay Pather, Dawn Langdown, Heinrich Reisenhofer and the Jazzart Dance Theatre company. Directed by Mark Fleishman, with choreography by Alfred Hinkel. Designed by Craig Leo.

1995 *The Sun, The Moon and The Knife*
A performance piece based on versions of /Xam poems, written by Stephen Watson, from the Bleek and Lloyd collection. Directed by Fleishman, with choreography by Alfred Hinkel. Performed by Dawn Langdown and the Jazzart Dance Theatre.

1996–97 *Soe Loep Ons…Nou Nog!* [This is How We Walk…Still!]
Dawn Langdown's embodied stories of Cape Town's coloured community, simultaneously disempowered and dispossessed, yet filled with the vibrant song and dance of the 'Kaapse Klopse.' Directed by Mark Fleishman, with movement direction by Jennie Reznek. Performed by Dawn Langdown.

Dawn Langdown in *Soe Loop Ons…Nou Nog* (1996).
Photo credit: © Magnet Theatre.

1997 *'I Do' x 22*

Based on the true-life story of Linda, the most married woman in the world, who dances her way through 22 failed unions. Directed by Mark Fleishman and designed by Craig Leo. Performed by Jennie Reznek, Mark Hoeben and Kurt Wustmann (Cape Town)/Joshua Lindberg (Johannesburg).

1998 *Pump*

A travelling piece about water as a precious resource that toured schools, prisons, community centres, beaches and streets throughout the Western Cape. Performed by Lara Bye, Gaeten Schmidt, Thembani Luzipho, Craig Leo, Alan Committee, Mandla Mbothwe, Warona Seane and Makhaola Ndebele. Directed by Mark Fleishman and Jennie Reznek.

1999–2000 *Vlam I* [Flame 1]

A collaboration between Southern Edge Arts (Western Australia), Jazzart Dance Theatre and Magnet Theatre, *Vlam* [Flame] was part of the Millennium Celebration in Cape Town. A symbol of transformation at once terrible and devouring, purifying and restorative, *Vlam* was performed by 500 community arts practitioners on Reconciliation Day (16 December 1999) in a large vacant lot in District 6, under the shadow of Table Mountain with the harbour and the lights of the city as a backdrop.

1999–2000 *Vlam II* [Flame II]

A Jazzart Dance Theatre/Magnet Theatre reprise of *Vlam I*, this time focusing on revelation and resurrection, death and rebirth. Performed by Celeste Botha, Ondine Bello, Sbonakaliso Ndaba, Hurgen Cornelson, Megan Erasmus, Rich Handler, Charles Maema, Amanda Lane, Thembanio Lusipho, Philani Mbana and Vumile Sitikosi, with choreography by Sifiso Kweyama, Sbonakaliso Ndaba and Alfred Hinkel. Directed by Mark Fleishman.

2001 *Cold Waters/Thirsty Souls*

The fifth collaboration between the Jazzart Dance Theatre and Magnet Theatre. A lively interplay between structure and improvisation, between form and freedom. Performed by the Jazzart Dance Theatre company. Directed by Mark Fleishman and Alfred Hinkel, with original music by Jane Rademeyer and James Webb.

2002–06 *Onnest'bo* [Upside Down/Topsy Turvy]

Timed to mark the return of the District Six land deeds in 2002 to those forcibly removed from the area by the apartheid government, this collaboration with the District Six Museum explored the legacy and impact of forced removals. The production included an educational curriculum and intergenerational workshops between original inhabitants of District Six and high school learners. Created and performed by Thami Mbongo (Mbulelo Grootboom/Thando Mthi), Jennie Reznek, Lulama Masimini (Mdu Kweyama/Luvuyo Mbuto), Craig Leo (Stefan Blignaut), Charles Tertiens (Gary Naidoo), Amrain Ismail-Essop (Jazz Levenberg/Jacqui du Toit), Riana Alfreds and Wiseman Sithole. Directed by Mark Fleishman, with movement direction by Jennie Reznek.

2002–03 *53 Degrees*

A three-phase event – including an installation, a performance and an exhibition – around the theme of Robben Island. The production positioned personal narratives against the context of the broader liberation struggle in South Africa: a mother tries to make a piece of theatre after years of absence from the stage; Florrie Berndt is trapped in an icy cold current as she attempts the first ever Robben Island swim; and Makana/Nxele/Links, a nineteenth-century Xhosa prophet, tries to free his people from the tyranny of British rule by taking a giant leap across an abyss. Performed by Jennie Reznek, Gosekwang Poonyane and David Johnson (Grahamstown)/Gary Naidoo (Cape Town). Directed by Mark Fleishman.

2004 *The Fire Raisers*

The Fire Raisers was a collaboration between Swiss troupe Théâtre Spirale and Magnet Theatre. It brought together Max Frisch's witty text with a Brechtian chorus sung under the musical direction of Neo Muyanga. It explored the consequences that face a world in which the gap between rich and poor widens daily. Performed by Jamie Bartlett, Jennie Reznek, Hamadoun Kassogue, Ivan Abrahams, Patrick Mohr, Sizwe Msutu, Mas Soegeng, Faniswa Yisa, Bheki Ndlovu and Gary Naidoo, with costumes designed by Illka Louw. Directed by Mark Fleishman.

2004–05 *Rain in a Dead Man's Footprints*

Based on /Xam stories from the Bleek and Lloyd collection, a Magnet/Jazzart collaboration that re-imagined South Africa's history through /Xam understandings of time, furthering the explorations they began with *The Sun, The Moon and The Knife* (1995). This was Neo Muyanga's first project with Magnet. Directed by Mark Fleishman, with choreography by Jazzart Dance Theatre. Designed by Craig Leo.

2006–present *Every Year, Every Day, I Am Walking*
A piece about dislocation and what home means, *Every Year, Every Day, I Am Walking* has become Magnet's most performed piece, tracing the story of a young girl who brutally and irrevocably loses her family and home, and is then forced to journey to a strange new country through many dangers and uncertainties. Featuring Reznek and Yisa, both in multiple roles. Directed by Mark Fleishman, with music composed and performed by Neo Muyanga. Designed by Julia Anastasopoulos. It has toured across Africa, Asia, Europe and America.

2007 *Cargo*
A performative engagement with the archive of slavery at the Cape, *Cargo* was the seventh and final collaboration between Magnet and Jazzart. Featuring Jennie Reznek, Faniswa Yisa and the Jazzart Dance Theatre, as well as members of the Jazzart Dance Theatre Young Adult Training and Job Creation Programme. Directed by Mark Fleishman, with set and costumes designed by Craig Leo, and music composed and performed by Neo Muyanga.

2008 *Isivuno Sama Phupha* [Harvest of Dreams]
Under Mandla Mbothwe's direction, this production was part of Magnet Theatre's Community Groups Intervention. It was Mbothwe's first major production for the company, weaving a lyrical story between places and spaces, between waking-time and sleeping-time. Costumes by Illka Louw.

2009 *ingcwaba lendoda lise cankwe ndlela*
[the grave of the man lies next to the road]
A stirring, vibrant multimedia work around the African notion of home, associations with the loss of the umbilical cord, as well as graves, histories, clans and ancestors. *ingcwaba lendoda* explored the physical, emotional, spiritual and intellectual dislocation of young black South Africans whose origins lie a long way down the N2 in the Eastern Cape. Directed by Mandla Mbothwe, with choreography by Xolani Rani and choral direction by Nolufefe Mtswabe. Featuring Faniswa Yisa and trainees from the Magnet Theatre Full Time Training and Job Creation Programme.

2010 *Die Vreemdeling* [The Stranger]
Devised by the cast from a short story by Frances Marek, *Die Vreemdeling* explores the impact of a stranger on an insulated and fearful community. Directed by Mark Fleishman and Frances Marek. Featuring David Johnson (Rudi Swart), Ephraim Gordon and Dann-Jacques Mouton.

2010–14 *Inxeba Lomphilisi – The Wound of a Healer*

A healer and her helper, Khehle, wander along the N2. Between sunset and sunrise they listen to the stories of the dead and those that have disappeared along the road, trying to help them find peace. Directed by Mandla Mbothwe. Featuring Faniswa Yisa, Asanda Rilityana, Thando Doni, Luvo Tamba, Thumeka Mzayiya, as well as Magnet Theatre trainees: Aphiwe Menziwa, Nolufefe Ntshuntshe, Thembekile Komani, and the drummer, Mzimkhulu Mtelekiso.

2011 *The Children and the Bees*

Directed by Mark Fleishman, assisted by Frances Marek, Alex Halligey and Faniswa Yisa, *The Children and the Bees* was created and performed as a companion piece to the opera *Brundibár*, based on a Czech folk tale, which was performed 55 times in the Nazi ghetto, Terezín, before its composer and many of the children in the cast were transported to the gas chambers of Auschwitz. *The Children and the Bees*, performed at the Artscape Theatre in July 2011, explored themes of displacement, migration and refugees, drawing on the testimonies of child survivors from across the world to weave together magic fairy tales and grim reality.

2012 *running with goldfish and gift wrapping the sea*

Physically inventive and sparkling with playful humour, this was the first production of the 2012–13 trainees in the Magnet Theatre Full Time Training and Job Creation Programme. The simple, practical problems of packing up and unpacking, of freezing and melting, became the starting points for this exploration of the wide-ranging experiences of a group of young South Africans. Directed by Brink Scholtz with The Magnet Theatre trainees: Asiphe Lile, Babalwa Makwetu, Bulelani Mabutyana, Dustin Beck, Jeoffrey Makobela, Lubabalo Nontwana, Marlon Swarts, Musa Silwana, Nomzamo Kula, Rozanne Holland, Siphenathi Mayekiso, Sisipho Mbopa, Sivuyile Dunjwa, Thukelo Maka, Thulisa Mayalo, Yonela Sithela, Stacy Malgarte, Eddie Newman and Lwando Sindaphi.

2012 *Kragbox* [Power Box]

Kragbox turns the spotlight on people who live in the shadows of contemporary Cape Town, in the dark forgotten corners of the Cape Flats. The piece explores notions of male identity and masculinity in communities dominated by gangsterism and violence. It tells a story of friendship, loyalty, betrayal and sacrifice; of poverty and violence and the struggle to survive. Originally created by Frances Marek, with Dann-Jacques Mouton and Ephraim Gordon.

2012 *Autopsy*

A detective thriller and multimedia feast featuring Faniswa Yisa as a high-heeled forensic investigator who excavates the current African landscape, unearthing shady deals, unsolved murders, Chinese landlords, traditional healers, shebeen owners and wealthy oil magnates. Directed by Mark Fleishman, and performed by Jennie Reznek, Faniswa Yisa, Dann-Jacques Mouton and Mandisi Sindo. Video images by Sanjin Muftic. Set and costume design by Illka Louw.

2013 *Beyond Vice*

A collaboration with a practice-based research project organized by Ola Johannsson from Sweden, *Beyond Vice* played at the Uppsala Stadsteater. The play explores questions of gender inequality as they play out within the dramatically different contexts of Sweden and South Africa, juxtaposing two narratives: in Uppsala a pompous Swedish professor falls in love with his ambitious South African student; while in Cape Town, a street-smart South African man falls in love with a naive Swedish aid worker. In a playfully provocative manner, these relationships offer an intimate and often uncomfortable view into the complex power relations of gender, but also of cross-cultural engagement. Directed by Brink Scholtz, and performed by Chiminae Ball, Björn Dahlman, Lise Edman, Dann-Jacques Mouton, Asanda Rilityana and Helena Sandström.

2000, 2014 *Voices Made Night*

An evocative assemblage of interpretations of short stories by Mozambican author Mia Couto, whose writing is rooted in the strange and often bizarre realities of life in contemporary African societies in transition. The original cast in 2000 were Gosekwang Poonyane, Rehane Abrahams, Mandla Mbothwe and Jane Rademeyer; the 2012 cast included Jennie Reznek, Faniswa Yisa, Mfundo Tshazibane, Dann-Jacques Mouton, Richard September, Thando Doni and Chiminae Ball. Directed by Mark Fleishman.

2014 *Passage*

A collaboration with The Baxter Theatre Centre and directed by Thando Doni, *Passage* explores how boys transition into men in a multicultural context. Looking at the rites of passage that boys undergo in South Africa to move from childhood to responsible adulthood, the production points to actions that men can take to redefine and reconstruct a positive notion of masculinity. Featuring Richard Tafane, Aphiwe Menziwa, Jeoffrey Makobela, Nicholas Campbell and Daniel Richards.

2014 *Ukhanyo* [I Am the Light of the World]
As the title suggests, this play explores aspirations and identity in the context of being young in an evolving democracy, as the youth of South Africa 'find their light' and express their voices. Directed by Thando Doni. Created with the 2014–15 trainees in the Full Time Training and Job Creation Programme: Loyiso Damoyi, Emmanuel Ntsamba, Meagan Booysen, Beviol Swartz, Tina Hashe, Mfundo Zono, Kay Smith, Luthando Mvandaba, Athenkosi Mfamela, Thando Suselo, Natasha Gana, Willmare Meloy, Lwando Magwaca, Zimkitha Mzimba, Ferdinand Williams, Zolisa Nkonyana, Zizipho Quluba, Anne Bosch and Livie Ncanywa.

2014–present *TREE/BOOM/UMTHI*
A delicate, tender performance about the relationship between a man, a tree and the seasons. Performed in three different languages (depending on the audience), *TREE/BOOM/UMTHI* uses song, image and the physical body to tell the story. It is designed for children aged three to seven years old. Directed by Jennie Reznek and designed by Craig Leo. Created by the company: Thulisa Mayalo, Sivuyile Dunjwa, Sisipho Mbopa and Lubabalo Nontwana.

2014 *Nomvula – The Girl of the Rain*
Created by the 2014–15 Expanded Public Works Placements – recent graduates of the Full Time Training and Job Creation Programme – *Nomvula* tells the story of a young girl's attempts to right the wrongs of man's destructive behaviour and its impact on the environment. Aimed specifically for five to ten-year-olds, it was directed by Thando Doni and created with the company: Lwanda Sindaphi, Asiphe Lili, Siphenathi Mayekiso and Sivuyile Dunjwa.

2014–present *I Turned Away And She Was Gone*
A poetic reworking of the Persephone story, written and performed by Jennie Reznek. Directed by Mark Fleishman, choreographed by Ina Wichterich, designed by Craig Leo, and with original music by Neo Muyanga.

2015 *Heart of Redness*
A forthcoming collaboration with the Cape Town Opera, based on Zakes Mda's novel. It will feature music by Neo Muyanga.

Current Youth Development Projects

Full Time Training and Job Creation Programme

Magnet offers 20 bursaried places in a two-year, full-time skills development and bridging programme for talented township youth from marginalized communities. The programme intends to bridge the gap between townships and tertiary institutions of education, as well as the professional theatre industry as a whole. The programme offers classes in play, imagination, physical theatre, voice, dance, singing, improvisation and play-making. Training takes place Monday to Friday between 9 a.m. and 4.30 p.m. There are organized visits to the theatre to expose the groups to mainstream and community performance. They are placed in internships to shadow various aspects of the theatre industry. The participants are encouraged to maintain their connection with their communities and with their groups. The programme is designed by Jennie Reznek, Mandla Mbothwe and Mark Fleishman, and the classes are taught by highly experienced theatre practitioners and teachers. As always with Magnet Theatre's work, the focus of the training is on the body as a universal language that can communicate across cultures and verbal language, while understanding that the teaching of physical theatre is one of the responses to violence and the violated body. The programme focuses on the development of skills and on the ability to generate new work. Each trainee receives a bursary (or stipend) to ensure that they have transport and food to attend the training. Magnet Theatre is currently busy with the fourth cohort of students.

Community Arts Development

Cape Town Townships

Culture Gangs

The Culture Gangs programme is a support programme for extant drama groups in Cape Town. There are hundreds of school-going and unemployed youth in the townships who are drawn to the theatre as a way of expressing and dealing with the harsh realities of their lives. The Culture Gangs programme exposes these young people to notions of creative thinking and play that will serve them in all aspects of their lives. It creates gangs of youth who are committed to culture and not to crime.

Magnet Theatre works with eight drama groups each year (involving about 250 youth), developing new products, running monthly skills workshops, organizing theatre visits, providing career guidance and assistance with identifying and applying for further education opportunities. The year ends with a community showcase. The current Culture Gangs Project is facilitated by Zwelakhe Khuse and Nolan Africa, and is operational in Khayelitsha, Nyanga, Langa and Manenberg.

Culture Gangs interventions in Khayelitsha (2014).
Photo credit: © Mark Wessels.

Cederberg Municipality

Clanwilliam Arts Project

The communities along the N7 are historically some of the most under-resourced and isolated in the Western Cape region. Magnet Theatre has been working in the area for the past 15 years, running the yearly Clanwilliam Arts Project with UCT and with the support of Fairheads Financial Services (until 2012). The project is a week-long arts residency including art, drama, dance, lantern-making, drumming and music, with 700 school learners focused around /Xam stories from the Bleek and Lloyd Collection. Magnet Theatre brings up to 40 young arts facilitators into the town, and the project culminates in a parade and performance to over 2000 people.

Farm Schools Project

Current rural arts facilitator Nolan Africa visits four sites in remote areas of Cederberg, working with farm children after school in order to teach them creativity, imagination and play – skills enabling empowerment and the ability to imagine alternative futures.

PART ONE

Concepts: Making Space for Ideas

Chapter 2

Making Space for Ideas: The Knowledge Work of Magnet Theatre

Mark Fleishman

Mark Fleishman is a professor in the Department of Drama at the University of Cape Town, as well as Magnet's co-artistic director. He is an award-winning director and has directed most of Magnet Theatre's productions since The Show's Not Over 'Til the Fat Lady Sings *(1991–93). His research is concerned with theatre-making in theory and practice, including physical theatre, interactive dramaturgy and site-specific community-based performance. His work has been published in the* South African Theatre Journal, *the* Contemporary Theatre Review, Theatre Research International *and various other edited volumes.*

The work that Magnet has produced over the past 29 years can be described as 'boundary work' in the sense in which the term is used by Henk Borgdorff (2012). In an interview on artistic research,[1] Borgdorff suggests that artworks that propose to be research projects are 'boundary objects,' a term he borrows from Thomas F. Gieryn (1983) and which he describes as objects 'that [change their] ontological and epistemological nature depending on the context in which [they are] used' (Borgdorff 2012: 177). He suggests that 'artistic research places itself on the border between academia and the art world' (2012: 177). To this extent, I am interested in using this chapter to explore the particular ways in which Magnet's performance practice – that which is produced for the art world, and which has its existence and a particular set of meanings within it – might be understood as quite consciously making space for ideas or generating a particular way of thinking, both about itself as performance and about aspects of the world beyond the theatre. In other words, the ways in which it can be understood as a research or knowledge practice in the academic world.

I would propose that Magnet's work is a process of research both in the sense of 'research for' theatre – gathering material for the making of work through intensive processes of information gathering that makes use of more conventional research methods, as well as somatic or embodied methods – and in the sense of 'research about' theatre – a self-reflexive interest in the methods and particularities of our practice; what in fact is actually going on in the multitude of individual moments and the flow of our processes. But it is also 'research by means of' theatre in so far as how we make work, and how that work functions in the world, is a way of thinking the world and the work. In this sense, it is hopefully performative in the way in which it enacts something, bringing something into being in the world through doing and making, as well as through the fabrication of concepts, ideas and speculative projections that might change attitudes and beliefs – a process I would describe as a project of active and creative citizenship in a transitional social context.

In what follows, I will begin by outlining the relationship between philosophy and performance broadly, before moving on to discuss the particular knowledge practice in Magnet's work using one production process to ground the argument. Finally, I will try to show how individual Magnet productions form part of larger research assemblages, with different modes of articulation, within our overall body of work.

Performance Practice and Philosophy

In a recent article in *Theatre Research International*, Laura Cull (2012: 20) asks the question: 'What is the relationship between performance and philosophy?' She suggests that in theatre and performance studies we need 'less philosophy per se' and more attention paid to 'specific philosophies' which 'provide us with the resources to rethink performance itself as a kind of philosophy, and indeed to reconceive what counts as philosophy' (2012: 21). She points out that what motivated her interest in this question was primarily a desire to articulate how the arts work in different ways; ways that value and express those aspects of performance practice, such as 'art's affective presence and material force' (2012: 21) and the 'seemingly ineffable' aspects of what we do that other discourses always fail to express (2012: 20).

According to Cull (2012: 21), this is not a question of simply applying philosophy to performance, but rather 'that the rare marriage between performance and philosophy is at its richest and most egalitarian if philosophy is willing to encounter performance as thinking.' In other words, performance practice avoids application 'when it conceives of itself as a way of thinking rather than the mere demonstration of existing ideas.' For Cull (2012: 23), the meeting of performance and philosophy must bring about 'new ideas [for] both on the basis of a mutually transformative encounter.' Her conclusion is that:

> [...] we need to move away from the application of the theoretical models we already possess and towards an embodied encounter with the resistant materiality of performance's thinking, its embodied-thinking, participatory thinking, or durational thinking – encounters that generate new ideas of what thought is and where, when and how it occurs.
>
> (Cull 2012: 25)

The example she uses to support this proposal emerges from practice as research, which 'has already gone some way to explore the nature of performance's kind of thinking, taking a particular and strategically necessary interest in how performance practice produces new knowledge' (Cull 2012: 25). However, she warns that:

Jennie Reznek in *Cheap Flights* (1987).
Photo credit: © Ruphin Coudyzer FPPSA. (ruphincoudyzer.com)

Jennie Reznek in *The Show's Not Over 'Til the Fat Lady Sings* (1991). Photo credit: © Ruphin Coudyzer FPPSA. (ruphincoudyzer.com)

Dawn Langdown in *Medea* (1994).
Photo credit: © Ruphin Coudyzer FPPSA. (ruphincoudyzer.com)

Heinrich Reisenhofer and John Linden in *The Sun, The Moon and The Knife* (1995).
Photo credit: © Garth Stead.

Heinrich Reisenhofer and Jazzart dancers in *The Sun, The Moon and The Knife* (1995).
Photo credit: © Garth Stead.

Dawn Langdown
in *Soe Loop Ons ...Nou Nog* (1996).
Photo credit: © Magnet Theatre.

Jennie Reznek as Linda, the most married woman in the world in *'I Do' x 22* (1997).
Photo credit: © Ruphin Coudyzer FPPSA. (ruphincoudyzer.com)

Warona Seane and Makhaola Ndebele performing outdoors in Hermanus in *Pump* (1998).
Photo credit: © Magnet Theatre.

Jazzart Dance Theatre and Magnet Theatre's *Vlam* [Flame] (1999) was part of the Millennium Celebration.
Photo credit: © Garth Stead.

Cold Waters/Thirsty Souls (2001) was the fifth collaboration between the Jazzart Dance Theatre and Magnet Theatre. Photo credit: © Garth Stead.

Onnest'bo [Upside Down/Topsy Turvy] explored the legacy and impact of forced removals in District Six. Photo credit: © Mark Wessels.

Jennie Reznek and David Johnson explore the legacy of Robben Island in *53 Degrees* (2005-6). Photo credit: © Garth Stead.

The Fire Raisers (2004), a collaboration between Swiss troupe Théâtre Spirale and Magnet Theatre based on Max Frisch's text, with a Brechtian chorus and musical direction by Neo Muyanga.
Photo credit: © Garth Stead.

Rain in a Dead Man's Footprints (2004) re-imagined South Africa's history through/Xam understandings of time.
Photo credit: © Garth Stead.

Rain in a Dead Man's Footprints (2004) continued the work begun in *The Sun, The Moon and The Knife* (1995). Photo credit: © Garth Stead.

A play about dislocation and what home means, *Every Year, Every Day, I Am Walking* (2006-present) has become Magnet's most performed piece.
Photo credit: © Mark Wessels.

Reznek and Yisa *in Every Year, Every Day, I Am Walking* (2006-present).
Photo credit: © Mark Wessels.

Jazzart and Magnet's final collaboration: *Cargo* (2007).
Photo credit: © Garth Stead.

Performers present their shoes in *Cargo* (2007).
Photo credit: © Garth Stead.

Reznek and Owen Manamela-Mogane in *Cargo* (2007).
Photo credit: © Garth Stead.

Part of Magnet Theatre's Community Groups Intervention *Isivuno Sama Phupha* [Harvest of Dreams] (2008) was directed by Mandla Mbothwe.
Photo credit: © R. Keith. All Rights Reserved. Robert4keeps@gmail.com.

ingcwaba lendoda lise cankwe ndlela [the grave of the man lies next to the road] (2009). Directed by Mandla Mbothwe. Photo credit: © Craig Leo.

Screen projections in *ingcwaba lendoda lise cankwe ndlela* (2009).
Photo credit: © Craig Leo.

Magnet's commitment to telling stories in multiple languages.
ingcwaba lendoda lise cankwe ndlela (2009).
Photo credit: © Craig Leo.

> [...] the production of knowledge is arguably only one definition of thinking, or specifically of 'research' [...]; indeed, rather than applying this definition of thinking to practice (as if it were the same as text-based research), perhaps we need to look to performance itself to produce new ideas of what thinking is.
>
> (Cull 2012: 25)

As Cull herself points out, the performance as research (PaR) movement has for some time now set out to investigate what 'performance as thinking' might mean. Having been involved with PaR both in the South African context and in the context of the International Federation of Theatre Research (IFTR) – where I have been a member of the PaR working group and its co-convenor for a number of years – my thinking has been shaped by the discourse generated in that context, while my work with Magnet has also contributed to that discourse. In other words, there has been a mutually beneficial relationship backwards and forwards between the practice at Magnet and the meta-theoretical ideas on PaR developed amongst international colleagues though workshops and conferences.

The general consensus is that PaR concerns research that is carried out through or by means of performance; using methodologies and specific methods familiar to performance practitioners; and where the output is (at least in part, if not entirely) presented through performance. I have previously argued that PaR is a form of creative evolution in the Bergsonian sense (Fleishman 2012a); not a progressivist building towards a finality, nor a mechanistic unfolding of a predetermined plan in search of something it knows exists before the search begins. It begins with energy (an impulse, an idea, an intuition, a hunch), which is then durationally channelled through repetition, on both micro levels (of bodies, movements, sounds, improvisations, moments) and macro levels (of events, productions, projects, installations), in variable and indeterminable directions, in search of difference. Such an ongoing channelling has been described by theorists of practice as a kind of 'tuning' (Pickering 1993: 564) or 'tinkering' (Knorr Cetina 1981: 34); a set of adjustments in the reciprocal encounters between different sets of human and non-human actors.

According to Joseph Rouse (2001: 190), 'the concept of practices is typically invoked to explain continuities or commonalities among the activities of social groups.' The particular practice Magnet has been involved in for 29 years is the making of performance works or productions – a practice I have described as dramaturgy.

I have outlined the features of this dramaturgical practice elsewhere (Fleishman 2011; 2012b). Following Tim Ingold, I have described it as a process that is more about dwelling than building:

> [T]he forms people build, whether in the imagination or on the ground, arise within the current of their involved activity, in the specific relational contexts of their practical engagements in their surroundings. [...] People do not import their ideas, plans or

> mental representations into the world, since that very world, to borrow a phrase from Merleau-Ponty, is the homeland of their thoughts. Only because they already *dwell* therein can they think the thoughts they do.
>
> (Ingold 2000: 186, emphasis mine)

According to this view, we build forms not as a consequence of having had thoughts, but as a consequence of dwelling, of being in the world, of being in ongoing action. And one kind of action we take whilst dwelling – one among many – is 'taking thought' or imagining ways of meeting our needs: 'In the process of dwelling we build' (Ingold 2000: 188).

In line with this view, in Magnet's dramaturgical process, we don't build a structure for the performance to dwell in; we dwell in the landscape over time in order to learn how to build there. It is not a case of building a container in the mind and then filling it; it is a case of allowing our embodied, active and participatory dwelling to reveal the right container. This is a methodological approach that reverses the cognitive model. It is not a Cartesian thinking to effect being; rather, it is an incarnated, participatory development of thought through creative discovery, and paying attention to the specific landscape of each individual project as it emerges. The dramaturgical view is from the inside rather than from a distanced perspective. By paying attention to the embodied encounters that unfold in the process, both content and a way of creating form suggest themselves. For example, when making *Cargo* (2007), we did not begin with the idea of using the inventory lists of household contents produced by the Master of the Orphan Chamber in the Cape Colony as a structural device for the performance fragments that were created. We discovered the lists and the research that had been generated from the lists as part of our dwelling in the slave archive. That discovery, alongside the ongoing generation of performance material, suggested itself as the most appropriate structural container for the final work produced.

Following Andre Lepecki, who points to the 'syncretic composition' of the word 'choreography' that fuses 'two apparently incongruous terms – movement and writing – into one single linguistic sign' (Allsopp & Lepecki 2008: 1), I have suggested elsewhere (Fleishman 2014) that Magnet's practice is a choreographic one. In other words, it is a process of writing with bodies in and through movement. Since our inception in 1987, it has been a feature of all of Magnet's work that theatre originates with specific bodies in specific spaces, rather than with words on a page. Indeed, there have only been few occasions over that time in which the script has been the starting point for a production, rather than a record of what has been created through processes of physical making.[2]

Furthermore, as a choreographic process it involves '*the making and modulation of assemblages* [...] the explorative associating or coupling of materially heterogeneous kinds of actions of humans as well as non-human performers' (Laermans 2008: 11, emphasis in original). Such choreographic assemblages involve a non-hierarchical collection of human and non-human bodies encountering each other in such a way so as not to favour the human bodies over, for example, bodies of light, sound or scenography. What emerges from such assemblages is a particular singularity that is more than the sum of the individual parts; a singularity characterized by a complex layering of movement(s), which engages the audience in a bodily and visceral way in a space that is beyond language. There are, for example, many consciously crafted moments or images in *Every Year, Every Day, I Am Walking* (2006–present): the swallowing of the origami flower by Ernestine; the plastic refuse bags that float through the space and that Mama eventually climbs into, becoming a cocooned figure rolling from side to side on the ground; the shoes and the sand on the table or on Mama's body in the refugee camp, where the body in movement, light, music/sound and material object combine to produce a cumulative effect that vibrates in the space, radiating outward and producing an affective intensity that engages the viewer in an immediate, sensual, felt and somatic way. These images are poetic in the sense in which Bachelard (1994: vx) employs the term 'a sudden salience on the surface of the psyche' that takes us by surprise; something which we have not been prepared for, but nevertheless requires us to be receptive in the very moment of its appearance, 'in the very ecstasy of the newness of the image.' These are not images that are easily translated into words or made sense of, but they are sensed by the audience, and they offer themselves as moments of exchange, of reciprocity, in which meaning and feeling are produced in an active way. Often in feedback sessions with audiences after performances, it is these images that stick and that are returned to over and over because of the impact that they have had that cannot easily be explained.

My argument here is that besides being a practice of making works, the practice of dramaturgy is also a knowledge practice. In other words, while making space for new works, Magnet also makes space for thinking, for raising questions, generating ideas and developing concepts. In this respect, Magnet Theatre is a particular 'knowledge setting' (Knorr Cetina 1999). As such, it has its own 'epistemic culture' that is defined as 'those amalgams of arrangements and mechanisms [...] which, in a given field, make up *how we know what we know*' (1999: 1, emphasis in original). Any such epistemic culture has its own knowledge-producing strategies that are not so much regulated as normative patterns of activities. In other words, while there is definitely no list of rules to be followed, there are certain normative behaviours that characterize Magnet's work processes. However, these are difficult to articulate in words. Instead, they are shared through observation and participation; through being alongside and within the work itself; and they are also not always the same or even required, but shift in relation to individual projects and circumstances.

While unpacking this 'epistemic culture' completely is beyond the scope of this chapter, I would like to highlight four features: the method of practice, the nature of the object of knowledge, the structure of participation, and the philosophical orientation. First, as I alluded to above, the body is the central methodological instrument in Magnet's knowledge practice. Knorr Cetina (1999: 99) describes the body as a 'black-box instrument.' By this she means two things. Firstly, that the body is silent; it provides 'no systematic description of sensory or bodily behaviours, no written instructions as to the appropriate bodily reactions in specific experimental situations, and no behavioural rules to be followed' (1999: 99). Secondly, through repeated physical and sensory activities, the body becomes experienced. A specific 'tacit knowledge' becomes inscribed in the body, which Knorr Cetina (1999: 99) describes as 'a bodily archive of manual and instrumental knowledge that is not written down and only clumsily expressed.' Stephen Turner (1994) has highlighted the fact that such body experience is difficult to share, and uses this to suggest that something like a coherent practice that is shared by a group may not be said to exist at all. I would suggest that such coherent practice is not impossible, particularly in a discipline like theatre that relies heavily, and as a matter of course, on the body-to-body transference of skills and knowledge (or the way one body affects, and is affected by, other bodies). In addition, while there is clearly nothing like a tacit rule book that must be followed when engaging in such a practice, there is an agreed upon set of values, principles and techniques that is not so much laid down through a linear process of instruction or a set of standing orders, but rather is produced collaboratively through ongoing, iterative conversation, in which parties feel their way towards a level of stable understanding and agreement.

Second, the nature of the knowledge objects (plays, projects, questions explored) in Magnet's knowledge practice (our work over the past 29 years) can best be described as what historian of biology Hans-Jörg Rheinberger calls 'epistemic things.' According to Knorr Cetina (2001: 181), Rheinberger is particularly interested in 'objects of knowledge that escape fixation,' that are less like things and more like projections and/or processes. She suggests that these are knowledge objects that are 'open, question-generating and complex' (2001: 181); that there is an 'incompleteness' about them and they unfold indefinitely over time and in unanticipated directions, never quite attaining a finality or fixedness. All we can hope for are representations that stand in for these knowledge objects as if they were able to hold together the object in time long enough for us to grasp its possibilities. Even when the project or production is 'finished,' there is a sense that it could have been otherwise; that it is never quite perfected or final or definitive. If we were to continue to work on it, the object would mutate and produce other meanings and significances. Furthermore, it would generate more questions, extend the practice, but it would remain unfinished, incomplete.

In my understanding, this description of a particular kind of research – that which is dynamic, creative, constructive and drawn from biological sciences – is close to what we are engaged in when performance practice becomes research practice. Even if productions emerge from such processes that have lives in the professional theatre context, and that end up as archival objects or traces in the company's historical record, as research objects they remain unfinished parts of a continually unfolding thinking process that expands in time and across space, intersecting with other unfinished objects and their thought processes along the way. As Knorr Cetina (2001: 184) reminds us, 'a stable name is not an expression and indicator of stable thinghood.' In other words, just because a Magnet project produces a production with a title – a *Cargo* (2007), an *Onnest'bo* [Upside Down/Topsy Turvy] (2002-6), or an *Every Year, Every Day, I Am Walking*, for example – does not indicate that the name represents a stabilized object. Over time that object is changing: either by virtue of its continual performance in a variety of diverse contexts, to different audiences and sometimes with different performers (various aspects of the production intensify and clarify over time); or by virtue of its shifting life in the somatic memories of those who encountered it, and who are then reminded of it or recall it for one reason or another at another time or compare it to other works by Magnet, or other performance-makers, thinkers, writers or artists engaged with similar themes and ideas. The production of *Onnest'bo*, for example, was clearly different when it was performed for school learners on the Cape Flats, who have strong personal and familial relationships with the removals from District Six and the aftermath thereof, and when it was performed at the National Arts Festival in Grahamstown, where the audience had no necessary connection with District Six at all. Again, when the performance moved to the District Six Museum building in what was once District Six, and many ex-District Six residents attended, both the effect and the affect of the production shifted. *53 Degrees* was initially designed to be performed on three floors of an old, abandoned power station on the outskirts of Grahamstown. When it performed in Cape Town, it was staged in the Intimate Theatre, which is a very small venue (as the name suggests), on only one floor. The whole production needed to be re-conceptualized for the small space. *Every Year, Every Day, I Am Walking* has been performed over an eight-year period in a diverse range of contexts around the world (to audiences that included refugee communities and audiences that did not). But the cast has also changed periodically over that time, with Nolovuyo Sam replacing Faniswa Yisa as partner to Jennie in the production. The fact that Nolovuyo is younger than Faniswa changes the feeling of the relationship between mother and daughter, and audience members who have seen both versions have reported sensing a difference in how they felt, without identifying the change in casting.

Third, each Magnet production has a project team which constitutes a 'repertoire of expertise' (Knorr Cetina 1999: 225) required to bring the production to fruition. There are two levels of participants at Magnet that I will loosely define as 'practitioners' and 'leaders.' The practitioners (performers, designers, technicians, composers) are passing through, making their particular contribution to the project (or perhaps a series of projects over time), while at the same time building up their own profiles. This leads to a certain tension between what the company is trying to do and what the individuals aspire to do. The practitioners are also more or less experienced, more or less involved, and have spent more or less time working with Magnet. On the other hand, the leaders (primarily Jennie and I), often fulfil specific practitioner functions, but are usually oriented differently. A significant part of our orientation as leaders is outward, away from the specifics of the work itself to the society broadly. As leaders, we have the responsibility for ensuring the sustainability of the company as a whole, as well as for ensuring that the work is disseminated successfully: whether in the form of performance on various platforms; or in the form of the discourse on the practice which is disseminated in both formal and informal ways through a variety of channels, both written and oral, analogue and digital. What this means is that, over time, and as the company has grown and become more successful, Jennie and I have been pulled away from doing the creative work to writing grant proposals, mentoring new people, attending meetings, and relaying information backwards and forwards between the company and the world. This means that new individuals – like director Mandla Mbothwe, for example – have taken on directorial functions on several productions. A kind of hierarchy has begun to develop at the practitioner level, with certain practitioners (like Mbothwe) absorbing greater leadership roles. Their own productions, while falling under the Magnet banner and suffused with the company's practice culture that has been built up over time, have begun to take on the particular intellectual concerns, aesthetic orientations and predilections of the new leader figure. For instance, Mandla's work on *ingcwaba lendoda lise cankwe ndlela* [the grave of the man lies next to the road] (2009) and *Inxeba Lomphilisi – The Wound of a Healer* (2010–14) are prime examples of his desire to create work in Xhosa around issues of migration and memory. There is a certain degree of play at work here, given that, while Magnet absorbs these new directions and ideas and they become part of the evolving practice culture of the company, an unacceptable tension would be produced if they were to deviate significantly from our core values and principles. Even where the absorption of the new directions does not produce a conflict in terms of the work produced, it might very well produce an internal conflict for the lead practitioner who begins to feel the need to individuate, to find a new space in which to develop independently from Magnet, at which point s/he leaves to take on a leadership role somewhere else. After many years of working as part of Magnet, and having been established as a co-director of the company with Jennie and I, Mandla left to take on the artistic direction of the Steve Biko Centre in King William's Town. And Faniswa Yisa, who was a resident performer in the company for many years, over time began to feel the need to separate and to develop her own projects, and take on roles outside of the company. This does not mean that the ties with the company are severed completely; it simply shifts the level of involvement, and in some senses expands the reach of Magnet's influence into other areas and other organizational contexts. What these growth dynamics point to is not a picture of a closed and stable structure, but rather a kind of rhizomatic structure with different entry and exit points; an entity that is open to the world and adaptable to new things, and in which a multiplicity of pathways and event nodes intersect, entangle and engage to produce a fluid and evolving practice, which is still sufficiently coherent so as to be recognizable as Magnet Theatre's work.

Fourth, if Magnet's practice *is* a way of thinking, another way of doing philosophy, then it is a philosophy understood in Deleuze and Guattari's (1994: 52) terms not as a set of concepts that are 'waiting for us ready made like heavenly bodies' to be applied to the world and our engagement with it, but rather as part of the 'art of forming, inventing and fabricating concepts.' Furthermore, it follows A. N. Whitehead (1978: 9) in understanding philosophy as 'an experimental adventure,' or 'an adventure of ideas' (1967). For Whitehead (1978: 11), every 'new idea introduces a new alternative,' a new way of approaching and understanding experience. As Isabelle Stengers (2011: 11) remarks in her book *Thinking with Whitehead*, to think with Whitehead today is 'to imagine, and to fight against "ready-made" models and above all, not to despair.'

> To think with Whitehead today is also to affirm that the success of a philosophical proposition is not to resist objections but to give rise to what he himself calls a 'leap of the imagination' (Whitehead, *Process and Reality*, 4) – and the point is to experiment with the effects of that leap: what it does to thought, what it obliges one to do what it renders important, and what it makes remain silent.
>
> (Stengers 2011: 22)

With these thoughts from Whitehead in mind, let us take the imaginative leap into a concrete example of Magnet's work: the production *53 Degrees* (2003–03).

Gosekwang Poonyane in *53 Degrees* (2002).
Photo credit: © Garth Stead.

The Leap: *53 Degrees* (2002–03)

I might have chosen any one of the many productions we have done over the past 29 years to illustrate our process, but I have chosen *53 Degrees* – a project based on the history of Robben Island, the low-lying, rocky outcrop situated some 10km off the coast of Cape Town that has been occupied in one form or another from before the first colonial arrival in the seventeenth century. It has been used as a place of exile, banishment, isolation and imprisonment for centuries, but it is most widely known as the prison in which Nelson Mandela was incarcerated for more than 20 years along with other leaders of the liberation movements resisting the apartheid regime.

53 Degrees, named after the Fahrenheit temperature of the water around Robben Island, featured Jennie Reznek as a contemporary mother of two small children trying to make a piece of theatre after many years absence from the stage. The piece she is making focuses on the historical figure of Florrie Berndt, who is trapped in an icy cold current as she tries to swim from Robben Island to the mainland in the first ever organized Robben Island swim in 1926. These two women's stories are woven into the context of the broader liberation struggle in South Africa through the character of Makana/Nxele/Links (played by Gosekwang Poonyane), a nineteenth-century Xhosa prophet who tried to free his people from the tyranny of British rule and who was imprisoned on the Island.

It is a production that sets out to engage dramaturgically with Robben Island in an attempt to construct a more inclusive historical presentation of this fraught space in the South African landscape. In this sense, *53 Degrees* proceeds as a kind of 'microhistory.' Giovanni Levi (2001: 101) defines microhistory as the reduction of the scale of observation for 'experimental purposes,' motivated by 'the belief that microscopic observation will reveal factors previously unobserved.' Carlo Ginzburg (1993), one of the foremost exponents of microhistory, in his article entitled 'Microhistory: Two or Three Things That I Know About It,' identifies a number of key features, including:

- 'the minute analysis of a circumscribed documentation, tied to a person who was otherwise unknown' (1993: 22). In our case, *53 Degrees* featured the story of Florrie Berndt, the daughter of the Robben Island baker, and one of the first women to swim from the Island to the mainland;

- a focus on the narration of an individual event rather than being restricted to its 'reconstruction' (1993: 23). In our case, we included the story of the first organized swim from Robben Island to the mainland in 1926;

- 'obstacles interfering with the research [are] constituent elements of the documentation and thus [...] become part of the account' (1993: 23). In our case, the staging of a contemporary woman's struggle to reclaim a creative life interrupted by motherhood and domesticity, and the personal and historiographical difficulties that this presented.

The latter is a kind of Brechtian distancing device intended to overcome the possibility that the narration 'could translate itself into an account that filled the gaps in the documentation to form a polished surface' (Ginzburg 1993: 23, emphasis in original). Ginzburg (1993: 28) the historian, 'who has only at his disposal fragments of things and documents,' accepts their limitations, while 'transforming them into a narrative element' on 'a terrain of invention.' He describes this work as a 'leap' over the 'inevitable gap between the fragmentary and distorted traces of the event [...] and the event itself' (1993: 28); a leap betwixt the past and the present, across the inevitable abyss that lies between.

It seems to me that such a leap, with all its impossible dimensions, is central to what I am trying to argue for here, as well as to the way of working that we at Magnet have been engaged in over the past 29 years.

In fact, one of the core images of *53 Degrees*, repeated over and over again, is Nxele's attempt to jump across Cove Rock. Nxele (or Makana) was a prophet who led the Xhosa nation in battle against the British in the nineteenth century, at a place now known as Grahamstown. I quote, at length, from Noël Mostert's account:

> For Nxele, the last act had come. He had fled with his followers eastwards along the coast. His final gesture of resistance created an extraordinary scene in an extraordinary setting. He chose a place known today as Cove Rock [...] a huge cliff-like slab, 86 feet high [...] at the extremity of a wide sandy beach.
>
> Cove Rock [...] is cleft by a deep, wide notch in the middle, through which the sea thunders, and is in fact two separate slabs. The one side adjoins the shore and the other the deep sea, and it was from atop the landward slab that Nxele declared that he would summon the Xhosa ancestors to rise from the sea and come ashore to help drive the white man from the land.
>
> To summon them, he said, he was required to leap from the landward slab to the seaward one, across the gap above the dashing seas that burst into the notch.
>
> [...] On the appointed day the sands surrounding Gompo [the Xhosa name for the sandy beach below Cove Rock] were packed by a multitude eagerly awaiting the miracle. Nxele ascended the rock from which he was to leap and sat atop it, contemplating the wide and dangerous gap. He sat thus through a long, weary day and made no attempt to jump. [...] From the crowds rose urgent cries, 'Nxele, the sun has set. We are tired and cold. Leap! Leap!' But he remained motionless.
>
> (Mostert 1992: 483)

In the end, the Xhosa were defeated and Nxele ended up being imprisoned on Robben Island. He drowned while trying to escape in a small boat, but his body was never found. Many Xhosa today believe that he will still return.

In the episode described above, Nxele stands poised, ready to take the leap. While ultimately he does not jump, at the precise moment of his potential jump everything is possible: all routes remain open and available, the miracle is still possible and the ancestors might still arise. What is required is a decision, a risk. It is this aspect of the decision that is central to the process of making and the emergence of novelty in Magnet's work; the way the virtual becomes actual in the process. Here, decision is used in the way it is understood by Whitehead (1978: 43), 'in its root sense of a "cutting-off".' It is an act of selecting or choosing from alternative possibilities, wherein such moments of decision are, at least primarily, felt rather than thought. They are suffused with what Whitehead (1967: 176) calls 'affective tone;' and this affective tone and our feeling of it exists prior to, and is in excess of, any attempt to cognize it. In fact, the feeling of the affective tone is a condition for any cognizing that might occur. Furthermore, such decisions are singular: they cannot be determined in advance or made according to any rule. It is what Étienne Souriau (cited in Latour 2011: 310) refers to as 'a case of instauration, a risk taken, a discovery, a total invention.'

The dramaturgical process in this early work was much less formed or conscious than it has subsequently become, but it produced a multitude of questions and initial tentative answers that we had to work through with greater clarity in the productions that followed.[3]

Some might raise the objection that to begin without a question in mind reflects a rather sloppy, unsystematic, perhaps random approach to conducting research. But I would argue that, far from being unsystematic or random, it represents one of the actual strengths of performance as a mode of research: its particular emergent character. As Baz Kershaw (2009: 112) puts it, 'even the most open and carefully expressed [questions] inevitably imply a more or less predictable range of responses, which flatly contradict the qualities of radical openness and excess that the creativity of performance practice at its best can produce.' Objections to this approach are based on a particularly orthodox sequentiality of knowledge production in which knowledge systems are vertically integrated. They involve the application of a pre-existent schema or concept onto the experience of the world. According to this view, we refer our immediate and fragmentary experience or sense-data (lower level) to the pre-existent schema (higher level) in order to render it coherent and intelligible. In other words, we produce a kind of cognitive map, defined according to a predetermined question or set of questions, before we use it to find our way. As we move in the real world, we refer back to the map to check where we are, and to see whether we are heading in the predetermined direction towards the predetermined destination, which is the answer to the predetermined question. This results in a closing down of the possibilities of the future. It reduces the potential for getting lost and for chance encounters along the way, thereby restricting adventurousness and novelty and the unexpected discovery. But it also assumes that the world represented by the map is fixed, rather than in a state of constant emergence; that the meaning that we seek is suspended awaiting our arrival; and that we are somehow detached from the world, self-contained, stable and fully formed, rather than in a constant state of our own emergence in the course of our embodied, practical engagement and involvement with the world.

Ingold (2000) argues, based on the work of David Turnbull (1989; 1991), that knowledge is not vertically but laterally integrated. It is in a constant process of formation as we move around in our environment. The knowledge that has brought us to one place is put to work in setting off towards another (Ingold 2000: 229). So, rather than applying a map that has been pre-made, the map is produced on the go. In other words, 'we know as we go, not before we go' (2000: 230). This is not map-making or map-using, but simply mapping; an ongoing process of attention and involvement. And if this gives rise to artefactual representation, these are merely 'stepping stones along the way, punctuating the process rather than initiating it or bringing it to a close' (2000: 231).

The experimental nature of performance as process involves the trial and error method of feeling one's way towards a goal, open to the possibility of bumping into new discoveries along the way, as well as the creation of imaginary or potential spaces within which to engage with specific questions. This is what makes performance able to 'articulate complexes of thought-with-feeling that words cannot name, let alone set forth. It is a way of accessing the world, not just a means of achieving ends that cannot be named' (Radley 1995: 13). The problem with this is that 'many academics do not see the world in this experimental way. For them it is already found before it is discovered. But in a world that has never been more mapped we surely still need to set out without maps every now and again' (Thrift 2003: 2003).

With *53 Degrees*, setting out 'without maps,' at first with just the desire to create something new, we became concerned with finding images of women doing extraordinary feats despite the difficulty of their circumstances. This was the starting point of the journey. This overarching interest led us to the first Robben Island swim, and that in turn led us to the site of Robben Island and its history as a political prison, an infirmary and leper colony, as well as a military fortification during World War II. To engage in the event of that first swim proved impossible without engaging in a heterogeneous history; one filled with contesting narratives, or at least fragments of narratives, some more visible than others. For instance, the history of incarcerations post-1962 is more visible than the history of incarcerations in earlier colonial periods; male narratives are focused on more than female narratives; the ANC history on the Island predominates over that of other political organizations like the Pan African Congress (PAC) or The Azanian People's Organization (AZAPO); and the Island as political prison is more visible than the Island as instrument of public health policy. Also, the swim suggested itself as another image of escape, another way to attempt to flee the bondages of the Island. In this way, we needed to bring the swimming narrative into relationship with the narrative(s) of escape attempts that are so much a part of the Island's various histories.

As we worked, the original impulse to find images of women transcending the limitations of female lives in a male-dominated world through physical activity (inspired/driven by Jennie's struggle to reclaim a creative life interrupted by domesticity) continued to interface with the emergent discoveries of the varied and complex history of the Island. And the difficulties of the research endeavour (both because of the complexity of the history and because of personal life demands) became part of the research itself.

Questions, or perhaps puzzles that required solving, emerged. Central to these was one regarding the relationship between the past and the present: How do they exist alongside, or perhaps entangled, with each other? How do they speak to each other, if at all? More specifically, we were engaged by the challenge of making the piles of paper drawn from the archive – the traces of the past – live onstage in the present. In other words, we had to find a way in which to embody or perform the archival fragments. What spatial image could we create onstage to contain the fragments of the past? How could we define the nature of the relationship between the body of the actor present onstage and the bodies from the past, absent except for their disembodied and fragmentary inscription/description in documents from the archive? Our dramaturgical questions of space, structure and character were all determined by the central question regarding the nature of the relationship between the past and the present.

As I engage in remembering the production, it is obvious to me that these questions did not lead to easy answers. In fact, in many senses the answers are, and continue to be, as paradoxical as the questions. The production reflects this in its uneasy and disordered character: the three storylines (Jennie's story; Florrie's story; Nxele's story) existing together uncomfortably, entangled in a complex meshwork of times and spaces; presences and absences that were not easily reconciled, and which required an active and engaged spectatorship that often resulted in a sense of incompleteness – a failure to produce a 'polished surface' (Ginzburg 1993: 23).

What I am trying to point to here is the way a process of thinking unfolds. It occurs at a variety of different levels or scales, which are woven into the making of the work. These give rise to questions and some proposed answers (however tentative these may be), which are picked up and developed further in other work. I would call this process a particular research assemblage that operates over an extended period of time. In the next section I will try to think through in more detail how such a process happens, with recourse, once again, to Whitehead.

The Corpus

While our production of *53 Degrees* exists as an entity on its own, with its own proper name, this does not imply that it is a fixed and finished thing. To describe a production as an entity is to suggest that it has achieved a certain level of 'objective immortality' (Whitehead 1978: 29 & 238); that it contains enough of a sense of 'integral satisfaction' to suggest something relatively stable has come into existence, even if there can be no suggestion of finality here because the 'pure thisness' (Deleuze & Guattari 1977: 7) of the thing produced is 'perpetually perishing' (Whitehead 1978: 29). This is both in the sense that all performance works have their existence only when they are being performed, and in the sense in which the existence of these performance works fades progressively in the corporeal memories of those who participated in the performances (practitioners and audiences), or becomes more and more imperfect over time. Or, on the contrary, the sense in which these works shift and expand as a result of additions to the overall landscape of productions over the lifespan of a company like Magnet.

At the same time, 'there is nothing that floats into the world from nowhere' (Whitehead 1978: 244): each individual production is related to all other productions, while not being determined by them. Each new production reacts – consciously or unconsciously – to the gestures, propositions, thoughts and questions raised in earlier productions, at the same time asserting its own singularity. The insertion of dance in *Rain in a Dead Man's Footprints* (2004–05) as a strategy to 'deterritorialize' language (after Deleuze and Guattari 1980: 174) – to break down the language of the sensible and replace it with, or relate it to, a language of sensuousness/sensation – and to 'reassemble the social' (after Latour 2005) through the bringing together of bodies in touch was picked up on and refined in *Cargo*, the production that followed. As Whitehead puts it:

> [Each] novel entity is at once the togetherness of the 'many' which it finds, and also it is one among the disjunctive 'many' which it leaves; it is a novel entity, disjunctively among the many entities which it synthesizes. The many become one and are increased by one. In their natures, entities are disjunctively 'many' in process of passage into conjunctive unity.
>
> (Whitehead 1978: 21)

Every production – which is ultimately an event, a process of becoming – is connected to what it relates to from before, and which it is also attempting to break away from: 'It both inherits everything that comes before it and breaks away from everything it inherits' (Shaviro 2012: 110). This is what Whitehead (1978: 279) calls a 'route of inheritance.'

Whitehead's ideas on routes of inheritance are applicable at various levels of scale in Magnet's work: at the molecular level of the process of making or of performing, as we leap from one moment of decision to the next; at the molar level of formations (i.e. how one production relates to others); and at the level of the corpus (the body of work as a whole). It is this third level that I am most interested in here.

Magnet's body of work is a 'conjunctive unity' of other bodies ('the many become one'). But this does not imply that the body of work is a simple totality:

> [If] we discover totalities alongside various separate parts, it is a whole of these particular parts but does not totalize them; it is a unity *of* all these particular parts but does not unify them; rather it is added to them as a new part fabricated separately.
>
> (Deleuze & Guattari 1977: 42, emphasis in original)

Nor does it imply a consistency or continuity whereby the body of work maintains itself by recreating the very processes that produce it, as Maturana and Varela's process of 'autopoiesis' might suggest (1980). Rather, creating a body of work over time implies a process of 'continual redefinition, or becoming other than what it was' (Shaviro 2012: 112, note 7).

There is, however, another intermediate level of organization at play in the work of Magnet Theatre that is central to its 'epistemic culture' (Knorr Cetina 1999). Early Magnet works tended to be random, opportunistic events that responded to various impulses and circumstances. For example, *Cheap Flights* (1987) happened because Jennie needed to create a show to make her visible again in the South African theatre context after studying at Lecoq in Paris. *The Show's Not Over 'Til the Fat Lady Sings* (1991–3) happened because The Dream Circus collapsed and Jennie wanted to make a theatre piece that incorporated the trapeze skills she had learned there. *Pump* (1998) was a response to the small houses we attracted for *'I Do' x 22* (1997) at the Market Theatre during the summer months, and the resultant idea that we should be taking theatre to audiences instead of waiting for them to come to us. Over time, a more considered relationship began to emerge between the work in the university and the idea of research and the practice in the studio. This led to conceptualizing a number of multi-year thematic foci around which different kinds of activities and outputs coalesced. The first of these themes concerned performing history or staging the archive. This involved four productions over the span of five years: *53 Degrees* (2002–03), *Rain in a Dead Man's Footprints* (2004–05), *Onnest'bo* (2002–06) and *Cargo* (2007), as well as our work in Clanwilliam with school learners on the Bleek and Lloyd Collection in the Clanwilliam Arts Project. This period in Magnet's history also engendered a number of journal articles and, ultimately, my Ph.D. thesis, 'Remembering in the Postcolony' (2012b). The second focus was on migration. Here again, there were four productions over the span of eight years: *Every Year, Every Day, I Am Walking* (2006–present), *ingcwaba lendoda lise cankwe indlela* (2009), *Die Vreemdeling* [The Stranger] (2010) and *Inxeba Lomphilisi – The Wound of a Healer* (2010). Additional journal articles followed, as well as a collection of play scripts, *The Magnet Theatre 'Migration' Plays* (Reznek, Fleishman, Yisa & Marek 2012), and a collection of academic essays, *Performing Migrancy and Mobility in Africa: Cape of Flows* (Fleishman 2015a).

In this way, I imagine our productions as arranged into what I will term 'research assemblages.' The concept of the assemblage appears in the work of Whitehead and Deleuze and Guattari, and while all use it to refer to a set of relationships between heterogeneous elements, it is Deleuze and Guattari who are most systematic in defining what is meant by the term. It is instructive that the French word that is translated as 'assemblage' in English is *agencement*, which is defined as a conjunction 'of bodies, of actions and passions, an intermingling of bodies reacting to one another,' and also 'of acts and statements, of incorporeal transformations attributed to bodies' (Deleuze & Guattari, cited in Shaviro 2012: 148, note 3).

Faniswa Yisa in *Autopsy* (2012).
Photo credit: © Mark Wessels.

Some of the elements that make up any particular assemblage take the form of an 'intermingling of bodies reacting to each other' at a variety of scales: the human and non-human bodies engaging each other in the molecular moments of each production; or one production reacting to another at the molar level of forms and formations. This is what Deleuze and Guattari refer to elsewhere as the '*production of productions,* of actions and of passions' (1977: 4, original emphasis). Other elements take the form of 'acts and statements, of incorporeal transformations attributed *to* bodies,' and these might be formal (as in journal articles or book chapters) or informal (as in interviews, rehearsal notes, post-performance discussions, reviews, etc.). Deleuze and Guattari refer to these as '*productions of recording processes,* of distributions and of co-ordinates that serve as points of reference' (1977: 4, original emphasis). Some of the elements are produced by Magnet and some are produced by others in reaction to what is produced by Magnet. To this extent, the assemblage is not entirely predictable or planned. It is not determined in advance, but emerges over time, revealing its properties and capacities in the process. It is a structural composition defined by its dynamic nature, shifting and adapting as it incorporates new elements. As Manuel de Landa (2006: 18) emphasizes, the assemblage is not based on relations of interiority in which the individual parts form the identity of the whole; rather, they are defined by relations of exteriority in which the whole is not reducible to its parts. The components that make up the assemblage are not essential to the identity of the whole, but can be replaced by other components (2006: 18). This does not mean, however, that the components do not interact with or relate to each other. The assemblage produces associative links between elements as a result of their contiguity in space and time, relations of resemblance, and relations of cause and effect. Together these produce a sense of coherence between the elements. This does not imply a sense of total agreement. The assemblage is characterized by difference, by the emergence of alternative possibilities. What is required is what Deleuze and Guattari (cited in Shaviro 2012: 114) call a 'disjunctive synthesis,' an affirming and 'positive relation among a multiplicity of [...] incompatible alternatives.'

The combination of these research assemblages make up the body of work, which, as Jean-Luc Nancy (1993: ix) suggests, 'makes sensible an insistence, if not an obsession [...] a certain way of thinking,' or as Cull (2012: 21) would have it, 'a kind of philosophy.' As a kind of philosophy, it 'does not consist in knowing and is not inspired by truth. Rather categories like Interesting, Remarkable, or Important [...] determine success or failure [and] this cannot be known before being constructed' (Deleuze & Guattari 1994: 82). I see this as an attempt to shift the focus away from the idea that this research involves the proving of any one thing, particularly in the positivistic paradigm that determines what is to be known or not known in advance. What emerges through the work as a form of thinking or philosophy is not a truth in the singular, monolithic and/or monological sense, but a collection of interesting, remarkable or important discoveries.

As a kind of thinking, Magnet's work can be considered to be 'unfinished' (Borgdorff 2012: 194; with reference to Hans-Jörg Rheinberger); it is 'a productive *not-yet-knowing* against the backdrop of an ever-receding knowledge horizon' (2012: 194). Our work at Magnet is a leap into the unprecedented and the unknown. Furthermore, it does not reveal the meaning of the work/world as if it had been hidden away, out of sight, awaiting our arrival and our sudden raising/parting of the curtain; the sudden capacity to see it or make it be seen as if for the first time. Rather, such thinking is a form of *poesis*: an 'action that is the cause of something to emerge from non-existence to existence,' which 'means both making and imagining' (Plato, cited in Seremetakis 1994: 15). Our work at Magnet brings something new into being: new concepts, new methods, new ideas, new questions, projections and possibilities. In this way it becomes a machine for thinking the future, even when, as is the case with much of Magnet's work to date, it works with material from a past that will not easily pass. To this extent, it is motivated by an ethical project: the concrete obligation to intervene in the present; to respond to the task that is before us in South Africa today, the task of being free.

References

Allsopp, R. and Lepecki, A. (2008), 'Editorial: "On Choreography",' *Performance Research: A Journal of the Performing Arts*, 13: 1, pp. 1–6.

Bachelard, G. (1994), *The Poetics of Space* (trans. M. Jolas), Boston: Beacon Press.

Borgdorff, H. (2012), *The Conflict of the Faculties: Perspectives on Artistic Research and Academia*, Leiden: Leiden University Press.

Cull, L. (2012), 'Performance as Philosophy: Responding to the Problem of Application,' *Theatre Research International*, 37: 1, pp. 20–27.

De Landa, M. (2006), *A New Philosophy of Society: Assemblage Theory and Social Complexity*, London and New York: Continuum.

Deleuze, G. and Guattari, F. (1977), *Anti-Oedipus: Capitalism and Schizophrenia* (trans. R. Hurley, M. Seem and H. R. Lane), New York: Viking Press. First published 1972.

—— —— (1987), *A Thousand Plateaus: Capitalism and Schizophrenia* (trans. B. Massumi), Minneapolis and London: University of Minnesota Press. First published 1980.

—— —— (1994), *What is Philosophy?* (trans. H. Tomlinson and G. Burchell), New York: Columbia University Press. First published 1991.

Fleishman, M. (2011), 'Cargo: Staging Slavery at the Cape,' *Contemporary Performance Review*, 21: 1, pp. 8–19.

—— —— (2012a), 'The Difference of Performance as Research,' *Theatre Research International*, 37: 1, pp. 28–37.

—— —— (2012b), 'Remembering in the Postcolony: Refiguring the Past with Theatre,' Ph.D. thesis, University of Cape Town.

—— —— (2015a), *Performing Migrancy and Mobility in Africa: Cape of Flows*, Basingstoke: Palgrave Macmillan.

—— —— (2015b), 'Dramaturgies of Displacement in the Magnet Theatre Migration Project,' in M. Fleishman (ed.), *Performing Migrancy and Mobility in Africa: Cape of Flows*, Basingstoke: Palgrave Macmillan, pp. 12–36.

Gieryn, T. F. (1983), 'Boundary Work and the Demarcation of Science from Non-Science,' *American Sociological Review*, 48, pp. 781–95.

Ginzburg, C. (1993), 'Microhistory: Two or Three Things That I Know About It,' (trans. J. Tedeschi and A. C. Tedeschi), *Critical Inquiry*, 20: 1, pp. 10–35.

Ingold, T. (2000), *The Perception of the Environment: Essays in Livelihood, Dwelling and Skill*, London and New York: Routledge.

Kershaw, B. (2009), 'Practice as Research through Performance,' in H. Smith and R. T. Dean (eds), *Practice-led Research, Research-led Practice in the Creative Arts*, Edinburgh: Edinburgh University Press, pp. 104–25.

Knorr Cetina, K. (1981), *The Manufacture of Knowledge: An Essay on the Constructivist and Contextual Nature of Science*, Oxford and New York: Pergamon Press.

—— —— (1999), *Epistemic Cultures: How the Sciences Make Knowledge*, Cambridge, MA and London: Harvard University Press.

——— (2001), 'Objectual Practice,' in T. R. Schatzki, K. Knorr Cetina and E. von Savigny (eds), *The Practice Turn in Contemporary Theory*, London and New York: Routledge, pp. 175–88.

Laermans, R. (2008), 'Dance in General or Choreographing the Public, Making Assemblages,' *Performance Research: A Journal of the Performing Arts*, 13: 1, pp. 7–14.

Latour, B. (2005), *Reassembling the Social: An Introduction to Actor-Network-Theory*. Oxford: Oxford University Press.

——— (2011), 'Reflections on Etienne Souriau's *Le differents modes d'existence*,' in L. Bryant, N. Srnicek and G. Harman (eds), *The Speculative Turn: Continental Materialism and Realism*, Melbourne: re.press, pp. 304–33.

Levi, G. (2001), 'On Microhistory,' in P. Burke (ed.), *New Perspectives on Historical Writing* (2nd edition), Cambridge: Polity Press, pp. 97–119.

Maturana, H. and Varela, F. (1980), *Autopoiesis and Cognition: The Realization of the Living*, Dordrecht, Holland & Boston: D. Reidel Publishers.

Mostert, N. (1992), *Frontiers: The Epic of South Africa's Creation and the Tragedy of the Xhosa People*, London: Pimlico.

Nancy, J.-L. (1993), *The Birth to Presence* (trans. B. Holmes et al.), Stanford: Stanford University Press.

Pickering, A. (1993), 'The Mangle of Practice: Agency and Emergence in the Sociology of Science,' *American Journal of Sociology*, 99, pp. 559–89.

Radley, A. (1995), 'The Elusory Body and Social Constructionist Theory,' *Body and Society*, 1: 2, pp. 3–23.

Reznek, J., Fleishman, M., Yisa, F. and Marek, F. (2012), *The Magnet Theatre 'Migration' Plays*, Cape Town: Junkets Publisher.

Rheinberger, H-J. (1997), *Toward a History of Epistemic Things: Synthesizing Proteins in the Test Tube*, Stanford: Stanford University Press.

Rouse, J. (2001), 'Two Concepts of Practices,' in T. R. Schatzki, K. Knorr Cetina and E. von Savigny (eds), *The Practice Turn in Contemporary Theory*, London and New York: Routledge, pp. 189–98.

Seremetakis, C. N. (1994), 'The Memory of the Senses, Part I: Marks of the Transitory,' in C. Nadia Seremetakis (ed.), *The Senses Still: Perception and Memory as Material Culture in Modernity*, Chicago and London: The University of Chicago Press, pp. 1–18.

Shaviro, S. (2012), *Without Criteria: Kant, Whitehead, Deleuze and Aesthetics*, Cambridge, MA: MIT Press.

Stengers, I. (2011), *Thinking with Whitehead: A Free and Wild Creation of Concepts* (trans. M. Chase), Cambridge, MA and London: Harvard University Press.

Thrift, N. (2003), 'Performance and…,' *Environment and Planning A*, 35: 11, pp. 2019–24.

Turnbull, D. (1989), *Maps are Territories: Science is an Atlas*, Geelong: Deakin University Press.

——— (1991), *Mapping the World in the Mind: An Investigation of the Unwritten Knowledge of Micronesian Navigators*, Geelong: Deakin University Press.
Turner, S. (1994), *The Social Theory of Practices: Tradition, Tacit Knowledge and Presuppositions*, Cambridge: Polity Press.
Whitehead, A. N. (1978), *Process and Reality*, New York: Free Press. First published 1929.
——— (1967), *Adventures of Ideas*, New York: Free Press. First published 1933.

Notes

1. There is little agreement over terminology for this kind of activity. Artistic research is the term preferred in non-anglophone European contexts, whereas practice or performance as research (PaR) is the accepted term in anglophone countries. Moreover, the International Federation of Theatre Research (IFTR) working group on the subject is called the Performance as Research Working Group, although some other jurisdictions and groupings prefer practice/performance-led research. In my view, these terms all refer, to a lesser or greater extent, to the same idea or set of practices.
2. An obvious exception is *The Fire Raisers* (2004), which was a production of Max Frisch's play. It was a co-production with Théâtre Spirale of Geneva, Switzerland, and the choice of the play was an attempt to find something to ground the collaboration (i.e. a Swiss play reconsidered from an African perspective). The production concept shifted the play quite significantly from the original. Both *Moby Dick* (1993) and *Voices Made Night* (2000–14) were adaptations of pre-existing literary texts, neither of which was intended as a performance text by the author. *Medea* (1994–96), meanwhile, appears to be based on an original dramatic text, but was in fact a collage of many texts, some dramatic, some poetic, some prose texts, and some material created specifically for the production.
3. For a more detailed discussion of how these questions and answers evolved in Magnet's work, see Fleishman (2012b).

Chapter 3

An Activist Company Inventing a Future: A Conversation with Neo Muyanga[1]

Neo Muyanga, an award-winning composer and a Magnet trustee, was born in Soweto, into a family of composers. Neo composes music for choirs and other ensembles. He has composed for contemporary dance (Jazzart Dance Theatre/Remix Dance Company), and cinema (Craig and Damon Foster's Cosmic Africa *[2003]) as well as television (*Architecture of Fear *[2012] by Nicky Newman). He was also responsible for the music in Magnet Theatre's highly acclaimed productions,* Rain in a Dead Man's Footprints *(2004–05),* The Fire Raisers *(2004),* Voices Made Night *(2000–14),* Cargo *(2007),* I Turned Away And She was Gone *(2015) and* Heart of Redness *(2015), as well as their longest touring piece,* Every Year, Every Day, I Am Walking *(2006–present).*

Describing Magnet Theatre as an 'activist company' because of the way in which they relate to questions of history and identity, composer Neo Muyanga says, 'For me, the attraction of working with Magnet is the storytelling aspect of their productions. I enjoy bringing music and musicality into telling a story. Also, it's usually a story that's based on historical fact. So it's about understanding some issue, some tension; about trying to explain ourselves – our identity now and how it's contingent on what came before. I guess, for me, it feels like a way of inventing a future, inventing an understanding of what new South Africanness is, in music theatre and physical theatre. I don't know many other production companies that work in the way that Magnet does.'

'Magnet is a devising company,' he explains, 'so the script comes to life as different exercises are shaped by the director. The music usually comes out of a similar process of investigation.' For Muyanga, the music in Magnet's productions serves multiple purposes: 'It accompanies the action, but it also gives an historical subtext. So the music is like another character in the piece, and the character speaks sometimes in the voice of the period and sometimes against the period.'

For example, in *Cargo* (2007), a work about slavery at the Cape Colony and its lingering effects in the new democracy, Muyanga extensively researched seventeenth-century music: 'I looked at old scores, trying to understand the relationship of that music to what later became brass music and techno, and what became *klopse*[2] music, so all of that tradition had to be present in the production,' he says. His musical choices provided a subtext for the content of the work: '*Cargo* opens with a piece on harmonium and sung in a pentatonic scale. I used a harmonium because of its association to Indian music. It links the Asian tradition with the African tradition. [Many slaves came from Asia to Southern

Composer Neo Muyanga live-scoring *Every Year, Every Day, I Am Walking* at the International Theatre Festival of Kerala in India (2009).
Photo credit: © Magnet Theatre.

Africa.] It's a five-note scale, and it's the dominant mode for indigenous styles of music. [...] I also used porcelain pots which were made by a visual artist, Katherine Glenday. The pots were made out of clay that comes from the beaches around here,[3] which was literally the first soil that the colonists would have stepped onto. And that relates to the idea of the soil that the indigenous people used to walk on.'

Neo serves as a Magnet trustee on their advisory board, along with Mark and Jennie, Mandla Mbothwe, entrepreneur Yolanda Methvin and Professor Sakhela Buhlungu, who is Dean of Humanities at UCT. Past trustees have also included Gillian Mitchell, who has a background in fundraising, activist and anthropologist Zayd Minty, and urbanist Edgar Pieterse, the head of the African Centre for Cities. 'The idea of the advisory board,' he explains, 'is that we also try to create links with other institutions, with access outside of Magnet's sphere. Different people come with different sets of skills and different networks, and we try to bring those networks to bear on the work that Magnet does, and to introduce people to what Magnet is about.'

Muyanga reflects on the work Magnet does to empower communities. Referring to their work in Clanwilliam, Muyanga asserts that one of Magnet's most important interventions in that community is activating the Khoisan mythology found in the cave paintings in the area and engaging with the history of the people of Clanwilliam: 'A lot of the stories that are told in [Magnet's outdoor procession at the end of each year's work in Clanwilliam] are actually inspired by Khoisan mythology, like Heitsi-Eibib,[4] the jester character. He's a character who has these mounds of stones, cairns, around parts of the country as commemoration of his burial site. Some people say this was a real character who existed, who told the first stories around the Eland. Finding a way to activate the mythology in the stories that would have been familiar to people who drew the cave paintings is, I think, educating people about their history.'

'My contention is that without imagination, without learning, a sense of self-confidence can't be given to someone.' For Muyanga, part of what Magnet contributes to the world is the empowerment of people. 'The spirit of that is that if you've got a sense of a compass, a sense of confidence based on your history and identity, and a means of creating or generating work that can feed you, then you become free from the oppressor.'

In reflecting on Magnet's key contributions to South African arts and culture, Muyanga enumerates the devised nature of their work, their archaeological process, and how their investigations of history speak to contemporary South Africa. According to Muyanga, Magnet's 'thinking around content and how content is dictated by fact, history and archaeology of a certain kind, and how that speaks to identity and our contemporary existence' is a signature of Magnet's work. The second major contribution is 'the devised element of the work. It doesn't come ready-made, prepared and scripted, which means that every time we come back to a production, we relook at the material; not from scratch, but with enough openness to make certain changes and adjust things and improve things. So that process of growing the work doesn't end with this run, or when the rehearsals are over.'

Neo believes that Magnet's work asks audiences to shift their existing perceptions. For example, he explains how seeing *Onnest'bo* [Upside Down/Topsy Turvy] (2002–06) and *Die Vreemdeling* [The Stranger] (2010) changed his relationship with the Afrikaans language, helping him to see beyond its status as a dominant language. 'That's when my understanding of the subversive nature of Afrikaans became apparent,' he says. He also comments on the political or activist impacts of Magnet's work: 'Some people might call that political theatre, since it was about forced removals in District Six, but it wasn't pontificating. It wasn't giving a point of view from on high. It was just trying to illustrate a reality on the ground. That dramatization allowed for a new dramatic imagination to happen because, you know, forced removals are still happening now, today. Refugee camps are being set up that are constitutionally questionable. Like Dunoon. If you look at all kinds of developments around asylum seekers, all these questions around health provisions for people who are marginalized, these are still, in a sense, contemporary [issues]. So the thing about going to history and talking about the archive is that it helps us refine our lens for looking at today.'

References

Muyanga, N. (2013), personal interview with A. Krueger, 12 June.

Notes

1. Interview quotes in this chapter are taken from Muyanga (2013).
2. The 'Kaapse Klopse' is a minstrel festival held in Cape Town on the 2nd of January every year, involving thousands of minstrels who participate in a street parade. They are typically from Afrikaans-speaking coloured communities, and compete against each other in self-organized *klopse* [clubs] that have preserved the tradition since the mid-nineteenth century.
3. The interview was conducted near the Magnet Theatre in Observatory, Cape Town.
4. In the /Xam tradition Magnet uses in Clanwilliam, this figure is called //Kaggen.

Chapter 4

'Being There': The Evolution of Performance Aesthetics from *Medea* (1994-96) to *The Magnet Theatre 'Migration' Plays* (2012)

Miki Flockemann

Miki Flockemann is a professor in the Department of English at the University of the Western Cape. Her primary research interest is the aesthetics of transformation, migrancy and citizenship. Her publications include comparative studies of diasporic writings from South Africa, the Americas and the Caribbean. Her work has appeared in collections such as The Routledge Reader in Gender and Performance *(1998),* The Routledge Reader in Post-Coloniality and Performance *(2000) and* SA Lit Beyond 2000 *(2011). She has also published widely in journals such as* Kunapipi, Tulsa Women's Studies, Ariel, the Journal of Commonwealth Literature, the South African Theatre Journal, Contemporary Theatre Review, AlterNation *and* English Studies in Africa.

> A stranger with a quivering mate,
> taken in with open arms.
> I am one of you now. Me.
> I have ripped the tongue from my mouth
> and lost it. I have washed the sweat from
> my body and hidden it.
>
> (*Medea*: Scene I)[1]

Magnet Theatre's 1994 production of *Medea* can be seen as a seminal work in terms of the distinctive aesthetic signatures that the company has evolved over the past three decades. While the production predates what Fleishman conceptualizes as the 'history' or 'memory' plays produced between 2000 and 2007, as well as the more recent 'migration' plays,[2] I argue that *Medea* not only prefigures, but even looks beyond, these other works by employing a 'thick' theatre aesthetic that produces a sense of 'being there.'

Medea was Magnet's first collaboration with Alfred Hinkel and the Jazzart Dance Theatre. The production used a powerfully visceral style of embodied and multilingual storytelling that marked a shift in the theatre landscape of the period, including Magnet's own work.[3] The epigraph above refers to a confrontation between Medea and Creon in which she defends herself against Creon's command that she must leave Corinth immediately for fear that her presence will jeopardize the new marriage of her husband Jason to Creon's daughter. During this encounter, Medea, the former Colchian princess, wears a sleek wig to cover her short-cropped hair, while her skimpy lingerie-style dress makes her seem vulnerable in the face of Creon's dark-glassed stare.[4] Medea's movements here are constricted by her high-heeled sandals, which keep sinking into the deep layer of sea sand covering the stage, while her awkwardness reinforces her claim that she has 'made over' her Colchian self to be 'one of you now.' The entire stage area was covered in sea-sand, evoking arrivals and departures and the connections between continents, across time and space. The sand briefly held the footprints of the performers as they moved across it, before being erased by fingers drizzling or raking rhythmically through it, or danced over by the feet of the chorus. At one end of the stage, Medea's sons perpetually build castles in the sand, apparently oblivious to the horror that awaits them. Juxtaposed against the ever-shifting but apparently timeless sand, however, is a stark brick wall at the back of the stage, with a metal roll-up garage door in its centre. Craig Leo's set design thus incorporates both the natural environment of Medea's homeland, Colchis, as well as the urbanized, built environment of Corinth. At the same time, the garage door suggests a space beyond ancient Colchis or Corinth: the city, the world of the here and now.

Medea's description of herself in the epigraph as a migrant stranger who unsettles the hostile hosts by becoming 'one of you now,' points to a process of violent dismemberment and apparent forgetting; however, there is also subterfuge involved in hiding what has apparently been washed away. The notion that the body's traces remain, ready to be revived and speak again, prefigures a number of thematic, dramaturgical and aesthetic strands in the works that followed. In tracking the evolution of Magnet's aesthetic signature, I will first explore the genesis of the *Medea* production, and then look at how the 1994 *Medea* looks forward to the more recent 'migration' plays (Reznek, Fleishman, Yisa & Marek 2012).

'Being There' as a 'Thick' and Inter-Subjective Performance Aesthetic

As noted earlier, the aesthetic signature of 'being there' in Magnet's work from *Medea* onwards is imbricated in the evolution of what I have termed elsewhere as a 'thick' performance aesthetic (Flockemann 2011). The notion 'thick theatre' is borrowed from Clifford Geertz's description of the practice of reading cultural events through 'thick description,' where a multi-layered contextual ethnography is created in order to encourage spectators to experience an approximation of 'being there' (Geertz, cited in Goldman-Seagall 1994: 8). According to Geertz (1973: 10), 'Doing ethnography is like trying to read a manuscript' which is faded and hard to decipher, 'and written not in conventional graphs of sound but in transient examples of shaped behaviour.' This speaks to the processes of play-making as described by Fleishman, since the meanings emerge through a process of physical images, a 'trying out.' Meanings are carried in and through bodies, sound and movement or 'shaped behaviours' (Geertz 1973: 10), rather than words. For Geertz (cited in Goldman-Segall 1994: 8), this 'encourages the reader [or spectator] to get close to the meaning of those who experienced what the author [or play-maker] is describing [...] the reader [or spectator] gets the sense of "being there."' At the same time, however, the sense of 'being there' is understood as a much-mediated, second-order experience, almost like trying to make sense of an obscure manuscript (the story of Medea and Jason) from another time. As a spectator, one is there in the virtual reality of the performance, but aware that one is also not 'actually' there in historical time.

The notion of 'being there' is integral to both the embodied and the inter-subjective aspect of performance. Fleishman (cited in Cooper 2007: 134) notes that the physicality of embodied performance denies simplistic meaning, and ideally, 'opens up potential for the audience to respond in an actively imaginative way to create new, individual meaning.' He argues that since performance involves both the body of the performer and the body of the other (the spectator) to whom the performance is directed, performance in this sense is 'always social and inter-subjective and the boundary between private and public is effaced' (Fleishman 2009: 123). The inter-subjective aspect of being 'attuned' to the performance is another way of experiencing the sense of 'being there.' In fact, being attuned is essential to the communicative function of embodied storytelling: as Peggy Phelan (2008: 136) puts it, live performance 'contains the possibility of both the actor and the spectator becoming transformed during the event's unfolding' – though obviously not all actors or spectators are capable of being attuned in the way she suggests. Nevertheless this potential 'is extraordinarily important because this is the point where the aesthetic joins the ethical' (2008: 136).

According to Yvonne Banning, who did a study of critical responses to *Medea* in 1997, some of the confusion felt by critics who seemed at a loss about how to respond to the work (which connected sensory, conceptual and emotional responses) was a product of the climate of the time, fraught as it was with complex cultural shifts. This unstable climate helps to explain the strong reactions elicited by the work, which was seen as a landmark production that ushered in a new dramatic language at a historical juncture in South Africa; a language characterized by both great uncertainty and momentous possibilities at the cusp of the transition to democracy that began in 1994. For Banning (1997: 72), responding to these shifts required a type of perceptual transformation, particularly in terms of negotiating cultural identities. Yet, for those who were attuned to its aesthetic, the play spoke directly to 'how living in SA made one feel in "its sheer complexity of emotion"' (Greig, cited in Banning 1997: 75).

In mapping how *Medea* prefigures thematic, dramaturgical and aesthetic strands developed in later works, it is important to foreground the storytelling processes that came into play in the production, as well as the role of embodiment in the inter-subjective process of meaning-making. Integral to my discussion of the play-making process is my 2013 interview with Fleishman, in which he situates the *Medea* production in relation to the works that came before and after it.

Embodied Storytelling: The Genesis of Magnet's *Medea*

Walter Benjamin's celebrated essay, 'The Storyteller,' provides a useful point of departure for looking at the genesis of the *Medea* production as germinal in the evolution of Magnet's aesthetic signature. According to Benjamin (2006: 364), the art of storytelling has run its course, partly because narrative has been removed from 'the realm of living speech.'[5] At the same time, he says, this makes it possible 'to see a new beauty in what is vanishing' (2006: 364). In listening and watching the often told (and re-envisioned) story of Jason and Medea, embodied and spoken in many tongues, the audience is also captivated by the 'beauty that is vanishing.' While we are bombarded with information from all quarters, a story, in the sense referred to by Benjamin (2006: 365), is not 'already being shot through with explanation.' This is particularly true of the story of Medea, the woman who does

Kurt Wustmann as Jason and Bo Peterson as Medea in *Medea* (1994).
Photo credit: © Ruphin Coudyzer FPPSA. (ruphincoudyzer.com)

the unspeakable; and yet, it is difficult to fully understand her actions or arrive at an ethically unambiguous judgement of her. This ambiguity is evident already in the original Euripides version in that Medea simultaneously regards herself a woman more sinned against than sinning, while nevertheless taking full responsibility for her unthinkable actions in killing her children. It is the type of story that, as Benjamin (2006: 366) puts it, does not expend itself: 'It preserves and concentrates its strength and is capable of releasing it even after a long time.'

There are several ways in which storytelling functions in the Magnet production of *Medea*. First, the myth of Medea, as a vehicle to think with or make sense of one's world – as outlined, for example, by Joseph Campbell in his *Myths to Live By* (1972) – is an example of a story that retains its power and unleashes it in the retelling. This is evident from ongoing revisions of the myth, even here in South Africa, the most recent being Brett Bailey's adaptation, *medEia* (2012).[6] One explanation for why such retellings persist is that re-envisioning a story from an ancient archive can disrupt the apparently overdetermined present through subversion and invention: as Emily Greenwood (cited in Hardwick 2010: 8) claims, 'the mythological imagination can constitute a form of knowledge that counters that of the imperial imagination in colonial literature.' In other words, by re-ordering events and contexts (in this case through embodied and spatial juxtapositions and linguistic code-switching), the mythological imagination is employed to show how 'unfinished' past traditions are carried into the future (Hardwick 2010: 8). For instance, the perception of Medea as a non-Greek 'other' or barbarian in the original myth points to the way xenophobic attitudes continue to be deployed to claim exclusive belonging (as in the spate of attacks on 'foreign' fellow Africans in South Africa which made international headlines in 2008). As Benjamin claims, the power of stories like Medea lies in their unfinished nature. Instead of merely returning us to the past, they are in fact pointing us to the present, and even to the future. Describing his re-envisioning of the Medea story, Fleishman (2013: 12) notes that the ancient stories carry continued power because of their structural assemblage, which 'in Deluezian terms operates in a very powerful way in the world, wherever you put it and whatever timeframe you put it in, whether Greece or South Africa.' It so happened that in the particular context of the 1994 election, Magnet's production of *Medea* hit a nerve; it found 'very fertile soil' (2013: 12) in the sociopolitical and historic moment of transition out of apartheid and into the new democracy.

In Fleishman's account of the impulse that led to the production, he describes a social gathering for students and teachers of Jacques Lecoq in Paris, where one of Jennie Reznek's former teachers asked him about his own work, even though he was not directing anything at the time:

> I said the first thing that came into my head, which was Medea. The reason being that we had recently been [to] the Edinburgh festival and saw a production directed by the Romanian, Andrei Serban, [his] *Medea* was very guttural sounding and it was a very

> short play and very intense, but entirely vocal and [with] very little physicality and I remember thinking at the time – how would this work if we made it in South Africa, would we make it more physical? And so when she asked what I was directing I said 'Medea' (which I was not at all thinking about) and she said, 'Apollonius of Rhodes.' And I said, 'What's that?' And then [the] conversation went on in French and I was lost again.
> (Fleishman 2013: 12)

This serves as an example of how the Medea story was unleashing its power in one form (Serban's guttural Greek version), only to strike the listener/viewer into speculating about the retelling of it, or putting it together again in a new (local, more physical) way. According to Benjamin (2006: 367), the listener is most struck by the story when in a semi-somnambulistic mode: that is when the story's power strikes, as if out of nowhere, such as when Medea popped into Fleishman's head unannounced. This is an example of how the *Medea* production prefigures Magnet's later work on recreating sites of memory, though in this case the site, as suggested by the amorphous sea-sand with its associations of arrivals and departures, was both nowhere (neither Colchis nor Corinth) and everywhere. At the same time, the sand also held memories and artefacts that could be retrieved. For instance, right at the start of the play, the nurse runs in and buries the Golden Fleece (emblematic of Medea's ancestral heritage) in the sand; at the end it is dug up again as part of Medea's ritual transformation back to Colchian princess.

Against this backdrop, retelling the ancient Greek story performs a memorializing function in the sense of remembering, or bringing together and reassembling bits of the story to make a new meaning. Magnet's *Medea* is not already 'shot through with information' of the accessible everyday kind, but communicates 'a dynamic expression of the intense life' (Chaikin, cited in Dolan 2005: 6). Dolan (2005: 6) notes how personal unsettlement is productive in making meaning, since it is when experiencing this 'partial vision' of the 'expressions of the intense life,' rather than the supposedly comprehensive vision, that one is able to 'see clearly.'

As already noted, the play originated with an apparently random spark: Serban's version of *Medea*, which prompted the listener/spectator (Fleishman) to become the storyteller; however, as suggested by the critical/audience response, it is the visceral style of embodied storytelling that created its strongly inter-subjective aspect. This also explains why it was seen as a landmark production that was speaking to its time. In discussing how the play's aesthetic developed, however, Fleishman notes that he and his collaborators at Magnet did not set out to speak directly to the political moment. Instead, this was largely 'an unconscious process. […] It was very much a case of working unconsciously, just following the work as it went. Just seeing what emerged. Trying out things and then trying out more things, and then things started to come together' (Fleishman 2013: 2).

The embodied performance that opens up a story or an image in this way involves 'a process of remembering. A remembering that is less about the need to forestall forgetting than it is about putting back together the body that is broken – an altogether more active process' (Fleishman 2009: 121–22). Here, Fleishman is referring to the body of work produced after the *Medea* production, which all deal with history and the reconstruction of memory.[7]

Medea also explores a process of recall and remembering, manifested in the re-ordering of the events in the version by Apollonius of Rhodes, who included the account of Jason and the Argonauts' voyage to obtain the Golden Fleece. At the same time, the actors also participated in creating the production through intensive workshopping of character and motive, while Alfred Hinkel worked on the gestural language with the Jazzart dancers as chorus. After the intensive rehearsal process, in which the ensemble tried out various approaches to the storytelling, Fleishman's/Magnet's *Medea* script gradually came together. This process of collective creation is another hallmark of Magnet's work. Fleishman's description of the processes involved – namely the unconscious, and trial and error to see what worked – is indicative of putting together, retelling and reframing.

A 'Ripped Tongue' and 'Buried Sweat': *Medea* and Memory

My earlier claim that *Medea* anticipates some of the methods and concerns of the 'memory' plays is also evident in Medea's claim, in the epigraph: 'I have ripped the tongue from my mouth' and 'washed the sweat from my body and hidden it' (Scene I). The 'ripped tongue' and 'hidden sweat' point to Medea's self-inflicted somatic disassociation from her own body described earlier in the way she assumes the trappings of Greekness by putting on the clothing, shoes and hairstyle of the Corinthians. In conforming to the social body of Jason's world, Medea must relinquish her own ways, where she moved freely on bare feet over the sand. In keeping with familiar racist and sexist discourses of otherness, Jason insists that she wear perfume to disguise her smell and put on make-up so she does not look like a boy (Scene XI). However, when Jason first encounters Medea in her homeland of Colchis, he says of her, 'She was beautiful. She smelt like coriander, like cinnamon, like cloves. She was of the earth and moved in its medium' (Scene IX B). Later he asks: 'Why do you not put on my country's dress/In Greece you should dress like a Grecian woman' (Scene XI). Despite Medea's apparent dismembering, and her dissembling heels and wig (when she looks into the mirror held up by the nurse, she claims mournfully, 'this is not Medea'), there is nevertheless an understanding – suggested by the 'hidden sweat' – that she still retains her own power, albeit latently (just like the Golden Fleece signifying Medea's stolen heritage that the nurse buries in the sand at the outset of the play, which is then resurrected in the retelling of Medea's story.) While Medea's tongue might be lost ('ripped out'), her body retains its story.

Magnet's power to shape events in the telling is foregrounded self-reflexively in *Medea*, which begins with Medea's prologue in which she addresses her children: 'Listen to my story children.' Later, Jason will mirror Medea with his identical injunction, 'Listen to my story children' (Scene IX B).[8] As mentioned earlier, Fleishman's decision to draw on Apollonius of Rhodes' prose version of *Medea* rather than Euripides' play meant that the narrative included the backstory of what happened before Jason and Medea arrived in Corinth. This was embodied spatially in the contrasting yet simultaneous worlds of the exotic Colchis of Medea's history, the in-between sea journey to Iolcus and the metropolis, Corinth. In Magnet's production, these spaces were evoked through bodies in movement (and accompanying soundscapes often created by the chorus), who mutated between Corinthians in the present – in uniform trench coats and Doc Martens boots moving awkwardly and violently across the sand – and the Colchians of the past, who were barefoot and travelling easily across the beach that is common to both locations. As mentioned earlier, the stark juxtaposition of the beach with the brick wall suggested both the natural and urban environment and, as Fleishman (2013: 7) points out, the shore is a kind of littoral space where the land and sea join. At the same time, the distinctiveness of these cultural landscapes was blurred by the chorus who transform from Colchians to Corinthians and back again. In the process, they deliberately subverted and played with notions of ethnically-marked body types; this was in fact a key feature of Jazzart's aesthetic, and at the time, the company had a policy of using dancers of diverse body shapes and cultural backgrounds in order to unfix cultural and gendered identities. Through their embodied mutations, the chorus thus prefigures a challenge to the distinction between those who are considered *authochthons* [belonging to the soil] and those considered *allochthons* [strangers], distinctions that have gained currency recently with the emergence of discourses of South African exceptionalism and exclusivity.

Medea as *Autochthon* and *Allochthon*: Indigenous Inhabitant and Stranger

When Medea and 'her quivering mate' Jason arrive in Corinth after their flight from Iolcus, they encounter a deserted beach and an old blind man looking for items of value with a metal detector. As Jason approaches, he is told, 'Fuck off. Fuck off… the beach is mine' (Scene XI). Here, the old man shuns Medea in ways that point forward to the xenophobic attacks starting in 2008. For instance, in his study of the rise of discrimination against Africans in South Africa, David Matsinhe (2011: 111) notes that for many African immigrants, 'Bodily looks, movements, sounds and smells are legible as evidence of imagined citizenship [and foreignness].' Although this is in keeping with pervasive xenophobic prejudices worldwide, there is nevertheless a sense in which the *Medea* of 1994 points forward to the xenophobic events of 2008. As the old man is blind, he 'sniffs' Medea out, 'that crazy woman,' and instructs Jason to 'take that woman with you sir. /Let her go. Leave her somewhere else/beneath a rock or underneath a bush' (Scene XI). The now familiar equation of the foreigner with a source of contagion is suggested when the old man turns to sniff Jason, claiming with jarring politeness:

> You smell a bit like her now.
> You have coupled with that barbarian
> explored her rivers, drunk her muddy pits.
> Sticky allegiance you have made, sir.
> We don't like her kind here, sir,
> with due respect. They take our jobs
> Muddle our language. Seduce our sons.
>
> (Scene XI)

It is in fact after this scene that Jason tells Medea to 'put on perfume' and repeats the old man's motto of 'Greece for Greeks.' While for audiences in 1994 these attitudes were familiar cautions against perceived cultural and ethnic contamination, they resurface now in the guise of South African exceptionalism (as indicated in *Die Vreemdeling* [The Stranger] [2010], one of the 'migration' plays in which a community builds a barrier around itself to keep out strangers).[9] Despite the fact that the old man regards her as a foreigner, a stranger, the play situates Medea less as foreigner than as an indigenous inhabitant whose identity has been overlaid by the prevailing values of the dominant social body, signified by the wig and high-heeled sandals she put on in Corinth. When the Nurse bathes Medea's head during a ritual ceremony, Medea's wig is removed, revealing Bo Petersen's cropped and shaved hair, which is styled to resemble an underlying Khoi identity. Her hair signifies Medea's 'hidden' cultural affiliation to the Nurse, who embodies more overtly an indigenous Khoisan/Griqua origin.[10] Medea's social unease in Corinth is manifested in the way she keeps checking her appearance in a little pocket mirror. When the nurse code-switches between English and Afrikaans, saying to a distraught Medea, who has just discovered that Jason has abandoned her, '*Staan op, Medea!* Get up and speak!' she does so to remind Medea of her 'indigenous' heritage:

> *Jy's n Colchian. Niemand lag vir 'n Colchian woman nie. Niemand mock die bloed van my ancestors nie.*
>
> [You are a Colchian. No one laughs at a Colchian woman. No one mocks the blood of my ancestors].
>
> (Scene IV)

The contrasts between the Nurse's use of *Kaaps* (a locally inflected creole of Afrikaans associated with those of mixed Khoi/San/slave/settler ancestry) and Medea's responses in standard English are indicative of Medea's sense of alienation at this point. In the course of the play, however, Medea reclaims an apparently 'uncontaminated' self by sacrificing her two sons, the embodiment of her union with Jason. This is suggested in the way she tenderly bathes them and removes the typical South African schoolboy uniform of short-sleeved white shirt and grey shorts to reveal their ancestral loincloths beneath, before leading them offstage. In hindsight, her infanticide feels almost like a Fanonian psychic upheaval through which the colonized subject frees herself from the mind-forged shackles of the social body she has felt compelled to inhabit, while simultaneously punishing Jason for his betrayal.[11]

In revisiting the 1994 *Medea* production 20 years later, it emerges how strongly it continues to speak beyond its time. This is partly because the power of a story like *Medea* is that it is ethically ambiguous; it is 'unfinished, and carrying into the future' (Hardwick 2010: 8). At the same time, the 'unconscious' process of the play's genesis resulted in a kind of intuitive foreshadowing. As Fleishman (2013: 2) notes (referring to how Medea as a stranger prefigured the later focus on xenophobia in the 'migration' plays), 'it's almost as if the country caught up with the themes of the work.' However, the foreshadowing in *Medea* operated almost on an unconscious level that anticipated (but also looked beyond) the Truth and Reconciliation Commission (TRC) processes that began in 1996, two years after *Medea* premiered. Medea is not just an outsider; she is also the 'other' within, a 'dark shadow-self' (2013: 13). In the first scene of the play, Creon commands Medea to 'Keep still! Look away!' When she asks him why, he rejoins:

> I fear you.
> You are the face I see in my dreams,
> In the mirror, a dark shadow.
>
> (Scene I)

Fleishman (2013: 13) notes that in making *Medea*, he and his collaborators were tapping into the legacy of the ravages of colonialism and apartheid, which engendered 'very twisted parts of ourselves,' and these 'really dark' undercurrents are what Magnet was 'tapping into.' Creon's fear of Medea is that she mirrors what he himself might become (or do). While the TRC was mandated to bring to light apartheid atrocities and human rights abuses – in other words, what They (the agents of the State) did to Us (the people) – the play appears to look beyond that, and asks instead what we are doing to ourselves. It anticipates what has now been termed the inward turn, where complicity is made visible and needs to be acknowledged. Yet this inward turn also has 'a dark side,' manifesting in 'the kind of violence that is emerging now in this country' (2013: 13). Nigel Gibson (2011: 24) describes the rising violence as symptomatic (again in Fanonian terms) of South Africa's Unfinished Revolution. The intersection of ethics and aesthetics referred to by Phelan (2008: 136) is demonstrated by the play's ending, where an apparently indifferent but splendid Medea, dressed again as a Colchian princess, is literally and symbolically distanced from culpability for her child-slaying.[12] Instead it is Jason, the opportunist with his realpolitik pragmatism, who is left with nothing but the hollow crown that is placed on his head as he clutches the clothes of his dead sons to his chest, his gaping mouth screaming her name, Medea, to the soaring chorus from Handel's 'Zadok the Priest: The Coronation Anthem.'

Drawing together the various ways in which the 1994 *Medea* production prefigured some of the conceptual dramaturgical and aesthetic signatures that have evolved in Magnet's work since then, it is clear that, like the 'history' or 'memory' plays which followed, *Medea* constituted a mode of remembering in the sense of putting things back together to make new meanings out of old stories, and also anticipated Magnet's later focus on migration. Moreover, by embodying the story through an aesthetic which involved complex, layered meanings, only decipherable by being attuned to the stage metaphors and physical images, the audience experienced a sense of 'being there.' This was achieved by turning the story inside out, before putting it together again so that an ancient text/story could speak to the present and future. Magnet's production of *Medea* involved not just retelling, but also 'telling the other side of the story,' through a self-reflexive storytelling process in which both Medea and Jason lay claim to the story: 'Listen to my story children.' In addition, Magnet's collaboration with Jazzart members Jay Pather and Alfred Hinkel, and with Craig Leo (who designed the staging of *Medea*), initiated a very productive series of continuing collaborations as part of an ongoing experiment around the intersection of dance and theatre. In contrast to the more 'unconscious' genesis and process of *Medea*, the body of work based on sites of memory that were produced as part of this collaboration (like *Rain in a Dead Man's Footprints* [2004–5] and *Cargo* [2007], discussed in the chapters by Lewis ['Performance Labours,' p. 203] and Hutchison ['Embodied Practice,' p. 175]) were far more carefully mapped, choreographed and researched, representing a shift in direction for the company over this period.

From the 'Memory' Plays to Performing Migration

Like the 'memory' and 'history' plays, Magnet's 'migration' plays – made between 2006 and 2012 – also developed out of research projects based in this case on three routes: the N7 along the West Coast up to Namibia; the N2 travelled by internal migrants from rural homes in the Eastern Cape to Cape Town and back (an ongoing legacy of the apartheid-era migrant labour system); and the route from Cairo to Cape Town, which encompasses the journeys taken by 'foreign' fellow Africans seeking a 'better life' in the mother city of Cape Town. Unlike the bulk of the 'memory' plays, however, the 'migration' plays — published as a collection, *The Magnet Theatre 'Migration' Plays* (2012) – were in-house productions (rather than collaborations with Jazzart) employing physical performance modalities, rather than being script or research based.

The first of these, *Every Year, Every Day, I Am Walking* (2006–present), was performed by Jennie Reznek and Faniswa Yisa and directed by Fleishman.[13] It has become Magnet's most performed production to date, running every year since its inception still with the original cast. Like *Medea*, *Every Year, Every Day, I Am Walking* anticipates some of the events of 2008, though in a more direct way, since the play was made in response to the issues faced locally by refugees from other parts of Africa. Given how this crisis

Reznek and Yisa as displaced mother and daughter in *Every Year, Every Day, I Am Walking* (2006).
Photo credit: © Mark Wessels.

has unfolded subsequently, both locally with ongoing xenophobic attacks, as well as in ethnically-based violence in other parts of Africa, it has become 'a story that needs to be told and retold' (Fleishman, cited in Reznek et al. 2012: 12). However, it is interesting to note the similarities in the way *Medea* and *Every Year, Every Day, I Am Walking* evolved. Fleishman (2012: 13) claimed that initially he did not have a clear sense of how the *Medea* production would speak to the historical juncture of the time, and he describes the genesis of *Every Year, Every Day* in his director's note in a similar way: 'This was a piece that was not meant to be. It was not planned for, thought about, wrestled with over time. It arrived unannounced, surprised us with its simplicity, its raw intensity and the urgency of its call.'

It is tempting to speculate that this partly explains why the play has retained such power, much like the intensity of the responses to *Medea* at the time. In the case of *Every Year, Every Day, I Am Walking*, subsequent productions performed here and abroad continue to generate fresh unsettlements because of the way the work encapsulates the 'intense life' of the journey of the two intrepid refugees, using an embodied storytelling aesthetic that provokes recognition and a sense of 'being there.'

The other plays in the *'Migration' Plays* collection act as companion pieces in that they offer alternative insider and outsider perspectives by, and of, travellers and strangers in our midst by drawing on local linguistic vernaculars and performance traditions. These plays are rooted in the locations and communities that generated these stories; stories with an archetypal core, but told in new ways. *Die Vreemdeling*, for example, draws on vernacular storytelling modes to recount what happens when a community's boundedness is breached by a stranger. Two plays directed by Mandla Mbothwe – *ingcwaba lendoda lise cankwe ndlela* [the grave of the man lies next to the road] (2009) and *Inxeba Lomphilisi – The Wound of a Healer* (2010–14) – take the evolution of the Magnet's aesthetic signature to another level in their exploration of the physically and psychically (dis)embodied experiences of internal migration along the N2 to Cape Town. These works employ performance modalities that unlock responses at the moment of performance, as in a sense of 'being there.' The two plays exemplify a 'thick' performance aesthetic wherein meanings are carried through bodies, sound and movement, as well as by occasional enigmatic surtitles projected onto a screen. The spectator is thus put in a similar position to someone trying to read a faded or obscure manuscript which is translated into 'transient examples of shaped behavior' (Geertz 1973: 10). As noted in my earlier reference to Geertz, through the act of deciphering, the reader or spectator comes close to a sense of 'being there.' There are of course implications for the way such performances can be recorded and scripted. At the same time, as I shall show, these works speak to and problematize the current preoccupation with notions of belonging and exclusion.

All the works in the *'Migration' Plays* collection are shaped by Magnet's physical theatre aesthetic, which is integral to their identity as a company: 'These productions reflect our commitment to the body, to mutilingualism and indigenous language theatre in South Africa and to taking theatre out of conventional spaces' (Fleishman, cited in Reznek et al.

2012: 8). A striking feature of the works is the way local language registers complement the gestural language. While *Every Year, Every Day, I Am Walking* uses French and English, *Die Vreemdeling* is performed in a richly inflected Afrikaans, interlacing both colloquial patois and standard registers interspersed with the occasional English word or phrase. This is a vernacular associated with geographically and politically marginalized communities living in small rural towns along the West Coast of South Africa (the Kaaps spoken by the Nurse in *Medea* is related linguistically to this vernacular, though of a more urban variety). On the other hand, Mbothwe's *ingcwaba lendoda lise cankwe ndlela* and *Inxeba Lomphilisi – The Wound of a Healer* were both groundbreaking for Magnet in the sense that they were performed entirely in Xhosa with English surtitles projected onto a screen.

Putting Bodies Back into the Landscape; Breathing Life into Them through Performance

According to Mbothwe (cited in Reznek et al. 2012: 154), 'Without the stories of the "disappeared" we are not whole […]. Inxeba Lomphilisi tries to place the stories of absent voices back into the landscape.' Mbothwe's attention to absent voices is supported by Magnet's work on memorialization and sites of memory, and has also helped to define them. Mbothwe asks what happens when, as in these two plays, the graves are at the side of the road and not in an official cemetery? As the Healer puts it:

> *Imihla ngemihla imiphrfumlo ihla inyuka,*
> *Izungeza amaqhosha angenamngxuma amagqobhoka*
> *ayithembisa ukuba ingcambu iluhlaza kwelinye icala*
> *Abanye baziyela ngeenyawo, babuye belele ngomqolo.*
> *Abaninzi sebeziintsmi kwizizukulwane.*
>
> [Day in and day out, the spirits up and down.
> Looking for the buttons without holes […] promised by Christians that the root is greener on the other side.
> Others went by foot, but came back on their backs;
> Many are folktales to their grandchildren.]
>
> (Reznek et al. 2012: 160)

In this case, where there is no locatable geographic or physical place of memory, the road itself stands in for the 'disappeared' or intangible site, as the site can also be an image or even a landscape (Fleishman 2009: 128). Memory is given presence and location (it is not just 'a folktale to grandchildren') only in the moment of performance. In a post-performance interview, Mbothwe (2010: 5) pointed to some of the challenges encountered in this performance modality, which "unlocks" meaning during the live event:

> It's painful to tell stories [...] it's choking for me to tell the stories, but it's also choking for you to listen to the stories. But if we run away from that stage, it means we are lying because that story hasn't disappeared and will come back more painful.
>
> (Mbothwe 2010: 1)

What is interesting here is the notion that the story, or the communal memory, appears to have a life of its own and that the effects of telling the story are also transmitted to the spectator. As pointed out by Benjamin (2006: 366), the story 'preserves and concentrates its strength and is capable of releasing it even after a long time.' Benjamin's assertion supports Mbothwe's claim that without the stories of the disappeared 'we are not whole.' His aim in the production is to try 'to place the stories of absent voices back into the landscape' (Reznek et al. 2012: 154). As Diana Taylor (cited in Phelan 2003: 205) puts it, 'Only through performance can disappearance be rendered visible;' it's not about going back she says, but about keeping alive.[14] In the local context, this 'keeping alive' involves creating space for those whose stories fall through the cracks of 'official' accounts.

Productive Incomprehension and the Evolution of an Aesthetic Signature

In conclusion, the evolution of Magnet's aesthetic signature over time reveals both what is gained and what might be lost in the process. For instance, Fleishman (2013: 9) observed in my interview with him that he now feels a little embarrassed by the *Medea* production because it feels very 'raw.' There is the danger, however, that in later productions where 'rawness' is avoided, one risks experiencing the works as over-thought, as too choreographed, and as a result the sense of 'being there' is muted (for me this happened at times in *Rain* and *Cargo*). On the other hand, when the 'rawness' of the sensory experience is given freedom to play itself out, this can slide beyond Artaudian theatre ritual into an ecstatic state, where notions of difference and exclusivity can – apparently paradoxically – appear to be entrenched by 'being there' in an unmediated way.

The most productive aspect of a 'thick' performance aesthetic is when spectators feel they can almost grasp the inscrutable otherness of the experience being performed, which almost seems recognizable, as if an invisible line emerges between cultural insiders and outsiders. This is in keeping with my earlier citation of Dolan (2005: 7) on the partial vision which provides a 'clearer' way of seeing. Fleishman explains how the notion of 'incomprehension' was integral to his dramaturgical strategy while working on *Medea*. On his return to South Africa to prepare for the production, he says that he was acutely aware of how South Africans, given our culturally diverse and divided society, are always only partly able to follow a story fully: there is always something incomprehensible, something missing. At the same time, this notion of incomprehension was already something Fleishman and Magnet had been experimenting with through workshopping methods, which explored the intersection of the body and theatre, as well as through

Lecoq's concept of collective creation, where the actors are not just interpreters, but creative collaborators. Fleishman (2013: 14) notes that the spectator needs to be willing to respond to that which appears 'incomprehensible,' as if in a language he or she does not understand: 'If you were resistant to the fact that you didn't understand everything, then you would block yourself from understanding, as it were. And that was a very conscious strategy.' Referring to the linguistic code-switching in *Medea* between English, Xhosa, Kaaps and Tamil, he says:

> We constructed it in such a way that the same story is told over and over again in the piece, but in different languages. I thought that was an important strategy to challenge the audience to be in a state of incomprehension, you know, non-comprehension, whatever it is.
>
> (Fleishman 2013: 14).

At the same time, he describes this strategy of trying to develop a concrete theatre language as also shaped by 'a kind of Artaudian tradition' (Fleishman 2013: 15). Looking back on the work produced at Magnet, Fleishman reflects on the way the Medea production foregrounded an attempt to find a language of the stage that was not tied to text, but in effect spoke its own language. In turn, each production that followed was an attempt to find an appropriate stage language and style for that particular work:

> [E]ach project that we do requires an investigation and a questioning of the whole basis of what theatre is, or what performance is, and to try and find the forms and the styles and the modes of performance that work for that project, not necessarily because they worked for a previous project. So that's what drives me, that's what interests me, as an actor, as a director. I certainly didn't know all [of what would follow] when I started with *Medea* now, 20 years later. Also being an academic at the same time, means that I get to reflect on my process in a way that most theatre people don't have to do.
>
> (Fleishman 2013: 15)

Fleishman's reflections suggest that the Medea production has not only been seminal, but indeed pivotal to the aesthetic signature developed by Magnet Theatre over the last 29 years. On the one hand, it was a crystallization of the embodied theatre practice developed by the company in previous productions like *Cheap Flights* (1987) and *The Show's Not Over 'Til the Fat Lady Sings* (1991–93). On the other hand, the experimentation with finding a gestural and physical language for the Chorus in *Medea* was instrumental in ushering in a series of works developed in collaboration with Jazzart, such as the 'history' or 'memory' plays, which like *Medea*, attempted to put absent voices back into landscape and place while also telling 'the other side of the story.' Simultaneously, Medea-as-stranger also anticipated the sustained focus of the later 'migration' plays, albeit looking beyond these (and the subsequent TRC discourses) in positing the notion of the stranger within, rather than focusing on perpetrators, victims and survivors.

In addition, the inter-subjective aspect of the performance aesthetic that has been developed by Magnet across the past two and a half decades situates the audience as secondary witnesses in the sense of an imaginative 'being there,' within which the performers and audiences 'jointly create liminal spaces and moments in which and during which sense-making is produced, if only partially and temporarily' (Kurasawa 2009: 100). If, for instance, one were to restage or publish the play now, it would communicate and create meaning rather differently. While the Nurse's use of Kaaps in the 1994 production caused a palpable *frisson* for cultural insiders on the threshold of a new dispensation (in that they recognized Medea as a Khoi princess of sorts, who is telling the other side of the story of those voices lost in the landscape), I doubt this would create quite the same effect today. Instead, the 'unsettlement' now might be felt much more powerfully in the shared complicity implicit in Creon's injunction that Medea 'Look away!' lest he see himself mirrored in her ('You are the face I see in my dreams'). Similarly unsettling would be the old man's xenophobic discourse about the contagion of Medea's presence, evoked by her 'muddy pits,' as well as her potential for 'muddling the language,' and thereby infecting the body politic. Just as Medea's body hides its sweat, the story's latent power endures, although it is in the moment of performance that it comes to life; a life that is shaped not only by the storytellers, but also by the witnessing audience in the sense of 'being there,' if only fleetingly, in the moment of performance.

References

Banning, Y. (1997), '(Re)viewing *Medea*: Cultural Perceptions and Gendered Consciousness in Reviewers' Responses to the New South African Theatre,' *SATJ*, 1: 1/2, pp. 54–88.

Benjamin, W. (2006), 'The Storyteller,' in Dorothy Hale (ed.), *The Novel: An Anthology of Criticism and Theory 1900–2000*, Malden, Mass: Blackwell Publishing, pp. 361–78. First published 1969.

Campbell, J. (1972), *Myths to Live By*, New York: Penguin Compass.

Cooper, S. (2007), 'Silent Cries of Protest: The Beginnings of Democracy and the Emergence of Physical Theatre in South Africa,' in Nigel Worden (ed) *Historical approaches. Volume 4, 2005-6: Research Papers by History Major Students at the University of Cape Town*, Rondebosch: Dept. of Historical Studies, University of Cape Town.

Dolan, J. (2005), *Utopia in Performance: Finding Hope at the Theatre*, Ann Arbor: Michigan University Press.

Fleishman, M. (2009), 'Knowing Performance: Performance as Knowledge Paradigm for Africa,' *South African Theatre Journal*, 23, pp. 116–36.

——— (2013), personal interview with M. Flockemann, 15 March.

Flockemann, M. (2011), 'Facing the Stranger in the Mirror: Staged Complicities in Recent South African Performances,' *South African Theatre Journal*, 25: 2, pp. 129–41.

Geertz, C. (1973), 'Thick Description: Towards an Interpretive Theory of Culture,' in *The Interpretation of Cultures*, New York: Basic Books, pp. 3–30.

Gibson, N. C. (2011), *Fanonian Practices in South Africa: From Steve Biko to Abahali baseMjondolo*, Pietermaritzburg: Palgrave Macmillan/Univ KZN Press.

Goldman-Segall, R. (1994), 'Whose Story Is It Anyway? An Ethnographic Answer,' *IEEE MultiMedia*, 1: 4, pp. 7–11.

Greenwood, E. (2007), 'Arriving Backwards: The Return of *The Odyssey* in the English Speaking Caribbean,' in Lorna Hardwick and Carol Gillespie (eds), *Classics in Post-Colonial Worlds*, Oxford: Oxford University Press, pp. 192–210.

Hardwick, L. and Gillespie, C. (eds) (2007/2010), *Classics in Post-Colonial Worlds*, http://www.oxfordscholarship.com/view/10.1093/acprof:oso/9780199296101.001.0001/acprof-9780199296101. Accessed 12 March 2014.

Kurasawa, F. (2009), 'A Message in a Bottle: Bearing Witness as a Mode of Transnational Practice,' *Theory, Culture & Society*, 26: 1, pp. 92–111.

Magnet Theatre (1994–96), *Medea*, Cape Town: Magnet Theatre (unpublished).

Matsinhe, D. (2011), *Apartheid Vertigo: The Rise of Discrimination Against Africans in South Africa*, Surrey: Ashgate Publishing Ltd.

Mbothwe, M. (2010), personal interview with the directors and cast of *Inxeba Lomphili*, Baxter Theater, August.

Phelan, P. (2008), 'Performance, Live Culture and Things of the Heart,' *Journal of Visual Culture*, 2: 3, pp. 291–302, http://www.academia.edu/8361293/interview_with_Peggy_Phelan_Performance_live_culture_and_things_of_the_heart. Accessed 13 February 2013.

Reznek, J., Fleishman, M., Yisa, F. and Marek, F. (2012), *The Magnet 'Migration' Plays*, Cape Town: Junkets Publisher.

Taylor, D. (2003), *The Archive and the Repertoire: Performing Cultural Memory in the Americas*, Chicago: Duke University Press.

Van Woensel, O. (2003), 'medEia,' *Theatre*, 33: 3 pp. 57–85.

Notes

1. All references to and citations from *Medea* refer to an unpublished script provided to me by Mark Fleishman (Magnet Theatre 1994).
2. The 'history' or 'memory' plays include *Onnest'bo* (2002–06), *Rain in a Dead Man's Footprints* (2004–05) and *Cargo* (2007). The Migration plays include *Every Year, Every Day, I Am Walking* (2006–present), *Die Vreemdeling* [The Stranger] (2010), *ingcwaba lendoda lise cankwe ndlela* [the grave of the man lies next to the road] (2009) and *Inxeba Lomphilisi – The Wound of a Healer* (2010–14).

3. *Medea* premiered at the Artscape Arena Theatre in Cape Town in 1994. The actors were Bo Petersen as Medea, Kurt Wustman as Jason, Jay Pather as Creon and Aetes, Dawn Langdown as the Nurse and Heinrich Reisendorfer as Aegeus.
4. Creon's dark glasses indicate his fear of Medea since he keeps telling her to 'look away.'
5. Benjamin (2006: 364) notes that 'the storyteller takes what he tells from experience – his own or that reported by others. And he in turn makes it the experience of those who are listening to his tale.'
6. Bailey has produced two versions of the Medea story based on Oscar van Woensel's script, *MedEa*: the first was a powerfully innovative site-specific outdoor performance at the Spier Estate in 2005; the latest was performed as a 'pop tragedy' at the Baxter Theatre in 2012.
7. The 'history' (or 'remembering') plays produced in collaboration with Jazzart include *The Sun, The Moon and The Knife*, *Soe Loep Ons…Nou Nog*, *Cold Waters/Thirsty Souls*, *Rain in a Dead Man's Footprints* and *Cargo*, as well as two in-house productions – *53 Degrees* and *Onnest'bo.*
8. In hindsight, this points forward to the role of testimony, of hearing different sides of the same story associated with the hearings of the Truth and Reconciliation Commission.
9. See Krueger ('Implacable Grandeur') for an analysis of *Die Vreemdeling* (2010).
10. A further layering to this performance of identity is that Bo Petersen is white, while Dawn Langdown, who plays the Nurse, is well-known as a performer and dancer who embraces her Khoi/Griqua (Nama) heritage (used to great effect in *Soe Loep Ons …Nou Nog* [1996–97]).
11. The idea of killing her children in order to reclaim herself, or to 'undo' her encounter with Jason, is a common trope. In Seneca's *Medea*, for instance, it is described as an attempt to reclaim her virginity.
12. Fleishman notes in the interview that the original idea was to have Medea lifted aloft in a golden chariot, as a *deus ex machina* stratagem that apparently absolves her in an about-turn at the end (as in the original Euripides, and in the Apollonius of Rhodes version).
13. See Hutchison ('Embodied Practice') for another analysis of *Every Year, Every Day, I Am Walking.*
14. Taylor's comments need to be seen in relation to the political intervention that was initiated by the 'Argentinian Grandmothers,' for instance, whose silent performances have been making the disappearance of their family members publicly visible.

Chapter 5

The Full Gamut of an Ideal Company: A Conversation with Jay Pather[1]

Jay Pather is artistic director of Siwela Sonke Dance Theatre and the director of the Gordon Institute of the Performing Arts (GIPCA), which is housed at the University of Cape Town, where he is an associate professor. He has taken his intercultural performances into public spaces across the globe, working with the architecture of Johannesburg, Durban, London, Zanzibar, Amsterdam, New York, Barcelona, Mumbai, Muscat, New Delhi, Copenhagen and Cape Town. In 2006, he was appointed onto the National Arts Festival Committee and elected as chairperson for the Performing Arts Network of South Africa. Pather performed a lead role in the seminal Magnet production of Medea *(1994–96), and has remained a close friend of the company for many years. He has also shared a collegial relationship with Mark and Jennie at the UCT Department of Drama.*

'Magnet have always been forerunners,' says Pather. 'On a broad infrastructural level, Magnet represents the full gamut of an ideal company.' For Pather, Magnet works start with a strong artistic premise and the kind of 'great artistic integrity' inspired by Lecoq and Barney Simon. The company has 'an unmistakable style' based on powerful images that 'really drain the theatrical spectacle of any excess of words; challenging that hierarchy [of language].' They are 'constantly questioning the form of the image or of their motivation and their intentions behind doing stage work,' he says. Their artistic commitment to their unique aesthetic of physicality, the body and image work later developed into their 'training ethos and the formation of the larger Magnet company and the trainee programme.' Over the 30 years of their existence, says Pather, Magnet 'have engaged in a steady, mediated process. They've maintained a vision that has evolved in a proper combination of infrastructure and inspiration; but also a lot of rational planning and a good sense of their vision. It's a company that has embedded itself in such clear ideas and which has then expanded systematically and methodically and with a great deal of social and fiduciary responsibility.'

Pather describes Magnet's way of working as allowing for freedom within a defined structure. Describing his work on *Medea*, he says, 'It was a free-floating workshop process, but with extremely defined ends. [They] knew what it was they wanted to do – they knew the boundaries, they knew the landscape. It was a common mission, playing within a very definitive sense and form.'

The devising process that Magnet espouses allows for much experimentation and play amongst the actors. Pather recalls the process of creating *Medea*: 'We were doing this

Jay Pather as Creon in *Medea* (1994).
Photo credit: © Ruphin Coudyzer FPPSA. (ruphincoudyzer.com)

improvisation, and Bo Peterson and I were going on forever doing all kinds of things. We were able to do that, and able to go that far because we knew that the people who were watching us were quite meticulous in their choices. We knew that they had a particular vision and that what they'd do with it would be very different to anyone else given the same material and the same ideas. That was something quite profound [...] For *Medea*, we spent long hours summoning the thoughts to build ourselves, our own chaotic selves, into what was going to be.' Pather also emphasizes that '*Medea* was very cross-culture. We were not dealing with an homogenous country, we were dealing with praise poets and religious references which go back to my childhood, and stuff which I had to draw from and bring into an unfamiliar space.'

For Guy Willoughby (2004), Jazzart's precision and Magnet's theatricality inform each other in their collaborative work. Pather agrees, claiming that *Medea* was a 'watershed moment' of collaboration between the two companies. Magnet's use of physicality complemented 'the movement vocabulary' of Jazzart 'without it becoming indulgent,' he says. He explains how 'what Mark and Jennie did – and what Mark in particular did – was to harness that and to frame it towards particular ends, towards a social premise. So that even though you were in the matrix of something kinetic, where the best of movement was coming through because of the physicality, it was never allowed to go on for two seconds too long. I remember them timing certain sections and making sure they were exactly the right length. I think that was quite amazing, it would have been hard work without a sense of a theatrical eye and the theatrical rhythm that they brought to it.' Pather believes Magnet was 'very good for Jazzart at the time, because they brought with them a sense of discovery – finding and developing new languages which drove and probed questions much deeper.' He adds, 'the actual quality of the productions are just astounding [...]. Their work is very rich, very layered; the colours and the spectacle are extremely well orchestrated.'

In describing Magnet's role in educating South African audiences to the potential and accessibility of physical theatre, Pather says, 'I think there may be a greater affinity now to physical theatre as a layered text in itself,' which he hopes has 'thawed the frost between physical theatre practitioners and champions of the convention of scripted dramas.' Magnet has contributed to 'a retraining of perception' about what Pather calls the 'absurd division, that goes back to Descartes,' between body and mind and thus between physical and intellectual theatre. 'Magnet has done a great deal to educate audiences and to destabilize these fundamentally flawed systems that are particularly dominant in a society riddled with all kinds of prejudice.' Historically, South African theatre has privileged written texts, predominantly those in English, and this has 'become a means to reinforce all kinds of exclusions,' says Pather. Physical theatre, on the other hand, 'asks of us another kind of intelligence and a response that many may feel fearful to accept.' Magnet has made this type of work accessible to a broad audience, without 'compromis[ing] the sophistication of all texts – literary, kinetic, proxemics,' and by offering up 'nuanced, layered' visions of our contemporary world.

'I think that Magnet are highly politically conscious,' explains Pather. 'It's the kind of world they live in, but it's not overt, not agitprop. The politics are embedded in their process of working, in the workshop strategy,' which Pather suggests allows 'the audience to take what they are, to make of it what they are.'

'What comes through is their embracing of social themes that do have a preponderance towards resolution, towards hope,' says Pather. 'There is an element of tragedy, of political tragedy, but there is a strong sense of resilience, of the human spirit, of the individual going beyond any tenacious political system.

'*Medea* is a political play: it's about the notion of violence begetting violence and that the language of violence rests as a responsibility within one's own culture. Those are very political ideas,' he asserts. But rather than an 'overt support for a particular party line or party affiliation,' Magnet's work is 'political in a very finely tuned way. Its politics are embedded within the form.'

References

Pather, J. (2013), personal interview with A. Krueger, 7 June.

Willoughby, G. (2004), 'Get Physical with /Xam Heritage,' *This Day*, 5 August, p. 9.

Notes

1. Interview quotes in this chapter are taken from Pather (2013).

Chapter 6

The Implacable Grandeur of the Stranger: Ruminations on Fear and Familiarity in *Die Vreemdeling* [The Stranger] (2010)[1]

Anton Krueger

Anton Krueger (co-editor) is an associate professor at the Department of Drama, Rhodes University. He is the author of Experiments in Freedom: Issues of Identity in New South African Drama *(2010), which won the Rhodes Vice-Chancellor's Book Award for 2011, and he has contributed articles to a wide range of journals, including* Scrutiny2, *the* South African Theatre Journal, Cross Currents, *the* English Academy Review, English in Africa, Literator, Liminalities *and* Safundi: the Journal of South African and American Studies. *He has also written several book chapters for Methuen, Routledge, Cambridge Scholars Press, Rodopi and Peter Lang on a range of performance topics, from indigenous dance to Zef. Anton has also written in a number of other genres, including a novella* Sunnyside Sal *(2010), a collection of poetry* Everyday Anomalies *(2011), and the play* Living in Strange Lands *(2003; 2009), which was nominated for the Olive Schreiner as well as for an FNB Vita Award.*

> ... a foreigner is neither the romantic victim of our clannish indolence nor the intruder responsible for all the ills of the polis.
>
> (Kristeva 1991: 1)

Diverse Unities

Since 1994, when the first democratic elections took place in South Africa, a priority for the new democracy has been finding ways of forging a new nation while negotiating issues of diversity within a multicultural population. There is clearly a danger in enfranchising one particular group's claims to tradition over those of another; and yet, flattening out differences in order to achieve the metaphoric melting pot of the 'rainbow nation' is also problematic. In the effort to be representative of all, there lies the danger of representing nobody, leaving one merely with the bland averaging out of generalization. The stranger is the way out of the general.[2]

In the same year as their first historic election, Magnet Theatre created their first large-scale production in collaboration with Jazzart Dance Theatre. This was the South African version of *Medea* (1994–96) – analysed in detail by Miki Flockemann in Chapter 4 – which embraced an astonishingly diverse, heterogeneous mixture of languages and culturally diverse performance styles. Magnet Theatre's ability to work within a broad range of performance languages has become one of the hallmarks of their work. Their approach to intercultural productions has tended to sidestep both the potential bigotry of a narrow-minded ethnicism as well as the compromise of homogeneity. Instead, their creative explorations have inculcated a growing awareness of cultural inclusivity while avoiding demands for conformity. As Mark Fleishman explains (drawing on the work of Bruno Latour), one of their principle aims has been to 'expand the collective.'[3] What this implies is not only allowing more people to be included within representations of culture, but to expand the very notion of what the social realm is considered to be.[4]

Medea was a groundbreaking production. The juxtaposition of different styles of dance and physical movement brought Indian *kathakali* onto the same stage as African gumboot dancing; and yet each form maintained its integrity and there was never a watering down of disciplines. This was a celebration of differences, which dealt directly with confrontational issues of strangeness both within and between its characters. For example, Miki Flockemann (2010: 133) points out how in this production, 'Creon [...] addresses Medea as "stranger," "foreigner" and "barbarian." However, it is Creon's own "other" self, his "dark shadow" that he fears he will encounter when looking at Medea.' This sounds very similar to Kristeva's (1991: 1) assertion in *Strangers to Ourselves* that 'the foreigner lives within us: he is the hidden face of our identity. [...] By recognizing him within ourselves, we are spared detesting him in himself.' Following this logic, the stranger is outside of us, and yet also part of our projection of who we think we are. In seeking our own identity (and that of a nation), we displace the foreigner, rejecting her from our circle. And yet, if one wishes to comprehend a society, the stranger may be able to reveal who we think we are precisely because she embodies what we think we are not.

After *Medea*, Magnet continued to deal with figures who are outcasts, abandoned and exiled from their traditions. For example, *Onnest'bo* (2002–06) is about forced removals from District 6; while *Cargo* (2007) deals with the slave trade in the early years of the Cape Colony. Then, one of their most widely travelled pieces, *Every Year, Every Day I Am Walking* (2006–present), is a play about two refugees fleeing an unnamed African country and coming to South Africa, where they are caught up in the cacophony of an alien environment. In all of these productions, Magnet Theatre engaged with the figure of the outcast, the slave, the refugee. In no other play, however, have they presented the figure of the stranger in quite as lyrical a fashion as in *Die Vreemdeling* [The Stranger] (2010). The ways in which the stranger is portrayed in this play might be helpful in reflecting on broader issues of strangeness, familiarity and fear.

Before approaching the specifics of the play, it may be worthwhile to be reminded of the very real dangers which a fear of strangers presents. These are not simply philosophical considerations, since fear of the unknown Other can have very real and terrible repercussions. In South Africa, an animosity towards outsiders led to horrifying consequences, when riots sparked by xenophobic violence tore through the country in 2008. (Sadly, these attacks continue to happen today, at the time of writing, in 2015.)

Stranger Danger – Xenophobia in South Africa

Although the conflict had been simmering for some time (and it would be difficult to pinpoint an exact inciting incident exacerbating the mounting tension), the drama of the stranger in South Africa erupted violently during the riots of 2008, when 'a wave of xenophobic attacks on foreign nationals around the country left more than 50 people dead' (Radebe 2013). Since the democratic reforms of 1994, the new South African government has insistently attempted to cultivate a sense of patriotism, and to develop pride in a newly formed national identity. This investment in a cohesive national body has, however, all too often been premised on the exclusion of the foreigner:

> [A] phobia about foreigners, above all from elsewhere in Africa, has been the illicit offspring of the fledgling democracy – waxing, paradoxically perhaps, alongside appeals to the African Renaissance and ubuntu, a common African humanity.
>
> (Comaroff & Comaroff 2001: 645)

The foreigner makes us notice ourselves in a different way. Derrida notes that the foreigner is a destabilizing presence in our midst (cited in Flockemann 2010: 246). The foreigner upsets the status quo, creating suspicion and fear, a theme lucidly elaborated by Zygmunt Bauman's *Liquid Times* (2007). Bauman's book concerns the crisis of refugees and the rising xenophobia in a world in which refugees are seen as human waste material: 'superfluous humans stripped of their assets, a [...] supernumerary and redundant population' (Bauman 2007: 28); ones not only outside of the nation, but also outside of economic systems, outside of recourse to the law. For Bauman (2007: 16), linked to this has been the 'recent rapid increase in the value of fear saturating the whole of societies.' One of the reasons for this, he notes, is due to the increasing heterogeneity of most countries. As cities grow and populations expand, as migrants move over the earth in search of safety, cities are no longer citadels. They no longer provide a safe haven. Instead, cities have become the locus of the foreign. From Pakistan to Brazil, the wealthy hide behind gated communities, increasingly withdrawing from the nation state. Bauman (2007: 37) notes that 'if we no longer have faith in the nation [...] we can then hire a private security company to keep the foreigners at bay. Making ourselves prisoners.' In this way, divisions between worlds have increasingly arisen within countries rather than between them. This fear of strangers both outside of a country and from within it is certainly evident in South Africa today. As levels of inequality in South Africa continue to rise, and security companies become an ever-present feature of urban life, our response to strangers has become increasingly driven by fear, and it is a short distance between fear and violence.[5]

The outbreak of the xenophobic violence which engulfed South Africa in 2008 led to the creation of a new media buzzword; something on which to focus the public's concerns, something to debate. However, there is now also, ironically, a growing fear of xenophobia itself. Bronwyn Harris, in her article 'Xenophobia: A New Pathology for a New South

Africa' (2002), shows how the language used to describe xenophobia is uncannily similar to the language used to describe foreigners:

> [X]enophobia as a term is described with the same language and images that are used to describe foreigners in xenophobic language. Indeed, the word 'xenophobia' is easily substitutable for the word 'foreigner' in many of these representations. For example, a xenophobic portrayal of the foreigner reads as 'stemming the tide of illegals,' while a depiction of xenophobia itself reads as 'stemming the tide of xenophobia.'
>
> (Harris 2002: 179)

There is thus a curious ambivalence about positions towards xenophobia, which is described as a kind of sickness similar to the unease expressed about foreigners. Both are mechanisms of fear, of separation, of distancing ourselves from others. Perhaps what is at stake here is the problem of anger, this destructive emotion which damages both the subject and the target it attacks. Ironically, fighting xenophobia can become yet another excuse for a consolidation of identity, an opportunity for refusal, for the rejection of the Other. As Harris (2002: 181) points out, a nation state 'is itself a means of violence.' Might it be that we have to give up being 'we' if we are to accept the migrant from outside and the stranger from within?

Staging Xenophobia

Societies prefer their refugees to remain invisible, which is perhaps why theatre-makers love putting them onstage. Ever sensitive to sociopolitical situations, South African theatre-makers have produced a great many plays about migrants, refugees and strangers in both the lead up to and the aftermath of the tragic attacks of 2008. In fact, there might now be enough plays about xenophobia for this to become recognized as the emergence of a new theme in recent South African theatre.

For example, award-winning choreographer Acty Tang's *amaQueerKwere* (2005) was located in an historical prison, the first building to be erected in Grahamstown, where the National Arts Festival is held every year. The title conflates the notion of being queer with the derogatory description of being *amakwerekwere*.[6] According to Tang's (2005) press release, this physical theatre production dealt with 'desires for love and freedom, and the costs that stand in the way.' Tang (2005) claims that: 'For a foreigner the cost to stay in this country may be a bribe; the cost of crossing borders may be his life.' The performance piece considers ways in which both sexual experience and belonging to a community can drive one into exile from all that is familiar.

Then, Jonathan Nkala's *The Crossing* (2009) is a play about his experience of becoming a refugee from Zimbabwe. It is the true story of Nkala's flight from the rural village of Kwe Kwe in Zimbabwe, and tells how he illegally crossed the border across the crocodile-infested Limpopo River to come to South Africa. In Nicholas Spagnoletti's *London Road* (2010), a feisty Nigerian refugee (Stella, played by Ntombi Makhutshi), befriends a reclusive elderly white woman (Rosa Kaplowitz, played by Robyn Scott). The two share a lonely estrangement from mainstream society and 'find themselves physically and emotionally marooned in Sea Point's flatland' (Thamm 2010).[7]

As already mentioned, Magnet Theatre has vividly explored the issue of forced migration in *Every Year, Every Day, I Am Walking*, which skilfully recreates the flight of two refugees using a vibrant sensorial landscape accessing the full gamut of sensations, including the acrid smoke of a burning house, provocative sound effects, and at times both startling and poignant physical images. *Every Year* premiered in Yaoundé, Cameroon in 2006, and has been running intermittently ever since, having toured 19 countries to date. The play's subject matter was made accessible to members of the refugee community in a special performance on 17 August 2007 during a run at the Baxter Theatre in Cape Town, when transportation and complimentary tickets were provided to refugee organizations, including the Scalabrini Centre for Refugees, Bonne Esperance and the Cape Town Refugee Centre. The play provides an excellent site for exploring the plight of refugees, and is discussed by Flockemann ('Being There,' p. 91) and Hutchison ('Embodied Practice,' p. 181). In this present chapter, however, I would like to look at what might be considered as a more figurative rendering of the predicament of the stranger in a strange land.

Die Vreemdeling [The Stranger]

Magnet Theatre's production of *Die Vreemdeling* was performed from 2010–11 and published in the collection *The Magnet Theatre 'Migration' Plays* (Reznek, Fleishman, Yisa & Marek 2012), from which all subsequent quotations, including translations, have been taken.[8] It is one of only a few plays they have staged in Afrikaans,[9] and it presents a rich ambivalence of attitudes towards strangers. Drawing on ideas presented by Georg Simmel and Julia Kristeva, I would like to consider what some of these attitudes might be, particularly notions of how exoticism can spawn both desire and dread. The plot of the play is based on a short story by Frances Marek,[10] which is described as 'a story about fences and borders; the things we construct to keep out what we fear' (Reznek et al. 2012: 95).

Die Vreemdeling is about a travelling troupe of three actors who re-enact a story by playing all of the various characters, as well as one or two inanimate objects, like a windmill, and a few farm animals. Much like the travelling troupes of medieval mystery plays, their characterization is exaggerated and the story takes on allegorical proportions. The story they tell is about the arrival of The Stranger, who collapses at a locked gate sealing off a fence around an isolated community which has gone into decline. The last girl in town, Ella, is referred to as '*die laaste dogtertjie*' ['the last daughter/girl'] (Reznek et al. 2012: 104). Ella (played by Ephraim Gordon) finds The Stranger unconscious on the

Dann-Jacques Mouton and Frances Marek wrestle with the concept of strangers in *Die Vreemdeling* (2010).
Photo credit: © Mark Wessels.

other side of the gate which cuts the village off from the outside world. She's afraid of this destitute figure, and her first words to him are:

> *Wie is jy? Wat soek jy hier? Gaan weg, dis nie veilig vir jou hier nie! [...] die mense van die dorp hou nie van vreemdelinge nie! Hulle gaan jou morsdood maak. Gaan weg!*
>
> [Who are you? What do you want? Go away, it's not safe for you here! [...] The people in this town don't like strangers! They will kill you! Go away!]
>
> (Reznek et al. 2012: 109)

At first Ella wants to call the other townspeople and to summon the police. But then, knowing what their response will be to The Stranger's intrusion of their community, she thinks better of it. Instead of reporting his arrival, she follows the promptings of her heart and fetches water to revive him. She then surreptitiously dresses his wounds and hides him in the chicken coop, saying: '*As die mense van die dorp uitvind ek gee 'n vreemdeling herberg, is ons altwee morsdood!*' ['If the people of this town find out I'm helping a stranger, we'll both be killed!'] (Reznek et al. 2012: 111). The beautifully poignant word *herberg* is repeated a few times in the course of the play. The literal meaning of the word is 'refuge.' His safety depends on her courage, on her being able to overcome her fear.

In deciding to help him, Ella has also unwittingly put herself in opposition to the community. Her father (Pa, played by Dann-Jacques Mouton) finds The Stranger, and discovers that he doesn't speak their language (Reznek et al. 2012: 112). Caught in a quandary, unsure about whether or not to report The Stranger's presence to the townsfolk, Pa consults the portrait of his dead wife, which is an ever-present feature of their kitchen. (The framed portrait is played by the writer of the short story on which the play was based, Frances Marek, who also assisted Mark Fleishman in directing the production.) Pa appears to be more afraid of the group's approbation than of The Stranger himself, and this is a clue as to where the greater fear resides. Worse than the fear of the stranger, is the fear of becoming strangers ourselves, of being cast out, exiled. The greatest danger which a stranger represents is in taking us beyond ourselves, outside of our community, questioning our allegiances and alliances. To underscore this fear of the unfamiliar, whenever a character says the word '*vreemd*' ['strange'], they struggle over its articulation, loading it with a sinister meaning. The word is repeated throughout the production, gaining an ever darker resonance as the piece progresses.

A neighbour, Gert, arrives unexpectedly, and Ella hides The Stranger with her own body (Reznek et al. 2012: 116). The Stranger stands behind her and mimics her gestures and actions to avoid detection. Later on, some of these moves are repeated in a romantic dance sequence and this mirroring might be seen as signalling attempts at communication, as the two identify with each other by means of similar gestures.

Ella moves The Stranger from the chicken coop to the garden to the kitchen, proving her commitment to his protection with each move closer to the home. Once he has been safely installed in their house, the previously barren farm mysteriously becomes fruitful – the chicken lays too many eggs to count, the orange tree produces luscious fruits, and the abundant water from the windmill encourages flowers to blossom. The presence of The Stranger has magically created a bounty. When he has recovered from his injuries, Ella wants him to leave for the sake of his own safety, but now Pa, who has noticed the connection between The Stranger's presence and the flourishing produce on his farm, sees an opportunity for gain and insists that The Stranger remain with them. Pa wants to sell the gifts which The Stranger has brought and Ella notices a change in her father as his greed takes hold of him. She says: '*Die idée van rykdom het my pa die horries laat kry. Hy's soos 'n monster. Hy maak my bang*' ['The idea of wealth has made my Pa demented. He's like a monster. He makes me afraid'] (Reznek et al. 2012: 124). Ella manages to convince him that selling their newfound goods will arouse suspicion among the townsfolk. Instead of making a profit out of the gifts, she secretly distributes the presents to all the houses of the town's inhabitants. The townspeople stay silent about these gifts, which appear on their doorstep under cover of darkness, since they do not want them to be taken away. The strangeness of the situation feeds their secrecy. Ella and The Stranger fall in love (which might be seen as the Self and the Other uniting to form a whole). This is expressed in a beautifully choreographed dance, full of tenderness and longing (Reznek et al. 2012: 132).

Thus, The Stranger in *Die Vreemdeling* evokes ambivalent affects: of not only fear and suspicion, but also mystery and the pleasures of the unknown. There's a curiosity about the potential he embodies. He brings gifts and understanding, and sympathy for Ella, as well as anxiety and uncertainty. In his essay 'The Stranger,' George Simmel (1971: 145) notes that, because they are outside society, strangers may receive 'revelations and confidences, at times reminiscent of a confessional.'[11] The stranger's very separation from the ordinary life in a group makes possible a 'positive and definite kind of participation' (1971: 145), in that they are able to dialogue and reflect on the accepted practices and habitual behaviours to which the group have been blinded by familiarity. Similarly, Kristeva (1991: 7–8) notes the aloofness of foreigners, their grandeur which draws people towards them. The Stranger in *Die Vreemdeling* is also enveloped in an erotic aura. An infectious ambivalence about romance and strangeness is described by Simmel:

> A trace of strangeness [...] easily enters even the most intimate relationships. In the first stage of passion, erotic relations strongly reject any thought of generalisation. A love such as this has never existed before; there is nothing to compare either with the person one loves or with our feelings for the person.
>
> (Simmel 1971: 147)

Lovers are initially strangers, and the first flush of romance is often accompanied by the excitement of having made a new discovery. When one encounters an unknown person for the first time, they appear to offer a multitude of possibilities. When one gets to know them better, one might argue, people become less strange, less mysterious. They become more specific, particular, limited. To be known is to become defined into a role, whereas the stranger is unlimited.

So Ella and The Stranger continue their dance of love and the townsfolk continue to receive their unearned gifts; but then Sheraton, a bombastic character who acts as a town Sheriff (comically played by David Johnson), starts to question why things have changed, and he begins to investigate the strange events that have been happening. In this atmosphere of secrecy and desire, dread grows, repeated in a refrain taken from Shakespeare's *The Merchant of Venice*: '*versoeking is die vuur wat die etter van die hart ontbloot*' ['Temptation is the fire that brings up the scum of the heart'] (Reznek et al. 2012: 133–34).

Every night, Ella goes around delivering the gifts – flowers, oranges, eggs – while The Stranger hides in the chicken coop. These gifts all convey a strong sense of a nourishing femininity, and might be read as signifying fertility and fecundity. But then, one full-mooned night, consumed with longing, The Stranger follows Ella and is discovered (Reznek et al. 2012: 138). A dog begins to bark and its owner alerts the town. Instead of being acknowledged as the source of the gifts, The Stranger is accused of being a thief. A woman (Tant Stiemie, played by Ephraim Gordon) fearfully cries out for him to be attacked. The women scream and the men ready themselves to shoot. The whole town circles around The Stranger in a scene which is captivatingly presented by means of three actors embodying different characters from the town leaving a hat (which has become identified with each character) in a circle around a crumpled African cape (which has come to signify The Stranger), while a strong drum beat drives their outrage. When he is asked who The Stranger is, Ella's father denies any knowledge of him, not wanting to be tainted by an unfavourable association. In this way, Pa betrays The Stranger in front of the ever-present portrait of Ma, Ella's mother; and now we find out the truth that Ma died because of the town's fear and because of their poverty of heart. Ella appeals to the mob:

> *Toe Ma so siek was, kon julle die hek oopmaak vir hulp, maar julle het nie. Nou het daar hulp vir ons dorp gekom. Kyk hoeveel geskenke het hierdie vreemdeling vir ons gebring, en julle het almal daarvan geëet en gedrink, maar nou vreet julle geheime begeertes julle binneste en vul julle harte met skuld. As gevolg van die skuldgevoel wil julle hom by die hek uitsmyt. Maar hy's klaar binne, los hom so. Hier's julle kans om die hekke van julle harte ook oop te maak.*
>
> [When Ma was sick you could have opened the gate for help, but none of you did. Now help has come to us. Look at all the gifts this stranger brought, and you all took and ate and drank those gifts, but now these secrets are eating away at you and filling your hearts with guilt. And because of the guilt you feel for taking him in, you want to throw this stranger out of town. But he's already here, just leave him. This is your chance to open the gates of your hearts.]
>
> (Reznek et al. 2012: 142)

Instead of being swayed by her plea, the townsfolk beat The Stranger to death. Hysterical, Ella attacks Sheraton with a knife, but he brushes her aside. She then turns the knife on herself, but relinquishes it before she's able to cut her own throat. After the murder of The Stranger, the town goes into decline – the dam dries up, the chickens refuse to lay eggs, the fruit trees fail (Reznek et al. 2012: 146). Eventually, Ella leaves via the same gate through which she allowed The Stranger in. She takes the portrait of her mother with her and abandons Pa to his hangover. Our last view of him is as a miserable failure who was unable to stand up for another man.

There seem to be two ways of viewing The Stranger here. On the one hand, he is complete in his mystery, having access to things – goods, knowledge, experience – which are not available to the community. He arrives from another world outside, bringing wonder. And then there's the other view of strangers, the view established by the community, the crowd. In their eyes, The Stranger is hardly human: he is barbarian, *amakwerekwere*. *Die Vreemdeling* neatly merges both of these responses into a poignant, bittersweet tragedy.

Conclusions

The title of this chapter comes from the introduction to Albert Camus' disarming novella of dislocation, *L'Etranger* [The Stranger] (1946).[12] The original citation from which I lifted the phrase 'implacable grandeur' reads: 'For if there is a sin against life, it consists perhaps not so much in despairing of life as in hoping for another life and in eluding the implacable grandeur of this life' (Camus 1946: 8).

In *L'Etranger*, the protagonist, Meursalt (the stranger of the title), is not connected to community and for this reason lives in the present – he does not mourn the past nor long for an imaginary future. He does not wish for more than he has. For him, the hope of any other life becomes a denial of the reality of his present conditions. In this sense, the stranger represents the plenitude, the rich mystery of every movement into the unknown. In contrast, the fear of strangers closes one off from new possibilities offered by the potential interdependence shared with as yet unknown others.

Perhaps separation from others would not be as damaging if difference were not inevitably hierarchized, if separation did not apportion rank. But foreigners, strangers and refugees are ranked lower than the citizen, and sometimes their very naming can become a means of elevating the citizen above them: 'The humiliation that disparages the foreigner endows his master with who knows what petty grandeur' (Kristeva 1991: 14). Instead of the 'petty grandeur' designating rank and file, *Die Vreemdeling* evokes a richer grandeur of the strange and mysterious.

As a thematic strain in recent South African theatre, the theme of the stranger appears to be particularly significant, reflecting as it does the dilemmas of being caught between poles of community and freedom. This theme is ideally situated to elaborate the *frisson* between feelings of belonging either to a polis or to a cosmos. There is a dangerous hypocrisy, as

Harris (2002) has discovered, in turning against and condemning both xenophobes and foreigners, of separating ourselves from others, whether these are inside or outside of our communities. Perhaps the myth that communication will solve all imaginable human conflicts is part of the problem. In other words, if one labels strangeness as a setback, one could try to make theatre which introduced and explained unfamiliar customs in order to compartmentalize the unknown in an effort to bring it to heel, to control it..

Attempts at familiarizing the constituents of various communities with aspects of each other's strangeness is a project which has typified much anti-apartheid South African theatre for decades; and yet this is an approach which stands in sharp contrast to views which see the role of art as being the encouragement of processes of *ostranenie* [defamiliarization], a concept first proposed by Victor Shklovsky in 1917, and taken further by Brecht with his theory of *verfremdung*. Shklovsky and Brecht saw the importance of art in making the ordinary unfamiliar, in being able to see the mundane in a new light, rather than in hoping to harness unfamiliarity in order to fulfil the underlying moral purpose of understanding the Other, which is what a number of apartheid era plays – such as *Sizwe Bansi is Dead* (1972), *Woza Albert* (1981) and *Sophiatown* (1986) – succeeded in doing so well. Each of these plays was created by a mixed race group of practitioners who attempted, amongst other things, to introduce white audiences at the Market Theatre to the circumstances and customs of black township dwellers. In contrast to these apartheid era plays, which often sought to familiarize one race with the traditions of another, for Shklovsky the aim is not to resolve, not to redeem, not to hope for a sense of familiarity; but to see in art an opportunity for wonder, for strangeness.

No-one operates entirely in isolation: one is always part of a group, even if one is not always aware of its exact parameters. Nelson Mandela (1995: 768) writes on the last page of *Long Walk to Freedom* that 'to be free is not merely to cast off one's chains, but to live in a way that respects and enhances the freedom of others.' This chapter has attempted to grapple with the questions of freedom and belonging, about who 'we' are; and whether we should try to identify this 'we' – we whites, we blacks, we South Africans, we humans – and tie it down by definition. Do we necessarily need to submit to the divisions of imaginary constructions which have allocated us into separate identities? Is it really inescapable to seek belonging in groups and categorized communities? Would it not be possible to accept being a community of strangers, and to see other strangers as guests who arrive, like The Stranger in *Die Vreemdeling* at '*die hekke van [ons] harte*' ['the gates of [our] hearts'] (Reznek et al. 2012: 142)? Would it not be possible to accept each other's incongruity, rather than seeing strangeness as something to be overcome, something which needs to be conquered by comprehension? In so many of their works, Magnet Theatre have revelled in the gloriously strange incongruities presented by the many strange cultures existing in South Africa today; mixing together styles, languages and physical forms without compromising any of them, but also without hierarchizing one above the other. In this way, the company has shown that we can enjoy each other's unfathomable peculiarity, and that it is possible to present strangeness without exoticism, and difference without judgement.

References

Bauman, Z. (2007), *Liquid Times: Living in an Age of Uncertainty*, Cambridge: Polity Press.

Camus, A. (1946), *L'Etranger* [The Outsider] (trans. S. Gilbert), London: Hamish Hamilton.

Comaroff, J. and Comaroff, J. (2001), 'Naturing the Nation: Aliens, Apocalypse and the Postcolonial State, *Journal of Southern African Studies*, 27: 3, pp. 627–51.

Deleuze, G. and Guattari, F. (1987), *A Thousand Plateaus: Capitalism and Schizophrenia* (trans. B. Massumi), Minneapolis: University of Minnesota Press.

Flockemann, M. (2010), 'The Everyday Experience of Xenophobia: Performing *The Crossing* from Zimbabwe to South Africa,' *Critical Arts: South-North Cultural and Media Studies*, 24: 2, pp. 245–59.

Fugard, A., Kani, J. and Ntshona, W. (1976), *Sizwe Bansi is Dead, and The Island*, New York: Viking Press.

Harris, B. (2002), 'Xenophobia: A New Pathology for a New South Africa?' in D. Hook and G. Eagle (eds), *Psychopathology and Social Prejudice*, Cape Town: University of Cape Town Press, pp. 169–84.

Kristeva, J. (1991), *Strangers to Ourselves* (trans. L. S. Roudiez), Hertfordshire: Harvester Wheatsheaf.

Mandela, N. (1995), *Long Walk to Freedom*, London: Abacus.

Mtwa, P., Ngema, M. and Simon, B. (1983), *Woza Albert*, London: Methuen.

Nkala, J. (2009), *The Crossing, and The Bicycle Thief*, Cape Town: Junkets.

Purkey, M. and Stein, P. (eds) (2003), *Sophiatown: A Play – Created by Junction Avenue Theatre Company*, Johannesburg: Witwatersrand University Press.

Radebe, H. (2013) 'Xenophobia in South Africa Alive Five Years After Riots,' *Business Day Live*, 13 May, http://www.bdlive.co.za/national/2013/05/13/xenophobia-in-south-africa-alive-five-years-after-riots. Accessed 13 April 2014.

Reznek, J. and Fleishman, M. (2013), personal interview with A. Krueger, 13 June.

Reznek, J., Fleishman, M., Yisa, F. and Marek, F. (2012), *The Magnet Theatre 'Migration' Plays*, Cape Town: Junkets Publisher.

Reznek, J. et al. (2010), *Die Vreemdeling* [The Stranger] (dir. Mark Fleishman), Cape Town: Magnet Theatre (unpublished).

Simmel, G. (1971), *On Individuality and Social Forms: Selected Writings*, Chicago: University of Chicago Press.

Tang, A. (2005), *Media Kit – amaQueerKwere*, Grahamstown: National Arts Festival.

Thamm, M. (2010), 'Unlikely Duo find Support in Shared Predicament,' *Sunday Times*, 21 March, http://londonroad.co.za/marianne-thamm-sunday-times/. Accessed 11 April 2014.

Notes

1. An earlier, shorter version of this chapter was published as 'The Implacable Grandeur of the Stranger: Ruminations on Fear and Familiarity in *Die Vreemdeling*' by Anton Krueger, published in *South African Theatre Journal*, 26: 3, pp. 303–10 (2012) © *South African Theatre Journal*, reprinted by permission of Taylor & Francis Ltd, www.tandfonline.com on behalf of *South African Theatre Journal*.
2. As Deleuze and Guattari (1987: 25) exhort: 'Don't bring out the general in you!'
3. See Introduction ('Plotting the Magnetic Field,' p. 4).
4. Fleishman adds: 'For Latour, what is expanded is the notion of the social – what can be considered to be part of the social realm at all. He argues for a "reassembling of the social" along newly conceived lines. This is interesting to me because it is exactly what we have been and continue to be engaged with in South Africa since 1994' (Reznek & Fleishman 2013).
5. One of the most common definitions for a 'xenophobe' relates to fear, whereas 'xenophobia' is more often linked to hatred. The two seem to be intimately linked.
6. The word *amakwerekwere* is similar to the word 'barbarian' in that it tries to imitate the nonsensical language of the unknown. In the same way that the ancient Greeks created the word 'barbarian' to describe foreigners whom they did not realize as having their own, separate language – and who were, consequently, thought to simply be bleating 'baa baa baa' – *kwerekwerekwere* is a mockery of other African languages, mocking sounds unfamiliar to South African blacks.
7. There are also many other plays that deal less directly with the topic of the stranger, such as Mpumelelo Paul Grootboom's plays, which often include foreign characters like the Nigerian pimp in *Cards* (2002) and the Malawians in *Relativity: Township Stories* (2006). Craig Higginson's *Girl in the Yellow Dress* (2011) also has to do with issues of foreignness and the acquisition of an unfamiliar culture. Perhaps there is a danger here in that often when embarking on a particular theme, it happens that the more one starts to search for material, the more evidence one finds for one's thesis, in the same way that studying psychology sometimes makes one discover what appear to be all sorts of neuroses within oneself. Soon it might begin to seem as though almost every play has something to do with strangers.
8. The visual descriptions of the play have been taken from a DVD recording made of the performance on 17 March 2011 at Magnet Theatre in Observatory, Cape Town.
9. *Soe Loep Ons Nou Nog* was mostly in Afrikaans.
10. See interview with Frances Marek ('Magnet's Recipe for Considered, Conscious Theatre-Making').

11. The stranger as confessor is also found in *London Road* (2011), in that the Nigerian exile Stella arrives as a stranger in South Africa, and acts as a sounding board for the memories and concerns of an elderly white woman.
12. The story was originally published in an earlier essay 'Summer in Algiers' (1936).

Chapter 7

Theatre That Can Organize, Mobilize, Conscientize: A Conversation with Mandla Mbothwe[1]

Before joining Magnet, Mbothwe directed a number of productions with strong community roots, such as Beyond Silence, Not a Prison *and* 9437 To Stadt. *He was the artistic coordinator for Sithi@Baxter and a director of the Garage Theatre Company. After studying with Mark Fleishman and Jennie Reznek at UCT, Mandla went on to play major roles in the creation and development of the Community Groups Intervention in Khayelitsha, which he ran with Jennie from 2002–08, and then the Magnet Theatre training programme (2008–present). Later, he directed the first Magnet shows in Xhosa:* ingcwaba lendoda lise cankwe ndlela *[the grave of the man lies next to the road] (2009) and* Inxeba Lomphilisi – The Wound of a Healer *(2010–14). After leaving Magnet Theatre in 2011, Mandla took up the directorship of the Steve Biko Foundation until 2014, when he took up a post as creative manager of Artscape, Cape Town. He is still a trustee on the board of Magnet Theatre.*

'It's through Magnet that most of my dreams have been realized,' says Mandla Mbothwe. Mbothwe's mission as a director and community theatre facilitator is to 'develop and empower people using performing arts and culture.' An activist as well as an artist, Mbothwe is driven by 'the idea of using performing arts and drama as a tool for mobilizing, organizing and conscientizing.'

'My first interaction with theatre,' he admits, 'was never inside the theatre. It happened in high schools, in community halls, clinics, hospitals, playgrounds. I wanted to use drama to educate people. And I started realizing that the work I'm trying to do – teaching and acting and all these things – it wasn't just for entertainment. [...] The experience reinforced the idea in me that theatre really needs to be political.'

In the 1980s, Mbothwe worked with a student organization called TOSCO (Township Student Congress); after matriculation, he briefly attended the University of the Western Cape (UWC) and met Alfred Hinkel through the New Africa Theatre Association (NATA). Then, Caroline Calburne of Theatre Arts Admin encouraged him to apply and audition for UCT. It was there that he met Fleishman and Reznek, who taught him acting, mime, movement and script analysis.

'Before I went to university,' he says, 'the only thing we knew was to improvise, the only thing we knew was poetry. We'd find a poem and divide it among ourselves and do a gumboot dance and create around it. At university was the first time I saw a script. This was new for me – analysing a script.'

Director Mandla Mbothwe working with CGI youth in Khayelitsha (2006).
Photo credit: © Mark Wessels.

But scripts, especially those from the European canon, frustrated Mbothwe. That was until 1995, when Mark and Jennie made the show *Sunjata* [based on the epic hero of the Mali Empire] with the UCT Drama Department. It 'was very African,' he says, 'And I was like – "O wow, there's Shakespeare in other places!"' Mbothwe was made to feel at home by what he calls 'the African theme' of *Sunjata*. 'It was unlike the forms I had done before,' he says, but 'I was, like – "Wow, it's possible, to be around here and still make theatre that speaks to me, not just to interpret." That inspired me and I really loved it so much. I thought – I want to work with these people, they're amazing. And then they also wanted to work with me.'

From there, Mbothwe began working with Magnet on a variety of projects, including the community-based annual lantern festival in Clanwilliam; the Community Groups Intervention (CGI) projects in Khayelitsha; and the Magnet Theatre training programme.

'Jennie and me ran the [CGI] programme for eight years,' he explains. 'She's passionate not only about creating, but also teaching. That says a lot about Magnet.' The CGI was a long-term investment in the townships, Mbothwe explains, aimed at empowering young theatre-makers. 'We understood what it means for intervention to develop and to educate a community,' he says, 'It was not hit-and-run. It's not like we're going to just do a festival and leave them.' Through the CGI, Magnet worked with local theatre groups in the township, training them in character work, physicality, research and storytelling, as well as offering workshops in directing and voice, and bringing in people like Mike van Graan[2] and Gay Morris[3] as guest teachers.

'Within those groups, we want to see the individual people developing,' he says. He describes how, over time, he started to challenge the township groups: 'They were doing all these plays about drugs and guns and shooting in *shebeens* [illegal township bars in people's private homes]. That's what drama means for them. There must always be violence. So we started challenging that, saying – "Do you think you're really helping your community?" Their way of thinking and their stories shifted through those interventions, and for me that's very important. They started looking at characters in a new way.'

'When we first started the [CGI], there were so many places we went to where there were community groups who needed help. After four years, Jennie said: "We need to find a way of training new black directors."' That led to the development of the Full Time Training and Job Creation Programme, which Mbothwe spearheaded with Reznek and Fleishman. For Mbothwe, the value of working with Magnet is not only about theatrical training, but also about the professionalization and encouragement of young artists. 'For example,' he says, 'when I did a second year production with students and community group members, I collected members from all the groups and my cast and they interacted. And half of those people were inspired to apply to come to UCT [...]. That year, for me, made an impact that's still affecting the community now. It takes time for people to discover their talent and it takes time for them to get to know theatre, to touch the intangible [...] and I think that's what Magnet did for me.'

As a director, Mbothwe says 'I watch and I feel what's going on in society. I'm interested in the humanity in the face of whatever happens. In all this suffering – what happened to humanity? That's my main interest. Where does violence come from? How do these things start? I'm not interested in rape [or AIDS] as a subject, [for example,] I'm interested in what happens to the inner person.'

He is also clear about his advocacy for and articulation of diverse voices in his work. 'We mustn't pretend we're all this big rainbow thing singing together; that's not true,' he says. 'It's not that everybody's wearing the same costume and doing the same things, and everybody's trying to be like each other. People are doing different things, and the unity is imperfect; but just the attempt, even if you try, it proves we are in it together, even if we're different.'

The inclusion of many voices, especially in languages other than English, is vitally important to Mbothwe. 'I was always interested in language,' he says. 'You know, in drama they speak in Xhosa only when they want to make people laugh. Even Xhosa people themselves. It becomes almost an estrangement of the audience, that's the only way it has been used.' To address this misuse of his mother tongue, Mbothwe says, 'I wanted to reclaim the idiom, to start a movement. I wanted people to find their own blood within them, to know the connections to their own lines. They need to connect to their own language, so that it can become part of their literature.'

Two of Magnet's more recent works, directed by Mbothwe – *ingcwaba lendoda lise cankwe ndlela* (2009) and *Inxeba Lomphilisi* (2010–14) – are in Xhosa. Mbothwe says that Fleishman, whom Mandla describes as 'a humble man, willing to learn, not taking himself too seriously,' always supported his vision and work as a director. 'He always gives space for people to exercise their signature within the space of creativity,' he says of Fleishman.

Language – both spoken and embodied – are two of Mbothwe's central concerns. 'Magnet as a company has shifted the landscape both intellectually and socially, and also in terms of their aesthetic,' he explains. 'Also, Magnet Theatre seeks to find a language beyond the spoken one. They've created a new kind of physical theatre. Yes, it comes from clown and all those kinds of things, but it's also because of their desire for theatre to communicate beyond language boundaries. They're always searching for a new language in physicality; and in that physicality they've managed to find metaphors that speak to people.'

References

Mbothwe, M. (2013), personal interview with A. Krueger, 9 June.

Notes

1. Interview quotes in this chapter are taken from Mbothwe (2013).
2. Mike van Graan is a popular South African playwright. He is a founding member of PANSA (Performing Arts Network of South Africa) and has played a leading role in numerous arts administration organizations.
3. See Morris ('Making Space for Community').

PART TWO

Collaboration: Making Space for Embodied Practice

Chapter 8

Performing the Language of the Body in My Mother Tongue: A Conversation with Faniswa Yisa[1]

Faniswa Yisa was a resident performer at Magnet Theatre from 2004–11, most often in leading roles. Graduating from the University of Cape Town with a Performer's Diploma in Speech and Drama in 2000, her first show with the company was The Fire Raisers *(2004). She has also performed in* Cargo *(2007),* ingcwaba lendoda lise cankwe ndlela *[the grave of the man lies next to the road] (2009),* Inxeba Lomphilisi – The Wound of a Healer *(which she co-directed with Mandla Mbothwe in 2010),* Autopsy *(2012) and* Voices Made Night *(2010–14). She has toured internationally with* Every Year, Every Day, I Am Walking *(2006–present). In addition to her work with Magnet, she joined The Mothertongue Project in February 2001, co-creating and performing in* Unkulunkulu the Sovereign One *(2001),* Beading My Soul *(2001) and* Indawo Yamaphupha – The Space of Dreams *(2003). Faniswa performed in Janice Honeyman's* Madiba Magic, *and starred in Brett Bailey's* meDia *(2005) and* Orpheus *(2007). She still works for Magnet in her capacity as a freelance actor.*

Faniswa Yisa believes the best theatre is 'a reflection of a society,' and that 'theatre-makers should have a sense of responsibility.' Across her work as a Magnet collaborator, she admires the company's approach to work, as well as their artistic sensibility. 'Magnet's shows are accessible to a wide range of people,' she says, emphasizing the importance of telling the stories of under-represented groups, particularly in the new South African democracy, and doing so in a carefully considered, ethical way. 'They're very socially aware,' she says, reflecting on how many of the shows she's worked on deal with poverty, for instance. At Magnet, 'we try to make people aware. I think the most dangerous people in the world are those who aren't aware.'

'What makes Magnet different,' she says, 'are the stories that they tell and the way they tell them. And the way their stories engage with the consequence of where we are, and who we are in South Africa.' Yisa recalls how she was drawn to Magnet's interest in telling stories about the migratory routes in, to and from South Africa: the N2 to Cape Town, the N7 between the Karoo and Namibia, and the Cape to Cairo route. 'For me it's the concept, it's the consciousness behind the stories they're choosing to tell, because they feel they're important,' she explains. Magnet is 'very committed to telling South African stories,' she says, 'and they want to do those stories in the languages that they come in; whether in Afrikaans or African languages [...] When we do work with text, it's in a non-mainstream language. I think the most text I ever had to work with was in Mandla [Mbothwe]'s[2] productions where we used Xhosa.' For Yisa, what distinguishes Magnet's work, and what

Magnet resident performer Faniswa Yisa in *Autopsy* (2012).
Photo credit: © Mark Wessels.

draws her to it, is its physicality and its linguistic choices: 'either using the body or using a language that's not really predominantly used in the theatre today. So I like that – using either the universal language of the body, and also being able to use my mother tongue.'

For Yisa, Magnet's devising process is very productive for her as an actor. 'For *Every Year, Every Day*,' she explains, 'we had an idea of what the show would be about, but we didn't really know where that idea was going to lead.' She explains what they knew going into the process: 'We were very clear we wanted to do a small show, just Jennie and me. And there was going to be music, and the set should be put in a suitcase – to be able to travel.' The show developed through a process of devising and play. Given 'tasks' by Fleishman as prompts for their improvisation, Yisa and Reznek would then do 'a lot of research, a lot of playing on our own.' Through this playful process, 'we'd start creating themes within the overall main theme and come up with specific things to do. Then Mark would look at what we've got and say, "I need you to work on this or that." For instance, Mark would prompt them: '"Home. I want you to create home. What do you think home is?" So we'd go out and think about it and take things from home that we feel are personal. And we'd play with the ideas and feelings and objects and actions, and then come back and play, on our own still, on the floor. Then Mark would come in and we'd show him what we had. And then maybe at the end of the week he'd say, "Okay, I like that, I didn't like this. How about you try and incorporate that into Jennie's movements..." And then we'd put it together.'

'[Once] we'd decided that *Every Year, Every Day, I Am Walking* was about home, we went to other sources. It was around the time of the xenophobic attacks and we were also reading a book called *The Suitcase Stories* [2005], which is about refugees. So we found material in what was happening around us, and also in what we were reading. Because we were playing children, we got inspiration from the kids in the book, and we mixed it with our ideas of home and the children we knew. We had to imagine what it would be like to be a refugee.'

In discussing what it's like to work with Mark as a director, she comments on the balance he strikes between empowering actors with the freedom to be co-creators of the work and shaping the material with his unique theatrical eye. 'I respect him as a director and as an academic,' she asserts, 'but first I respect him as a man. That respect is important.' While she acknowledges that 'Mark's voice comes through in his directing. His voice is huge in our stories,' she also asserts that 'he gives you space. We often come to rehearsals and he says, "I don't know what it's going to look like." Or he'll say, "I have an idea about what I think the show should look like, but I want to hear from you what you think or feel it should look like."'

Yisa believes Magnet serves as a space in which the diverse voices of South Africa find a home: 'In every community there are all sorts of different people, so it's a bit naïve to assume that everyone in the community has the same ideas or that they're interested in the same things. I love approaching characters from a personal angle [...]. What I like about working with Magnet is that they'll say: "we want to know what you have to tell us."'

References

Clacherty, Glynis (2005), *The Suitcase Stories: Refugee Children Reclaim Their Identities*, Johannesburg: David Krut Publishing.

Yisa, F. (2013), personal interview with A. Krueger, 12 June.

Notes

1. Interview quotes in this chapter are taken from Yisa (2013).
2. See interview with Mandla Mbothwe ('Theatre That Can Organize, Mobilize, Conscientize').

Chapter 9

Magnet Theatre and the Moving Body

Jennie Reznek

Jennie Reznek (actress, teacher, director) is a graduate of the University of Cape Town's Drama School and studied in Paris with Jacques Lecoq for two years. She has worked as an aerialist and clown in the circus; a movement director, choreographer and teacher; a puppeteer with Handspring Puppet Company; and has performed in many productions of new South African plays. She is a founding member of Magnet Theatre and, together with Mark Fleishman, is responsible for the creative life of the company.

The training that I received as a performer at École Jacques Lecoq in Paris from 1984–86 has influenced much of Magnet Theatre's work. Equally important, though, has been the political and social context of South Africa itself. Because of both my Lecoq training and the South African context, the moving body of the individual has been the central obsession and driving exploration of the company Mark Fleishman and I founded in 1987. This can be seen in our production output, as well as in the training component of Magnet Theatre.

The body that Magnet is concerned with is a body threatened, one that faces erasure in the face of mortality; a body that is subject to oppression, to racial categorization, embattled through being immersed in social and political environments that are systemically violent; and a body that is subject to classical dualisms that leave it somehow subordinate to the animating intentions of the mind (Grosz 1994: vii). Magnet's work, then, can be seen as a response to a context of violence.

The Pendulum Swing

Magnet was born during the late 1980s in South Africa, a period marked by the intensification of the struggle against apartheid. The violence of that era has continued in different forms and varying levels of intensity to the present day. Magnet Theatre's focus on the body in our teaching and production work can be seen to have responded 'pendulum like' to the violence that existed in our context. For Lecoq (2006: 35), such a pendulum swing response to violence is 'inevitable.' Referring to the resurgence of a focus on the moving body after World War II, he states, 'The return to nature and spontaneity of gesture is an inevitable result of the overwhelming limitations that suppress life' (2006: 35). The overwhelming evidence of death (as a result of war and violence) forces a focus on the living body, and the way it invests in the future and in individuality through movement and action.

The images that saturated the landscape during the 'struggle years' in South Africa were of resistance, of young people insisting that the structures of power would and could be changed. Destruction and creation; repression and resistance – these were binaries set up within the social landscape which the theatre responded to in both form and content. Co-director of Magnet Theatre Mark Fleishman (1997: 202) states: 'Life in South Africa, filled as it had been with desperate struggles for change, or power and simple survivals, has a physically dynamic nature which feeds physically dynamic images on the stage.' The culture of violence in South Africa has turned the body into a marked site.

All forms of violence – be they physical or symbolic, violence as power, overt or covert – impact on the body. Violence imposes stillness, erases identity, and ruptures both the normal functioning of the body and existing perceptions about the world, knowledge, acceptable human behaviour and religious systems. If the body is the place where apartheid and other forms of violence made their mark, then the body can also be the site on which to offset this unmaking/destruction with making/creation (Scarry 1985).

Magnet's Response

So what are the strategies that are the defining cornerstones of Magnet's work, as it exists in response to the context and particularities of racism and violence in South Africa? At the risk of simplification, I would like to suggest that Magnet's work with the body springs from four notions, which I will explore in greater detail in the following pages:

1. Everything Moves ('*tout bouge*'), or the Body as Bridge.
2. The Body as Subject.
3. Transformation and Play.
4. Collective Creation.

Everything Moves ('*Tout Bouge*')

> Tout bouge. Tout evolue, progresse. Tous se ricochette et se revebere. D'une point a une autre, pas de ligne droite. D'une port a une port, un voyage. Tout bouge, moi aussi!
>
> [Everything moves. Everything evolves and progresses. Everything rebounds and resonates. From one point to another, never in a straight line. From port to port, a journey. Everything moves, as do I!]
>
> (Lecoq, cited in Keefe & Murray 2007: 192, my translation)

Magnet's emphasis on the body has been evident from their earliest productions, including *'I Do' x 22* (1997).
Photo credit: © Ruphin Coudyzer FPPSA. (ruphincoudyzer.com)

If everything moves, then everything can change. Inherent in the understanding of this continuously moving body and continuously moving life is a political understanding of the notion of constant change. Simon McBurney (cited in Jenkins 2001: 4) sums this up: 'The acceptance of constant movement flies in the face of all conservative dogmatism because it acknowledges that nothing is fixed, and it leads to the development of tolerance.' This vision of the world and body in constant motion is a challenge to all types of hegemonies, be they political, ideological or personal. To understand movement politically is to understand that structures of power can change, and if they can change, then alternative political futures can be envisioned. Without an understanding of movement, life in a political arena may seem immutable, and the political structures become a prison that has no possibility of alteration. This was, and continues to be, a crucially liberating notion in relation to the power structures that had remained in place in South Africa for the 45 years of apartheid, and in relation to the current crisis of confidence, with rising corruption and a lack of leadership under the ANC government.

By creating work that focuses the audience's attention on the human body, and by locating the meaning of the theatrical moment in the moving body, Magnet Theatre continually affirms this notion of the possibility of change. In Magnet productions, bodies shift from earth-bound weight to air-borne aerial artist, as in *The Shows Not Over 'Til the Fat Lady Sings* (1991–93), a metaphoric story of liberation around the central image of a fat lady who dreams of flying. Bodies move from being contemporary dancers to slaves and back, as in *Cargo* (2007), a collaborative project with Jazzart Dance Theatre, which embodied the fragments of the buried history of slavery in the Western Cape. And bodies move from being long-distance swimmers to nurses to the lepers on Robben Island, as in *53 Degrees* (2002–03), which intersected the personal narrative of a woman returning to creative life after leaving to be a mother with the history of Robben Island and long-distance swimming. Movement is also from past to present, and onwards to an imagined future. In *Onnest'bo* [Upside Down/ Topsy Turvy] (2002–06), created in collaboration with the District Six Museum, the cast of actors returned to an empty space to enact an imaginary return to a land from which they were forcibly removed during the apartheid regime. In each of these productions, our central thematic images affirm the possibility of change and transformation.

On a more personal level, to teach a body that always moves is to accept fundamentally the possibility of changes and nodes of growth and development that can occur at any time within an individual. Our training has always been longitudinal, and our interventions with young people occur over extended periods of time: seven years in the Community Groups Intervention; a two-year full-time intensive training programme currently busy with a fourth intake; three years of the Culture Gangs Project; 14 years in the Clanwilliam Arts Project. Giving substantial time to these projects allows for personal changes and development in skill to be nurtured and noted. Broadly speaking, Magnet's educational processes teach bodies to move, but they are also *about* movement in a broader sense: movement away from feelings and thoughts that imprison; movement away from the restricting confines of substandard education; movement out of the geographic and economic prisons that are the legacy of apartheid; movement towards a greater visibility of themselves; movement towards opportunities. The 40 young graduates of the full-time training programme have had a huge impact in terms of both role modelling (opening up possibilities for others), as well as on the industry itself. The change in the quality of product that is, for example, being produced on a platform like the Baxter Theatre's Zabalaza Festival is directly related to the skills upliftment that occurs in the training programme.

Everything Rebounds and Resonates ('*Tous se ricochette et se revebere*')

Lecoq suggests connectivity as a causal aspect between all the moving parts, which allows for events and people to have an impact on each other. This refers not only to the world outside the theatre, but also relates to the fundamental relationship that is created between performer and audience. In the theatre, performance sets up resonances and echoes in an audience, which is also an opportunity for movement. These are the shifts and changes in feeling and perception that occur as a result of the moving presence of the performer in space. The body in space has affect: it has the ability to impact on its environment both in terms of space and the people who witness it. To know this is to invest individual bodies with a sense of agency and power in their environment, which is a profoundly affirming notion. Magnet's Vision/Mission statement succinctly expresses this notion as a desire 'to challenge participants in our activities, performers and audience, through experiences that shift bodies, assumptions, feelings, beliefs and understandings' (Magnet Theatre n.d.). Magnet strives to be 'a moving force in the lives and minds of people in relation to changing local and global contexts' (Magnet Theatre n.d.).

Every Year, Every Day, I Am Walking (2006–present) – Magnet Theatre's longest running and most travelled show – sets out to move people towards an empathetic understanding (avoiding judgement) of the inner emotional landscape of the story of two refugees in Africa. It is a story told very much from the inside out. The actresses (Faniswa Yisa and myself) are ourselves extremely emotionally engaged, which along with the power of the story, 'moves' the audience and has an impact on their level of emotional engagement with their feelings. For example, we have sometimes performed to an audience of exclusively teenage boys, which was probably the most difficult audience to 'move.' The boys started the performance restless and destructive, but by the end of it they were silent and tearful, having surrendered to the feeling landscape of the story. To move people, to affect, to change them in this way is to assert life over death, movement over stillness, freedom over entrapment. Like a pendulum, the continuous movement of *tout bouge* insists on the continuation of life in the face of violence and death.

Another important point to take into account here in relation to the multicultural, multi-linguistic context of South Africa is made by Alain Gautré (2009, my translation), who told me that '*Quand Lecoq dit "tout bouge" il dit que la verité n'existait pas*' ['When Lecoq says "everything moves" he is saying that truth does not exist']. If all is in motion,

Reznek's image work *in 'I Do' x 22* (1997).
Photo credit: © Ruphin Coudyzer FPPSA. (ruphincoudyzer.com)

as Lecoq suggests, then there can be no single overarching truth or perspective that dominates. In this respect, Lecoq's vision is anti-fascist, since it contains an affirmation of diversity of perspective. An admission that, as a result of the continuity of movement, 'truth' does not exist explains the tendencies towards the multiplicity of voices that Magnet Theatre encourages in our collective creative processes. Magnet Theatre is not interested in employing people in the production work who simply affirm one particular vision or perspective. We deliberately choose people who can complement the gaps we have in understanding our own context. We seek out diversity in our choice of performers, as we are historically allergic to any cultural hegemony.

Furthermore, *tout bouge* is an image that moves beyond its time. It contains within it an understanding of the notion of migrancy that is embedded in contemporary thinking. As Edward Said (cited in Chambers 1994: 2) has said, the movement of people in the world has been transformed 'into a potent, even enriching motif of modern culture.' The constant movement – the nomadism of people, objects, and ideas – makes up one of the iconic images of contemporary society, prefiguring the inevitability of my own journey with Lecoq's ideas to South Africa and their impact on the life of the company. Indeed, the global tendency to the migratory movement of populations has served as one of the major thematic preoccupations of Magnet's recent work, and has resulted in the creation of four productions that have been published together as an anthology of work around this theme. What is unique about this collection of work – *The Magnet Theatre 'Migration' Plays* (2012) – is that the plays are in four different languages: English, French, Afrikaans and Xhosa. Language diversity is one of the major elements contained in the story of the movement of people from one place to another.

Committed to the spirit and practice of *tout bouge*, Magnet's current home houses a small training theatre, but we have always been committed to providing opportunities for theatre to move to where people are. In addition to this venue, Magnet Theatre also takes the theatre out of the more conventional, less accessible spaces (both geographically and economically) to ensure that people who do not have easy access to theatre are included in the experience. This movement of the theatre into less conventional spaces – crèches, school halls, sports fields, beaches, community centres – ensures that the legacy of the architectural structuring of our cities by apartheid does not continue to exclude people. Apartheid's racism, and the accompanying geographic policies that were established, rendered individuals and communities immobile. Apartheid sought to 'introduce between state power and its targets a relationship of capture, indeed of captivity' (Mbembe 2001: 9). Our decision to take theatre to the areas where people had been confined far away from the centres actively opposes the sense of imprisonment created by distance and economic inequality.

For example, *Pump* (1998) was the first production that Magnet created that was specifically designed to maximize access both in terms of style and mobility. This was an outdoor theatre production, created in the style of the popular tradition of the clown using the little red nose and extended physical characterization, but which did not use any recognizable language. It was performed to over 16,000 people in outdoor spaces throughout the Western Cape, on school playing fields, streets, beaches, prisons courtyards and public spaces in the townships. *Pump* dealt with the theme of water as a precious resource.[1]

Onnest'bo and *Die Vreemdeling* [The Stranger] (2010) were two other outdoor productions that were designed to be performed anywhere, unconfined by remoteness or access to resources. *Onnest'bo* and *Die Vreemdeling* were also thematically engaged with the notion of movement: in *Onnest'bo*, this was the movement back to District Six after the forced removal of people during apartheid; *Die Vreemdeling* was about the impact of a migrant stranger on a small rural community. Both also made use of popular styles of performance and relied heavily on music (*Onnest'bo*) and song (*Die Vreemdeling*).

Now, in our own theatre in Observatory, the movement across boundaries continues through a bus subsidy, which allows us to bring communities into the city centre in order to access the experience of other fully equipped mainstream theatre spaces in addition to our own. This ability to move people from the margins to the centres has impacted importantly on young people's comfort in, and 'ownership' of, those spaces where they would previously have felt like outsiders.

The Body as Bridge ('*D'une port a une port*')

To choose to perform in one or another language is not only divisive in South Africa (with so many languages in use), but it also has the potential to marginalize and exclude certain audiences. In addition, the continued use of English as the most common language that performers rely on to reach multilingual audiences is in itself problematic in the post-apartheid contexts, where indigenous languages are still being relegated to a minority status. This devaluing of indigenous languages has continued post-1994 in the primary and secondary education system, as well as in public arenas. It could be seen to form part of South Africa's ongoing 'imperial legacy' (Kruger 1999: 19).

Even before my training at Lecoq, I suspected that in South Africa, as a result of the colonial relationship to certain languages, the power to cross boundaries and the ability to avoid the pejorative aspects of spoken language could be delegated, to a certain extent, to the body. Therefore, to train the body for the theatre, and to continue to explore the body in performance, is to refine its language: to investigate its reach and the body's ability to circumnavigate the ruptures created by the multilingual culture within the context of colonial attachments to language. This is not to reduce the dense syntax of the body, which has complexities that include its own set of colonial attachments and which also necessitates a process of analysis and decoding; rather, the investigation of the practice is precisely a means by which to uncover and explore the articulation of that language.

At Magnet Theatre, we have long acknowledged that the physical, visual image is one that proliferates meaning, rather than defines or pins it down. It is a means of communication that allows for the creative, imaginative participation of each audience member, and, as such, is subject to the individuality and uncertainties of a multiplicity of responses. As Mark Fleishman (1997: 207–08) says, '[Physical images are] multivalent, ambiguous and complex [...] but precisely because they do not reduce to simple meanings, they demand that the audience be actively involved in making individual choices.'

This understanding of the physical image as something that defies fixity as one or another thing echoes my earlier discussion about perpetual movement antagonizing overarching truths. Through our engagement with the physical image, Magnet Theatre encourages a diversity of responses, an active listening and feeling that is the conversation we hope to have with each and every member of the audience. There is no right or wrong in each individual's attempt to decipher the image; there is only the desired active participation in grappling with meaning.

For example, in *Every Year, Every Day, I Am Walking*, Ernestine, the older sister, quietly disappears from the stage. It is never stated what happens to her. The only clue is a visual image of her childhood picture burning in a fire. Frequently, audiences ask for clarity in the Q&A sessions after the production as to what exactly happened to her. When prompted to 'read' the image on the stage themselves, the process of diverse imaginative engagement kicks in and some say she was burnt in the fire that attacked their house. Others say the attackers killed her. Some say Mama and Aggie (her sister) could never find her body or get clarity themselves, which is why the details are mysterious in the play.

If the image – and this is where the work of Magnet happens – is a good one, it will open up many layers of meaning without obfuscation. Again, in *Every Year, Every Day, I Am Walking*, there is an image which represents the moment where Mama is raped in the refugee camp. It does not deal with the rhythm or physical action of a realistic rape; rather, the image is of a pair of large black boots on top of the uncomfortably and precariously balanced body of a woman, while the soundtrack plays a delicate, repetitive, mechanical riff. This image feels successful, as it speaks to the heart of the relationship between rapist and victim, which is one of power and control. The image allows us to understand a layer of meaning in the experience that would not be apparent had we attempted to graphically represent a realistic rape.

So in our multilingual context then, the sense of the body as bridge not only opens up the most inclusive notion of who an audience could be, but also drives many of Magnet's choices, including our choice of collaborators. For example, we welcomed the opportunity of working with the Jazzart Dance Theatre, since dance is in many ways a universal language, more accessible than dialogue. Our collaboration with the company resulted in eight new creations during a 13-year journey. We also actively seek out strategies of translation, including physical and visual images, as well as English translations of poetic Xhosa texts, as in *ingcwaba lendoda lise cankwe ndlela* [the grave of the man lies next to the road] (2009) and *Inxeba Lomphilisi – The Wound of a Healer* (2010–14). We have also employed broad popular physical styles, such as the use of clown in *Cheap Flights* (1987),

Tout bouge/Everything moves. Jennie Reznek and Faniswa Yisa in *Every Year, Every Day, I Am Walking* (2006).
Photo credit: © Hennie Coetzee.

The rape scene in *Every Year, Every Day, I Am Walking* (2006).
Photo credit: © Hennie Coetzee.

Magnet's performance of Frances Marek's *Die Vreemdeling* [The Stranger] (2010) in a rugby stadium in Citrusdal in the Western Cape.
Photo credit: © Mark Wessels. No images may be used for print or electronic purposes without consent from the copyright holder.

Die Vreemdeling [The Stranger] (2010).
Photo credit: © Mark Wessels.

Director Mandla Mbothwe explores migration along the N2 highway in *Inxeba Lomphilisi – The Wound of a Healer* (2010).
Photo credit: © Hannes Thiart.

Wounded spirits in *Inxeba Lomphilisi – The Wound of a Healer* (2010).
Photo credit: © Hannes Thiart.

Faniswa Yisa and Thando Doni in *Inxeba Lomphilisi – The Wound of a Healer* (2010).
Photo credit: © Hannes Thiart.

A companion piece to the opera Brundibár, *The Children and the Bees* (2011) explores displacement, migration and child refugees.
Photo credit: © Mark Wessels.

Kay-Lee Esterhuizen & Lusanda Dayimani in *The Children and the Bees* (2011).
Photo credit: © Mark Wessels.

Directed by Brink Scholtz with the Magnet Theatre Full Time Training and Job Creation Programme, *running with goldfish and gift wrapping the sea* (2012).
Photo credit: © Mark Wessels.

Kragbox [Power Box] (2012) addressed masculinity in communities dominated by gangsterism and violence.
Photo credit: © Mark Wessels.

Dann-Jaques Mouton & Ephraim Gordon in *Kragbox* [Power Box] (2012).
Photo credit: © Mark Wessels.

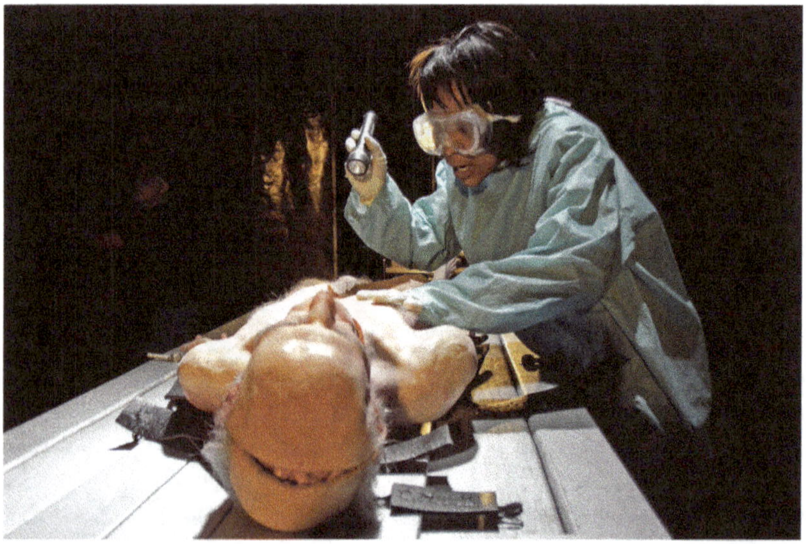

Faniswa Yisa excavates the current African landscape in *Autopsy* (2012).
Photo credit: © Mark Wessels.

Faniswa Yisa and Jennie Reznek in *Autopsy* (2012).
Photo credit: © Mark Wessels.

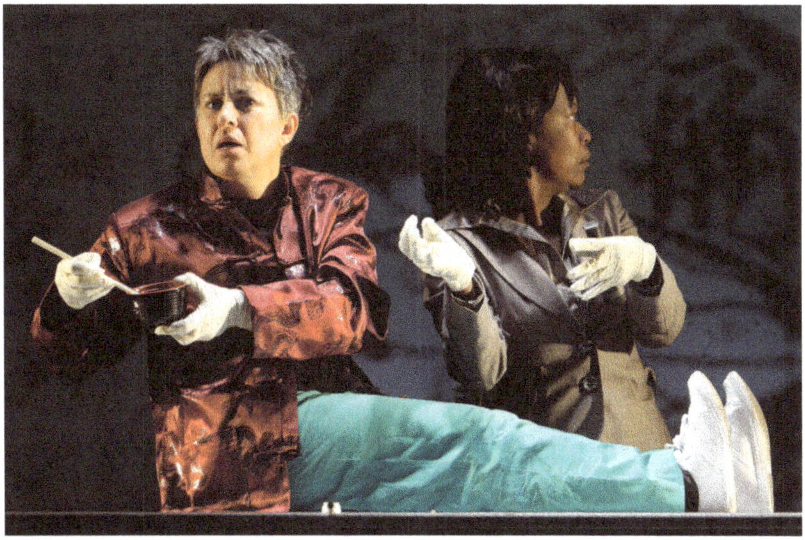

Yisa and Reznek in *Autopsy* (2012).
Photo credit: © Mark Wessels.

Nkosinathi Gaar in Magnet's interpretations of short stories by Mozambican author Mia Couto, *Voices Made Night* (2000, 2014).
Photo credit: © Mark Wessels.

Faniswa Yisa, Thando Doni, DJ Mouton, Chiminae Ball, Richard September, Mfundo Tshazibane & Jennie Reznek in *Voices Made Night* (2000, 2014).
Photo credit: © Mark Wessels.

Reznek and Yisa with Chiminae Ball and Dann-Jaques Mouton in *Voices Made Night* (2000, 2014).
Photo credit: © Mark Wessels.

Yisa in *Voices Made Night* (2000, 2014).
Photo credit: © Mark Wessels.

Directed by Thando Doni, *Passage* (2014) explores how boys transition into men.
Photo credit: © Oscar O'Ryan.

Doni's *Ukhanyo* [I am the Light of the World] (2014) explores being young in an evolving democracy.
Photo credit: © Jesse Kate Kramer.

Loyiso Damoyi & Athenkosi Mfamela embrace in *Ukhanyo* (2014).
Photo credit: © Jesse Kate Kramer.

Meagan Booysen writes her story in *Ukhanyo* (2014).
Photo credit: © Jesse Kate Kramer.

TREE/BOOM/UMTHI (2014) is performed in three different languages.
Photo credit: © Mark Wessels.

TREE/BOOM/UMTHI (2014) is designed for children aged three to seven years old.
Photo credit: © Mark Wessels.

In *Nomvula — The Girl of the Rain* (2014) expanded public works placements address human impact on the environment. Directed by Thando Doni.
Photo credit: © Mark Wessels.

A poetic reworking of the Persephone story, *I Turned Away And She Was Gone* (2014) was written and performed by Jennie Reznek.
Photo credit: © Mark Wessels.

Reznek in *I Turned Away And She Was Gone* (2014).
Photo credit: © Mark Wessels.

A collaboration with the Cape Town Opera, and based on Zakes Mda's novel, *Heart of Redness* (2015) features music by Neo Muyanga.
Photo credit: © 2013 Johan Bernard Bruwer.

The Show's Not Over 'Til the Fat Lady Sings, *Pump* and *Onnest'bo*, and developed detailed gestural languages and images particular to each production that can actively engage different audiences (to some extent regardless of spoken language), which were used in *Every Year, Every Day, I Am Walking*, *Die Vreemdeling* and *running with goldfish and gift wrapping the sea* (2012).

The Body as Subject ('*Tout bouge, moi aussi!*')

For Lecoq, the body as subject is both the 'starting and finishing point of all live performance' (Murray 2003: 5). His teaching reflected and referred at every point to the body as being at the centre of the theatrical endeavour. For Magnet, this awareness of the subjectivity of the body has been deepened by a response to the erasure of individual subjectivity through the systemic violence and laws relating to racial classification that were part of the legacy of the apartheid project. For us, the focus on subjectivity was part of the need to affirm the complexity of diversity.

In Magnet's teaching of the body, we attempt to restore the person's body to its subject position; and central to that subjectivity is the fact that the body can move. In this way, the individual body is reconfigured as the primary source of knowledge, identity and creative action in the world. The underlying assumption is that the body as object should be challenged. The position of body as object was established through racial classification during apartheid. It has also been established as object by the nature of violence, and the particular impact and relationship that violence has to the body. Moreover, the body has been subordinated to 'the mind' through the weight of the history of philosophical thinking since Descartes. For women in particular, there is an ongoing socially constructed objectification of women's bodies in sexist societies (hooks 2000: 149). In teaching the body, focusing on it as the primary source of creativity and developing exercises which allow the body to 'lead,' Magnet initiates processes that could reply to the oppressive nature of objectification that occurs through both actual violence and the symbolic violence of prejudice and political or economic expedience.

Prioritizing the body in performance shares a tendency in modern philosophical thinking of freeing the body from its inherited negative characteristics, which had been established as a result of the Cartesian splitting of the mind and body into 'distinct, mutually exclusive and mutually exhaustive substances' (Grosz 1994: 10). Value judgments are attached to these oppressive oppositions that have been responsible for relegating the body to a minor role in philosophical thinking, leaving it relatively absent from discussions of what it means to be a human being. According to Johnson (2008: 159), the body only became a subject of philosophical thinking about 30 years ago. Phenomenologists seem to have been singularly responsible for initiating a consideration of the body as lived experience, at the very centre of human knowledge, and not merely as an object interacting with the controlling subject of the mind and other objects.

For me, the sense of motion is at the heart of descriptions of the living body. As a subject, the corporeal being is not configured as a fixed, unchanging thing. In teaching the body, I am choosing to teach that which is constantly changing: moving, resisting, accepting and growing. The body as a subject also has a 'performative power' (Lepecki 2006: 8); it has the ability to move into a space, to create action and to affect one's own becomings – what Foucault (1988) termed the 'technologies of self' – which are fundamental to establishing the status of a free, empowered subject.

The sense of the body as a subject that is dynamic within itself and dynamic in relation to space/field/environment (Bourdieu 1990) is useful to Magnet in several ways. It allows us to respond directly to the fixing of identity through the mechanism of the Population Registration Act, the echoes of which are still being felt today. It establishes a body that moves, as something that is never fixed, but which has power through its capacity to affect and impact others in the space and, therefore, in the world. It also justifies the impulse to teach the body, since it provides a theoretical frame for believing that the subject of the body has potential; that it can learn, develop, grow and change both itself and the world. Finally, it provides a basis for a theory of transformation that I discuss in more detail later, and that relies on defining the body's relationship to others and to the world as a dynamic exchange.

Case Study: Exercising the Subject Body

There is an exercise I use that reveals how power and creativity can be realized when the body becomes the central modifier in the moment of movement. It is an exercise that I use to create language or material for new work, as it yields up a richness of original language that feels rooted in the domain of the individual, rather than artificially copied from elsewhere. The exercise is called 'shift.' It needs time, and I would typically not introduce it during the first six months of training. It requires a certain sinking into the landscape of one's own body; a certain trust and surrender; a 'being' in the body that doesn't happen immediately, even with the most experienced practitioner.

What is important about this exercise is that the body completely becomes the subject of the movement. The mover allows the body to take the lead. This can sometimes take a while, which is why I wait to introduce the exercise until students are more confident and less caught up in wanting to please me. They need to be patient and prepared to engage in the exercise for their own sakes. It is very easy to see when the body is not the subject. There is a rupture in shape and rhythm, and the person acts out a predetermined decision that leaves the body behind as something that is being acted upon. The movement feels willed, known, calculated and constructed. When the mover manages to stay with the body – to wait, to listen, to follow the changes – then the movement shifts gradually, initially, and begins to feel organic, unknown.

Preparing future physical performers through the Training Programme.
Photo credit: © Jesse Kate Kramer.

This elevation of the body to a subject position can result in an extraordinary release of energy. Students report feeling that they can go on for hours and hours. My sense is that, if this exercise is done properly, it frees the body from its object position as emphasized by the violence of society. The traditional devaluing of the body (especially for women) is momentarily lifted and this lack of oppression generates a great deal of vitality.

Fundamental to all the training that Magnet has been involved in is this emphasis on the subjectivity of the body and the particularity of the histories contained in the body of each student. In the full-time training, we start with a teaching beat called Performing Identity, which involves research into the identities of all the participants. We ask certain direct questions: Where do I come from? Who are my parents? Where do they come from? Often for students this involves, for the first time, a conversation with their families about their own histories, and it remains one of the most grounding, most commented on and most significantly empowering aspects of the training we offer. In a similar way, the

Clanwilliam Arts Project reinterprets stories from the history of the area, reconnecting young people and the community at large with the cultural richness of their own past.

Towards a Theory of Transformation

Lecoq ('*tout bouge*') seems to perceive the human being as caught up in a landscape of which s/he is a part. All aspects of the material world are equal and become potential 'teachers,' provocations for mime, copying, imitation. Lecoq reinvented and reinvigorated the notion of 'mime,' turning it away from the *mime du forme* [a fixed style of codified physical language occurring in silence] towards the *mime du fond* [mime of source] (Lecoq 2000: 46). *Mime du fond* finds the actor recreating and replaying the world through the gestures of his/her own body (Gautré 2009). This becomes a profoundly philosophical exercise, since '[t]he human ability to mime enables us to recognise everything that moves; man [sic], with his entire being, identifies himself to the world by recreating it' (Lecoq 1973: 117). Contained in the human body, then – in its ability to move – is the capacity to recreate the whole world, and this has implications for the way that we perceive ourselves and others, as well as our relationship to the world. If contained within our moving bodies is a capacity to identify with the rest of the world, then there exists the potential for understanding, for inhabiting difference, for embracing 'otherness' and other realities. This then becomes a powerfully liberating premise that allows an empathy that can transport one beyond the physical boundaries implied by the delineation of the material body. As Gautré (2009) says, '*C'est trés Zen*' ['It's very Zen'] – containing the whole world in the human moving body. For Magnet, this approach to the body within the sociopolitical context of South Africa is very important. The body is a place where otherness and the diversity of human and material experience can be engaged.

The openness to the world required for transformation to take place is important as it counteracts a kind of modernist splitting off from the world. As Lepecki (2006: 11) suggests, this splitting off can have disastrous consequences. It opens the door to a particular kind of relationship with the natural ecologies of the world, dogged by excessive self-serving consumerism through which the human being's destructive relationship to the natural ecologies can be justified.

The global pillaging of natural resources, along with the presence of the 'other' implied by global migrancy, suggests a need to teach the empowerment of the individual. Furthermore, it intimates raising levels of agency simultaneously with a theory of transformation that respects others and the world outside the subject. Physical transformation involves a readiness to accept a complicity that the body has with all matter, as well as a belief in the possibility of that interactive flow. Rather than Buber's 'I–it' relationship (Friedman 1954: 268), where the human is viewed as the subject while the rest of the world (animals, the landscape, nature, objects and other human beings) are seen as merely objects to be sublimated, I argue for physical transformation that is predicated on and allows the 'I-Thou' (Buber 1970) relationship to develop towards creative conclusions.

The groundwork of Magnet's teaching follows Lecoq's trajectory of working first with the elements – air, fire, water, earth – and then with animals, matter, objects and colours as impulses for transformation. In all, the external world becomes the teacher, and the student/performer makes a significant shift to learn from the external world, rather than to engage with it in a relationship of usage. In *TREE/BOOM/UMTHI* (2014), Magnet's latest work for two to six-year-olds, a tree is created out of four performers. The animated life of the tree leads the children through the four seasons of the tree's life and its relationship to a man. We've seen several little people leaving the theatre afterwards pointing out the trees in the street with delight, transferring their newfound experience from the dark of the theatre to the tree in the world. In this way, *TREE/BOOM/UMTHI* has shifted their relationship to the world outside. Character transformations are predicated on allowing empathy across the borders of human otherness. For instance, Faniswa Yisa and I play all the characters in *Every Year, Every Day, I Am Walking*, regardless of race, age and gender. This is so as not to ghettoize the experience of forced migrancy, but to focus on the reality of the emotional landscape of the play, which could in fact belong to anyone. For us at Magnet, these transformations are fundamentally important.

Transformation and Play

Magnet's practice of transformation requires an understanding of play. Improvisation as Jacques Lecoq taught it, is embedded in a practice that is designed to reveal the specificity of identity and subjectivity as expressed through the action of play. As such, it responds directly to violence and war, which succeeded in erasing the body's action and thus performances of identity. Play is the antidote for the mechanical and fascist body. Play is what resurrects the body and delivers it from the confines of the fixed discipline of the gymnastic body. It is what allows forms and ideas to change and transform. Play announces the future. As Chamberlain and Yarrow (2002: 113) say, 'The spirit of invention is the spirit of play.'

This tool of improvisation or play was precisely the element that helped to affirm the diverse creative identity of the students I studied with at École Lecoq, which then later informed our work at Magnet Theatre. It can be seen as a 'psychological and political intervention' (Frost & Yarrow 2007: 194), a site where, because of the particular kinds of openness and readiness that it demands, the identity of the person and the form can be made and remade. Frost and Yarrow (2007: 194) see improvisation as a 'challenge to the closed, the received and the repressive and protective mind sets.' It is a process and 'an operational mode of generating structural and attitudinal change' (2007: 194); a pedagogical tool for the express purpose of growing the creative voices of students.

Whenever I am asked in interviews about my two years at École Jacques Lecoq and what I learned there, I always reply that I feel that he gave me the gift of myself. What I mean is that he allowed me to recognize my own historical and physical contexts and stories as the creative source of my theatre-making. Having come from a theatre training that was predominantly interpretive (University of Cape Town's Drama School 1979–83), this was a fundamentally liberating notion. Once I understood that within my physical reality lay the tools to make theatre, I could then operate as a completely independent entity in the creation of work. This sense of value, and its consequent sense of independence, was deeply empowering. In a political historical context where control of bodies, space and movement were isolated within the structures of fascism, totalitarianism or the apartheid state, this notion of control of the 'means of production,' as it were, radically shifted agency onto the individual as creative being.

This gift then that Lecoq gave me – and which Magnet tries to pass on to our trainees and other participants in our educational processes – is a political and creative act. The encouragement of human distinctness through play has consequences for human social behaviour and opposes any form of racism, sexism or ageism. This act of empowerment – a creative release of difference through improvisation and play that Magnet continues to practice – insists that students and performers become visible to their distinctly unique selves, experiencing themselves as particular in all ways: culturally, creatively, sexually, socio-economically, ideologically, intellectually.

Embodied play is the central impulse that allows for the generation of new work, and a tool that Magnet Theatre continues to use exhaustively in its creative processes. Mark Fleishman's process as a director initially involves the setting of improvisatory tasks around particular themes. The material thereby generated by the performers on the floor is then accepted, rejected or adjusted for incorporation into the final product. It has been our methodology of creation since the very beginning, and continues to be redefined and practiced with developing complexity and understanding.

In Magnet Theatre's teaching practice, I incorporated another aspect of play at a more foundational stage and in a slightly different way. I explored playing childhood games because this allowed participants to release, listen and trust, particularly at the initial stages. Magnet has borrowed from, and been inspired by, other practitioners who were using games in different ways in the training of actors, such as Clive Barker's *Theatre Games* (1997) and later Augusto Boal's *Games For Actors and Non Actors* (1992). I use games to 'socialize' participants into participating in the behaviours that I need in order to proceed with the teaching. These include an ability to listen, focus, trust and respond to the diversity of other bodies and space, and also to allow for physical release.

One of the most important things about play is that it generates pleasure as a group, which impacts on the release of tension and creating trust. In 2010, I worked with a group of refugee women from the Whole World Women Association in Cape Town, who wanted to create performance around their experience for World Refugee Day (20th of June every year). They were diverse in every possible way – age, language, culture, size – but they had all experienced being foreigners in South Africa. I wondered how I was going to move them. Some of them were fully shrouded; others, it seemed, stayed permanently glued to their seats and were reluctant to stand. We started by playing silly games from childhood: clapping games and gentle running games. There was an immense amount of laughter and forgetting. Their comments afterwards revealed how the play had managed to create an island of holiday space, where they were able to drop their guard, to just relax and enjoy their bodies moving. They were able to experience each other's company and the space in a way that was regenerative – both as a moment of forgetting the trauma of their relocation and as a reminder of a state of play relating to the joy and carefreeness associated with childhood. Play determined a space in which who they were as human beings could be defined by their own imagination, as opposed to their being defined by others as victims of violence, or as *makwerekwere*.[2]

Collective Creation

Because the body is creating text through active play and improvisation, the direction of the performance is determined by the individual creator-bodies that form part of the creative collective. Magnet Theatre's focus on collective creation was informed both by Lecoq's pedagogy and the history of workshop theatre in South Africa; a process whereby a new piece of performance is created 'on the floor' (as opposed to 'on paper') by a group of people, rather than an individual author. Workshop theatre became a place where the fundamental assumptions on which the apartheid regime was built were challenged through the kinds of stories that were told. It also became the place where the specificity of human life – a 'multivocality' (Sitas 1996: 8) – could be championed, and a sense of 'solidarity and communality' (Orkin 1991: 226) could be affirmed. For Fleishman (1991: 1), the workshop process 'foregrounds collectivity and physical making as opposed to individuality and writing.' Workshop theatre as a process of play-making was most prominent in the 1970s,[3] and was used as a means of creating performances at many different levels of theatre in South Africa: from community theatre to the professional arena, from trade union movements to protest theatre (1991: 1). In South Africa, workshop theatre as a form has been seminal and its impact on play-making and Magnet Theatre has been long-lasting (Larlham 1991: 206). Certainly for Magnet Theatre, the workshop method has been an essential part of our process.

Workshop theatre also has its roots in the carnivalesque, and, as such, it plays out power struggles that exist between dominant and emergent forms. In workshop theatre, the body takes on an equal weight with text, and is not seen as something that supports or marginalizes the word. Instead, workshop theatre is 'engaged in a power relationship with the dominant form not in order to replace it as the dominant form but in order to revitalise its exclusive claims to truth and superiority' (Fleishman 1991: 156).

In almost every Magnet Theatre production, we have started out by gathering together the performers, dancers, choreographers, musicians, videographers, set and costume designers (and everybody else involved with the production) to ask them to embark on the project with us as collective collaborators. Mark has always said: What's the point of asking someone to be part of a process and then not listening to what they have to offer? He made this comment specifically in reference to a set designer who had proposed a radically different design than the one that Mark himself had imagined, but it has reference for every level of the creative process at Magnet. This invitation to 'offer' themselves from all the different people that are engaged in the processes is what makes the Magnet work full of diversity and multi-vocality. This doesn't mean that the work ends up without a driving vision or central core. I think that is the particular talent of Mark as a director: his ability to encourage and hold on to that diversity while at the same time delivering a production that is focused and coherent.

Conclusion

For Magnet Theatre, the training of young people – and creating access and movement for people that have been historically marginalized, or economically and educationally trapped – is driven by a commitment to redress past inequities. By inviting active participation in the development of new work through improvisation and play with the collaborators in the space, we continually affirm a more equitable and ethical relationship in the creative process; one that creates space for contributors to offer themselves, and in the process affirm the wealth and richness of their own experiences and imaginations in the creative product. This awareness of inequalities has also driven the choice of subject matter and the approach to particular themes. For example, *Cargo* highlights the forgotten, shameful history of slavery in South Africa; *Onnest'bo* brings back the community that was removed; and *Every Year, Every Day, I Am Walking* places on the centre stage those nationals that the xenophobic actions of certain South Africans would seek to remove. Magnet Theatre asks: Whose voice, perspective, body or story is not present here? And how do we redress that balance in order to help them to become more visible?

Magnet Theatre has created production work and a pedagogy that responds to violence in content, form and methodology of creation, particularly the violence of the South African context. It counters the stillness and immobility imposed by violence, death and the ongoing legacy of the restrictive legislations of apartheid, with a focus on the moving body. The emphasis on physical images also cuts across the boundaries that confine people into linguistic enclaves in South Africa. Through our commitment to physically taking theatre outside of the confines of conventional theatrical space, Magnet Theatre defies the geographic and economic restrictions that continue to lock people into particular areas. We strive to counter the oppression of violence and racism with notions of play, and by developing work directly from the subjectivities and differentiated identities of the collaborators in each particular production. Our teaching profile creates exercises that elevate the body to a subject position, freeing it from its object position emphasized by violence and the traditional devaluing of the body. Magnet counters ruptures between people through our teaching, outreach and development work, as well as by means of collective creation. Through a focus on creative transformation, we hope to repair a dislocation between the human subject and its environment.

References

Barker, C. (1997), *Theatre Games: A New Approach to Drama Training*, London: Methuen.

Boal, A. (1992), *Games For Actors and Non-Actors* (trans. A. Jackson), London: Routledge.

Bourdieu, P. (1990), *The Logic of Practice* (trans. R. Nice), Cambridge: Polity Press.

Buber, M. (1970), *I and Thou* (trans. W. Kaufmann), Edinburgh: T&T Clark.

Chamberlain, F. and Yarrow, R. (eds) (2002), *Jacques Lecoq and the British Theatre*, New York: Routledge.

Chambers, I. (1994), *Migrancy, Culture, Identity*, London: Routledge.

Fleishman, M. (1991), 'Workshopped Theatre in South Arica in the 1980s: A Critical Examination with Specific Relevance to Power, Orality and the Carnivalesque,' MA thesis, University of Cape Town.

—— —— (1997), 'Physical Images in the South African Theatre,' *South African Theatre Journal*, 11: 1, pp. 199–214.

Foucault, M. (1988), 'Technologies of the Self,' in L. H. Martin et al. (eds), *Technologies of the Self: A Seminar with Michel Foucault*, London: Tavistock, pp. 16–49, http://foucault.info/documents/foucault.technologiesOfSelf.en.html. Accessed 1 May 2011.

Friedman, M. S. (1954), 'Martin Buber's Theory of Knowledge,' *The Review of Metaphysics*, 8: 2, pp. 264–80.

Frost, A. and Yarrow, R. (2007), *Improvisation in Drama*, Hampshire, NY: Palgrave Macmillan.

Gautré, A. (2009), personal interview with J. Reznek, 26 September.

Grosz, E. A. (1994), *Volatile Bodies: Toward a Corporeal Feminism*, Bloomington: Indiana University Press.

hooks, b. (2000), *Feminist Theory From Margin To Centre*, London: Pluto Press.

Jenkins, R. (2001), 'Prophet of Gesture Who Got Theatre Moving,' *New York Times*, 18 March.

Johnson, M. (2008), 'What Makes a Body?' *Journal of Speculative Philosophy*, 22: 3, Pennsylvania: Pennsylvania State University.

Keefe, J. and Murray, S. (2007), *Physical Theatres: A Critical Reader*, London and New York: Routledge.

Kruger, L. (1999), *The Drama of South Africa: Plays, Pageants and Publics Since 1910*, London: Routledge.

Larlham, P. (1991), 'Theatre in Transition: The Cultural Struggle in South Africa,' *The Drama Review*, 35: 1, pp. 200–11.

Lecoq, J. (1973), 'Mime Movement Theatre' (trans. K. Foley and J. Devlin), *Yale Theatre*, 4: 1, pp. 117–20.

——— (2000), *The Moving Body: Teaching Creative Theatre*, London: Metheun.

——— (2006), *Theatre of Movement and Gesture* (ed. D. Bradby), London and New York: Routledge.

Lepecki, A. (2006), *Exhausting Dance Performance and the Politics of Movement*, New York and London: Routledge.

Magnet Theatre (n.d.), 'Home Page,' http://www.magnettheatre.co.za. Accessed 25 March 2015.

Mbembe, A. (2001), 'Ways of Seeing: Beyond the New Nativism,' *African Studies Review*, 44: 2, pp. 1–14.

Murray, S. (2003), *Jacques Lecoq*, London and New York: Routledge.

Orkin, M. (1991), *Drama and the South African State*, Johannesburg: Witwatersrand University Press.

Reznek, J., Fleishman, M., Yisa, F. and Marek, F. (2012), *The Magnet Theatre 'Migration' Plays*, Cape Town: Junkets Publisher.

Sitas, A. (1996), 'Description of a Struggle: South African Theatre Since 1970,' *World Literature Today*, 70: 1, pp. 83–88.

Scarry, E. (1985), *The Body in Pain: The Making and Unmaking of the World*, New York and Oxford: Oxford University Press.

Notes

1. 'Five clowns arrive in a space looking for water with a windmill and a tank and a shower. There is drought and flood and drought again and waste and fierce competition for the last drop of water. And a woman that searches for water for her family and always arrives as the tap runs dry. A story told through physical comedy and image without an identifiable verbal text' (http://magnettheatre.co.za/productions/pump/).
2. A derogatory slang word for foreigners, usually referring to illegal immigrants. For a fuller explanation, see Krueger ('Implacable Grandeur').
3. In the 1950s, Fugard had created *No Good Friday* (1958) and *Nongogo* (1959) through a form of workshopping; in the 1960s, Fugard, Kani and Ntshona created *Sizwe Banzi is Dead* and *The Island* in a similar way.

Chapter 10

Ideas Dying to Be Born: A Conversation with Craig Leo[1]

Craig Leo is a puppeteer, performer and designer who has collaborated on set design and construction for numerous Magnet productions, including Medea *(1994–96),* 'I Do x 22' *(1997),* Onnest'bo *(2002–06),* Rain in a Dead Man's Footprints *(2004–05),* Cargo *(2007) and* Voices Made Night *(2000–14). He is known internationally as a performer, playing a lead role for a number of years in Handspring Puppet's production of* Warhorse *at the National Theatre in London.*

'Designing at and working for Magnet Theatre is like falling in love,' says Craig Leo. 'It's exhilarating and exciting, but a touch frightening at the same time. As when in love, the journey begins as a landscape of possibility inside your mind; initially, it doesn't really exist outside. Magnet Theatre is not only a family of creators existing in physical place, but also a mental realm. As with the character of 'The Writer' in Mia Couto's *Voices Made Night* – where the stories and the words are swimming around and haunting him – ideas are dying to be born.'

Leo was trained as a puppeteer under Keith Anderson, and went on to work in the Zip Zap Children's Circus and at a big circus extravaganza in Sun City. He also worked with Nina and Sascha Gerasimov from the Leningrad State puppet theatre at CAPAB (Cape Performing Arts Board). 'I was very lucky,' he says, 'because I came into the institution when they still had wig-makers, shoe-makers, cobblers, props-makers. All the departments were still functioning. It was a great experience to watch them put together a show in a way that very few theatres still work in the world today.'

Leo was introduced to Magnet by his best friend Kurt Wustmann who was working with Mark and Jennie and Jazzart on *Medea*. Craig says 'They were looking for a designer. I had done some work with Alfred Hinkel before, helping with lighting, and so I got onto that production. That was my first large-scale show with Mark and Jennie. One thing led to the other and I'm still with Magnet today.'

Leo believes that Magnet's success is a combination of an ensemble approach that strives to make high-quality work focused on images and the body: 'I think the work that Magnet makes is absolutely world-class,' he says. 'In terms of quality, I don't think of working with Magnet as in any way inferior to working with the National Theatre in London. The end products are the same, and sometimes even more refined and beautiful than what you see on a massive stage at the National.'

Designer and puppeteer Craig Leo in *Pump* (1998).
Photo credit: © Magnet Theatre.

For Leo, their image work is their signature: 'Images, like puppetry, inspire our imaginations rather than fix meaning,' says Leo. 'For example, when the puppet stands dead still, in that moment of stillness they let us in. As soon as they're moving or talking they're telling us what they're thinking; but when they're still, then each person in that auditorium will have a different thought about what they're feeling or contemplating. I think that's why images are very powerful.'

Magnet's way of working is also a key element to their success: 'When you work again and again with the same people, you develop an understanding and you start to speak the same language. Then you can build on the relationship, rather than going back to square one every time. By now, I know Mark: I know what he's talking about, I know what style he works in and I enjoy that style. When I go and do other work, I tend to compare it to the way that he does things.' Describing Fleishman's style, Leo says, 'He cares about you and the work and isn't trying to prove himself, which makes him very secure. Mark cares deeply about you first and foremost before he cares about the work. The play is just a play. That's the essence of the Magnet ethos.'

As a designer, Leo says he is 'careful not to impose the design onto the work. You have to take part in the process, to go on the journey with them.' He explains that when they were devising and researching *Rain in a Dead Man's Footprints* and *Cargo* 'we worked for months with just ideas and themes [...]. With the historical pieces, like *Cargo* [...], you have references you use. There's the architecture of the time, the stories and clues from the past. You have different pieces of information that can be embroidered into ideas [...]. With those pieces, we were working with the thematic ideas and historical information before beginning the work on the rehearsal room floor.'

Leo describes how the play emerges through the devising process: 'You walk into the room and you don't know what you're going to make. We very rarely work with a text that already exists, be it physical or scripted. It's all generated within the rehearsal process, which does make it difficult and a little bit scary – you can't plan in the same way you would plan with a script or predetermined plot or text. You've got to be on your toes, you've got to be in the moment with them. Often the work that we do only comes into existence as it's being rehearsed on the day.'

'I like things to be slow and contemplative and well-researched,' he explains, 'I think it's very important to really delve into the world that you're going to put onstage. You have to start right at the beginning – with digging, with information, with asking questions. There's no handbook for that sort of thing. You have to just make a start and everything evolves quite naturally. I think I'd find it quite difficult if the process was too prescriptive from the start.'

Magnet's spirit of working is open to not knowing, as well as to exploration and play: 'I can't tell you how many times Mark has said to me "I don't know." For somebody with his status and position to be able to say that is a wonderful thing. It's very rare, because then you suddenly go, "Oh great. Thank God! If Mark doesn't know, then I don't have to feel the need to pretend that I know." So he levels the playing field, which I think is incredibly useful.'

Magnet often works with sand as a design element: 'We started our relationship with sand right at the beginning with *Medea*. And it's been very difficult to pull myself away from that. Once you do work with sand as a material, it becomes a character in a show and it's very difficult to replace. You just can't go back to the bare floor, or a cloth, or whatever. Once you've actually had sand onstage, that's it – you've got to have it again.' But, he adds a caveat: 'It's a mess and it's bloody hard work. There's always a bloody hairdryer or a light to position. You always have something to sort out with sand. Either you're trying to get it to stick, or you're trying to get it to harden, or you're just trying to get it dry, or you're trying to get it wet because it's too dusty. Our relationship with sand has been quite extraordinary, and very much a part of almost every production we've ever done together.'

For Leo, 'a design is successful when the audience doesn't actually notice it, when it really merges with the performance, when it doesn't sit on top of the work itself. It's a recipe for disaster adding a design at too late a stage in the rehearsal process, especially with Magnet.' He explains that, because 'their work around the physical body and the images they make with their bodies is so beautiful and so eloquent,' to add design elements is at times a real challenge. 'I fall in love with what I see in the rehearsal process and don't want to change it. Even the artist's own rehearsal gear begins to me to seem like the only costume they should ever wear in that moment! When you do add your design input to the mix, they will need the object or design sooner rather than later because they'll work with it, integrate and include it. You can't add it later, because if you do it's going to throw everything off kilter. [So] I aim for integration of design and performance – for them to become inseparable from each other. That's really important for me.'

Magnet includes designers as part of the devising process right from the start: 'It's about ownership,' says Leo, 'you also get to own part of the process.'

References

Leo, C. (2013), personal interview with A. Krueger, 11 June.

Notes

1. Interview quotes in this chapter are taken from Leo (2013).

Chapter 11

The Creative Flow of Arresting, Exquisite Fabric: A Conversation with Illka Louw[1]

Costumer designer Illka Louw has worked on designs for numerous Magnet productions, including Voices Made Night *(2000–14),* Autopsy *(2012),* The Fire Raisers *(2004) and* 'I Do' x 22 *(1997). She has also worked with the Royal Shakespeare Company and won Fleur du Cap awards for design in 2006 and 2010, and has received numerous nominations in other years. She currently works and teaches at Rhodes University.*[2]

As a designer, Louw says that her 'first love is fabric [...] its movement and its flow.' Trained as a fashion designer, Louw started working at CAPAB[3] as a junior costumer in 1994, then at Artscape under the mentorship of Eva Parsons. After this, she 'had the opportunity to run the wardrobe for the Drama Department at UCT, and that's where [she] really started working with Mark and Magnet Theatre.' Illka says, 'The first production I met the Fleishman's on was *'I Do' x 22*, for which I was a junior costumer,' creating garments designed by Craig Leo. The first production on which Illka worked with Magnet as costume designer in her own right was the original incarnation of *Voices Made Night* [in 2000].

Magnet's 'format of design, where you sit in on rehearsals, is very rare in this country,' explains Louw. She describes how Magnet's devising process includes designers:

> Whoever has an idea about what's happening can share their idea, not only in one's own discipline. If you have something to say about the lighting for example, then fine. So it's invigorating. It feels authentic and shared. But also everybody knows that you have your area of expertise that you're trusted with and a rhythm of how you work. There's the communal thing, then you go on with your own thing and then back to the communal thing. Mark is very good at making sure that cycle works. He's never disappointed in you because you're not delivering; he's never freaking out because he doesn't know. It's always about the show. [...] Maybe in some cases people don't ask enough questions because they don't want to expose what they don't know. But that's not the case [with Magnet] – *jy vra* [you ask].[4] Look, the productions are always an extension of the people involved. It's always a reflection of that. It goes through their bodies and their souls.

For Louw, 'Each costume tells a story, and you create something that the character as well as the actor requires.' One of her favourite pieces was Rosa Caramela's dress which she created for *Voices Made Night*: 'I loved *Voices Made Night* in its various incarnations. The text itself by Mia Couto is absolutely beautiful, and the humour of [...] that particular production is wonderful, it's magical.' Paired with the humour of the piece, for Louw, is also 'the tragedy of how we cling to our old symbols, and how the symbols themselves are stagnant.' The character of Rosa Caramela (played by Jennie Reznek) falls in love with a statue because it will not leave her. 'I enjoy making the "character" of a costume merge with the character of a play,' says Louw. 'Rosa Caramela has a wedding dress that took me many, many hours to make because it was hand-painted and hand-sewn, and it was so heavy to work with!' The dress is meant to look very old: 'it sort of drags from the mud and seepage! She was in the *malhuis* [madhouse] with this thing on as well. The weight of that particular dress needed to work for Jennie. It needed to help her with the body and embodiment of that character, the body language.' Describing how she develops a costume with and for a particular actor, she says, 'It's a very one-on-one process. It's in the service of the production, but you need to make sure that the person who's wearing the costume and who develops the character is also served by this beautiful thing you are making. And painting onto it is like an act of love, because it takes very, very long, and because it is a form of artistic expression.' With Magnet, Louw says, 'the preciousness of our craft [as designers] is taken to heart.'

She describes her work on *Autopsy* as 'hectic, because of the intricate storyline. It had to make forensic sense. There were so many challenges. The design needed to have a corpse, a completely realistic body, down to the last follicle, because it was being filmed from close-up. And it needed to cost under 10,000 rand. Miniature landscapes had to be created which were going to be filmed during the performance, and that created different challenges which influenced the rehearsal process.' This was because the story was 'like a murder mystery, all the little strings needed to be connected in a way that *Voices Made Night*'s magic realism didn't need at all.'

'So, you know, it's quite a lot of work,' she says, 'but you do it, because it's necessary.' Her designs need 'to serve exactly what the production needs. It cannot overwhelm the performer, it can't overwhelm the character [...]. It has to be *verruklik* [exquisite].' Then she clarifies the translation: 'more arresting than just exquisite. It has a sensate effect on the one who is experiencing the *verrukking* [ecstasy]. It has to make you go – "Oh my God, that's beautiful!" That's actually what I'm after.'

References

Louw, I. (2013a), personal interview with A. Krueger, October.

—— —— (2013b), 'From Designer Through Space to Spectator: Tracking an Imaginative Exchange between the Actants of a Scenographic Event,' MA thesis, University of Cape Town.

Notes

1. Interview quotes in this chapter are taken from Louw (2013a).
2. Illka's MA in Theatre and Performance (2013b) was completed under Mark Fleishman's supervision and was awarded a distinction by the University of Cape Town in 2013.
3. The Cape Performing Arts Board (CAPAB) was one of four provincial Arts Councils. These bodies were heavily subsidised under the former South African government; however, this funding mostly came to an end after 1994 in the lead up to the creation of the NAC (National Arts Council) in 1997, which sought to distribute government funding more equitably.
4. During the interview, Illka sometimes used expressions in Afrikaans, which is her mother tongue.

Chapter 12

Embodied Practice that Troubles Fixed Narratives of Identity, History and Memory

Yvette Hutchison

Yvette Hutchison is an associate professor in the School of Theatre Studies at The University of Warwick. Her research and teaching interests focus on theatre in the African context, particularly South Africa, and intercultural theatre practices. Her interest in theatre in the contexts of history, myth and memory has resulted in several essays on contemporary South African theatre that have been published in journals and edited collections, including the Contemporary Theatre Review, *the* South African Theatre Journal, A History of Theatre in Africa *(Cambridge University Press, 2004) and two Palgrave books on documentary drama. She recently published a monograph entitled* Performance and the Archive of Memory *(Manchester University Press, 2013).*

The focus of this chapter is an exploration of how Magnet Theatre has created work that troubles, discomforts or disturbs dominant narratives related both to the past and the present – particularly regarding identity, history and memory – while at the same time negotiating the place of narrative in the work. I look at Mark Fleishman's (2011) search for 'a dramaturgy of displacement,' which involves making rather than telling; which is about embodiment, where the dramaturgy must find ways of including silence and absence; and of telling stories without co-opting the narratives of people who cannot or will not participate themselves. I compare Magnet productions, specifically *Rain in a Dead Man's Footprints* (2004-05) and *Every Year, Every Day, I Am Walking* (2006-present), with strategies employed by other arts practices to critique how audiences make meaning from Magnet's embodied dramaturgy.

Throughout its history, South Africa has been dogged by the issue of belonging, which has profoundly informed claims to various rights: to land, to citizenship and to particular kinds of representation. As apartheid was primarily concerned with defining racial borders, and degrees of belonging and rights, these issues continue to haunt South Africa, as evidenced in Mbeki's 'I am an African' speech[1] to the constitutional assembly in 1996. Using an oral mode evocative of Nguni praise poetry,[2] Mbeki associated the various peoples of South Africa with particular landscapes. This association is significant when one understands that, for many first world nations, any claim to belonging in a country is profoundly linked with narrative and storytelling, encapsulated in the question, 'If this is your land, where are your stories?' (Brown 2006: 1). When read against the Truth and Reconciliation Commission (1996–98), Mbeki's speech illustrates how important narratives of belonging and memory are to this divided nation, and how the state has attempted to use narrative to effect national unity.

The effect of these initiatives has, however, been limited, as evidenced by the shocking wave of violent xenophobic attacks in 2008, which saw tens of thousands of the several million refugees in South Africa displaced, and over 50 murdered; with sad repetitions still occurring. Such events provoke the question of how one addresses the legacies of apartheid which foregrounded particular narratives to the exclusion of others, resulting in privilege for some and subjugation for others. How can one negotiate history, memory and identity, and avoid constituting new grand narratives? These questions are both ideological and aesthetic, and involve the thorny problem of how to engage with marginalized people who are unwilling or unable to speak for themselves.

In their attempts to answer such questions, Magnet Theatre has facilitated non-hierarchical ways of exploring multiple identities, histories and memories in South Africa. In his master's thesis in 1990, Fleishman argued for a shift away from focusing on text towards exploring 'core images' in theatre. Writing on physical theatre, Fleishman (1997: 200) challenged the binary between word and 'other meaning-making processes such as the physical and the oral, which have been marginalised by the dominant.' He argues that the complexities of South Africa require 'a complex treatment [...] in which the written word, the spoken word, and the transformative material body, amongst others, are in a constant state of dynamic dialogue,' without any 'essential hierarchy where one mode of expression or one process of making meaning can be seen to be more important than another' (1997: 200). The truth of this argument can be seen in the history of theatre in South Africa, which has been characterized by improvisation and collaborative theatre workshop processes that have consistently placed corporeal storytelling alongside text, thereby facilitating diverse audience engagement with complex issues (Sichel 2010).

As a physical theatre company, Magnet Theatre consciously engages with the somatic potential of oral and embodied performance to signal 'transformation in the art of theatre' (Fleishman 1997: 203). Transformation here refers to two things: the process whereby an actor visibly changes into a character before the spectator; and the process of metamorphosis, where an action or gesture begins as one thing and becomes something else, 'passing through a range of possibilities in between' (1997: 204). This range of possibility is important insofar as it 'opens up a plural field of possibility for the spectator. Each image is in this sense dialogical: a play of open-ended possibilities interacting between two fixed poles which exist in some form of dialogue with each other' (1997: 205). These two fixed poles could include a spectator's perception of identity and history, with the spaces between them opening up other, contested perspectives and possibilities. This dialogue between people's held views and the new perspectives being suggested onstage challenge fixed narratives of identity and history, and thereby facilitate possible change in mainstream perceptions of them. It is for this reason that Fleishman (1997: 206) argues that this 'field of possibility' demonstrates both 'the possibility of change in an active way,' and 'what Mihkail Bhaktin [...] would call the "grotesque realism" of the South African theatre.' Fleishman (1997: 206) argues that the process of refashioning and re-inventing the material body into often grotesque forms 'subverts, parodies and unsettles "given" social positions and interrogates the rules of inclusion, exclusion and domination which structure the social body.'

First, I consider how Magnet Theatre has made space for these 'fields of possibility,' by juxtaposing marginalized stories within mainstream discourses. Secondly, I analyse how Magnet's dramaturgy has facilitated creative responses[3] that destabilize fixed narratives of identity, history and memory; facilitating audiences' ability to make meaning imaginatively from a facilitated dialogue between text and embodied images.

Since 1994, theatre practitioners have been profoundly engaged with how South Africa is revising history and engaging with disavowed memories in the postcolony. Drawing on Achille Mbembe (2001), Fleishman (2011: 8) describes the postcolony as 'the multiple, contradictory moments of everyday life in Africa read against the persistent accretions of slavery, colonialism, apartheid and neo-liberal forms of democracy.' These latter discourses have been concretized through performative events and culturally encoded forms – including commemorative days, specifically designated archives and memorial sites – which have been profoundly implicated in redefining the nation post-1994.[4] Fleishman (2011: 14–15) has argued that specific sites, such as Robben Island, District Six and the Bleek and Lloyd collection of /Xam records, are part of what has been termed 'sensitive sites [...] that embody a history of "extreme events".' What is significant about Magnet's productions is how they trouble fixed ideas associated with these sites as they juxtapose these ideas with images of everyday, individual experiences and embodied memories.

I would like to begin by analysing such troubling in Magnet's collaborative production with Jazzart Dance Theatre, *Rain in a Dead Man's Footprints*, hereafter referred to as *Rain*. South African poet Antjie Krog (cited in Brown 2006: xix) has suggested that while '[w]e have had many years of telling stories,' only 'some were heard; others went underground; some were written; some were oral; some were trapped in neglected mother tongues [...].' Increasingly, scholars and artists have recognized the importance of re-engaging with such marginalized stories and disavowed memories, including the colonial experiences of the original indigenous inhabitants of Southern Africa – the Khoi/Khoe and Bushman or San peoples.[5]

Rain takes as its starting point stories told primarily by /Xam elder //Kabbo, as recorded by German linguist Wilhelm Bleek and his sister-in-law Lucy Lloyd in the 1870s in Cape Town.[6] These stories profoundly connect the people to the land and to one another (Fleishman 2005). //Kabbo, /Han#kass'o,!Kweiten ta //ken and Dia!kwain (among others) cooperated with Bleek and Lloyd's linguistic research because they were aware that San culture was endangered, and they wanted their peoples' stories to survive for future generations. Often all that remains of a culture are material artefacts, but these stories allow us the rare opportunity to access the thoughts and ideas of a people. It can thus be argued that 'Without Bleek and Lloyd's pioneering efforts, very little would be

Dancers and stiltwalkers in *Rain in a Dead Man's Footprints* (2004)
Photo credit: © Mark Wessels.

known about the myths, legends and fables of the Cape Bushmen, few of whom survived beyond the 1920s' (Loos 1997: 199). However, as Fleishman (2005: 44) poignantly notes, until the 1970s this archive all but disappeared from view and it is still limited, as the myths remain only as texts, never to be performed again, which Fleishman argues 'is surely another kind of death.'

However, anyone who attempts to translate transcribed and already translated material like this into performance faces many challenges. Firstly, oral texts tend to be halting, discontinuous and include much repetition. Secondly, serious ethical and political issues arise 'from attempting to translate narratives from a culture that has been exterminated into forms alien to that culture' (Fleishman 2005: 46). These issues signalled the need for a dramaturgy that could engage with absent peoples and cultures without speaking for or about them. Many of the issues involved in this process are inherent in much intercultural theatre (Knowles 2010), but it is more complicated here because all Magnet was left to work with from this culture were traces; as such, the company had to find ways of representing stories, absences and silences.

For Schleiemacher (cited in Fleishman 2005: 49), there are two modes possible for such a translation project: either '1. the author [San narrative] is brought to the language of the reader [contemporary audience]; [or] 2. the reader is carried to the language of the author.' The problem of the first option, as outlined in contemporary intercultural theory, is that the social, cultural and economic conditions of the source material are excluded or concealed to make the content intelligible for its intended audience (in this case, contemporary South Africans).[7] The second option involves finding a means of formulating and communicating a San world-view; that is, renegotiating approaches to and representations of time, space and oral narrative, without speaking for or misrepresenting the culture. Fleishman worked on his research with Pippa Skotnes, who has been researching San rock art and the Bleek and Lloyd archive for some time, as well as curating the 'Miscast: Negotiating the Presence of the Bushmen' (1996) exhibition. They concluded that in San narratives:

> the sense of consequence is unexpected;
> the past is brought into the present unproblematically;
> there is no distinction between the magical and the banal; and
> linear, chronological development is replaced by an almost perpetual present.
> (Skotnes & Fleishman 2002)

As the project's director, Fleishman responded to these dramaturgical challenges by merging these various planes of reality – coexisting time-bands;[8] the sacred and profane; shifting senses of spatial relatedness, signalled by 'here' and 'there' – into the performance. This results in a spatial principle that challenges the temporal progression of Lucy Lloyd's narrative from 1870–84: the audience sees not only the embodied figures of the Colonial Time, but also (and sometimes simultaneously) those of the Early Time (through the figures of the Therianthropes) and Contemporary Time (through the male figure in a suit [played by Neo Muyanga]), who walks through the action, or sits and reads on the side (*Rain* 27.35 mins);[9] yet they also see the cameraman, who projects images throughout the final movement. Here, Fleishman signalled the ethical and political issues of reconstruction – and the literal absence of the San people – by resisting a coherent, single narrative. Instead, he juxtaposed 'three different threads, [...] stanzas, [...] moods or moves that interweave over time' (Fleishman 2012: 108). The first one is 'a nostalgic, melancholic thread that is about the task at hand, the project of collecting and interpreting stories [...] for future generations' (2012: 110). The second is 'a celebratory thread,' which gives the audience 'a different sense of place, an "other" place,' and finally, 'a biographical thread that becomes increasingly political' (2012: 111).

All three threads were woven simultaneously through the piece by juxtaposing recurrent core images and motifs – both physical and musical – against fragments of narrative taken from the Bleek and Lloyd archives. For instance, Lucy Lloyd (played by Jennie Reznek) represented the colonial perspective, although not one that we are used to. Instead of a powerful man, we see a vulnerable woman, wearing what looks like Victorian underwear, a corset and crinoline. She represents European colonial attempts to understand indigenous experience rationally and then record these in writing; hence her association with a writing desk and book placed centre stage. She does not present the usual imposing figure of European history; rather, she struggles to translate the moving bodies of the male dancers performing //Kabbo and Dia!kwain[10] and, increasingly, her own narrative is of exhaustion. She speaks of growing 'weaker and weaker,' having a sense that 'the sand of my life is running to an end' (4.14–4.16 mins).

Another image that metaphorically and somatically communicates the complexities of this endeavour is suggested by a jar of buttons. //Kabbo requests thread in order to sew buttons onto a coat that Lucy has given him, because, he says, 'Without thread, they will get lost' (6.26–6.28 mins). Lucy drops the jar and the buttons are strewn across the sand. As she and the two men desperately try to collect and return the buttons to the jar, more bodies enter the space. The endeavour becomes chaotic, and we sense that not all the buttons will be found. In the second movement of the play, which is a celebratory group dance, Lucy incorporates gestures of sewing into her dance, suggesting her attempt to somehow preserve this experience that is intrinsically embodied and ephemeral. We understand from this image that while some things from this culture have been preserved, much has been lost. The visual metaphor of sewing stands as a reminder of the impossibility of weaving a coherent thread through history, and the limitations of attempting to capture complex aspects of a culture in a written text.[11]

Another core image is a San man dancing with a therianthrope figure (half man, half animal) reminiscent of San rock art.[12] The first movement ends with a slow, gentle *pas de deux* between //Kabbo and the therianthrope (10.03–10.58 mins). The only sound we hear is their breath as they connect in an embodied way, and then they leave the space. During the second phase, Lucy and the cast narrate 'that place, far off, where //Kabbo once lived,' where 'sorcerers, dancing, would fall into trance and become birds' (12.33–13 mins). Once again, the therianthrope figure dances with the contemporary youths in a dream-like sequence that incorporates modern dance and the kick-stamp of the *isicathamiya* form,[13] here performed in slow motion, as if time has slowed down. A little later (20.57–24.35 mins), they tell the titular story of the Rain Bull who brings rain. The use of a steadily increasing rhythm – established by the dancers' choral singing, clapping and stamping alongside the sound of the rain-makers and the circular movements of the individual dancers and group – invoke a ritual dance experience that suggests the merging of time and space, of the sacred and the banal. The repetition of phrases and their juxtaposition to the clapping, moving bodies, both human and therianthrope, suggest a contemporary interpretation and experience of these ethnographic narratives from another culture and another time, particularly through the eclectic dance movements and music. This eclecticism of style is an important device used in this piece to avoid any claim to reproduce the past authentically. In both the second and third phases, these repertoires are expanded when the embodied performances of the San narratives are accompanied by the music of Neo Muyanga, which combines San instruments and sounds, particularly the *shungu* [percussion] bow, with contemporary jazz music. Instead of attempting to understand what these stories might have meant in the past, the repetitive phrases and clapping has an hypnotic effect on the audience, which allows them to shift between rational consciousness and a more subjective, affective response, not unlike that evoked by the music in Noh theatre. In this way, it permits the audience to imagine what these stories could mean for them in the present.

The third movement of the play is biographical and increasingly politically critical. It relates the effects of the displacement of San women and children on the San informants and their relationship with Lucy. //Kabbo's struggle between wanting to record his peoples' stories and his longing for his wife and his 'place' is communicated in a dream encounter with his wife, !Kwaba-an. She is small and alone in the space; her movements suggest struggle and pain. The cost of his absence is conveyed indirectly in her request for a smoke and in //Kabbo's response: 'I gave her my pipe but the tobacco was all gone' (34.20–37 mins). When he wakes from his dream, the sun is up and his wife and son are gone. The dream is conveyed through a dance that communicates struggle, particularly through the dancers' laboured breathing.

In another scene, Dia!kwain relates the Story of Ruyter, who 'was near beaten to death,' because he 'had not herded well.' Dia!kwain says:

> The Boer has broken my body's middle [...] I fear the string has gone from me. That things have changed and cannot call me. Sleeping, I cannot hear it, I cannot hear it. There is silence now where a song would ring, there is nothing now where it once sounded.
> (38–40.30 mins)

While he is saying this, Dia!kwain's movements convey indescribable pain. Once again, the text is translated into a discordant song that conveys the distress caused 'by the others [...] who came, breaking the strings for me,' and between Lucy's narration of the men's loss of family members, Dia!kwain sings 'this place has changed [...] the earth's not earth' (40.30–42.40 mins). This narration goes beyond words, physically conveying the psychic damage done to this man, including his separation from his family and culture, which makes him unable to hear the stories of the land, thereby resulting in his profound dislocation from a sense of self and belonging.

The play's finale suggests that *Rain in a Dead Man's Footprints* is about more than the past. As Lucy Lloyd submits her Third and Final Report to the Secretary of Native Affairs in London, concerning the progress of the Bushman Researches from 1875 to 1884, darkness falls across the stage, suggesting the close of an era. To the soft sounds of a bow song, two young women enter the space carrying flames at the end of a cord that they spin hypnotically. On the margins of the playing space, the Victorian women help Lucy and each other out of their corsets, thereby signalling a release from the symbolic colonial/western lens that has constrained them. More people enter the space and a young woman narrates the story of a falling star that came to tell of a death. She says that 'as we stand at the water's edge, we see all things. The things in the sky we see in the water' (46.22–46.34 mins). Time, space and perception shift as a fabric scrim appears in one corner of the space, and shadows of the performing figures are projected from behind: surreal moving figures, both human and therianthrope. This finale of about 20 minutes increases in intensity as the figures dance, clap and sing in syncopation, with glowing rain sticks made from dried cacti or gourds filled with seeds or pebbles and strings of fluorescent lights creating the sensations often described by people who have been in a trance state. The title song, 'Rain in a dead man's footsteps,' combines the sound of the San *shungu* percussion bow with the jazz piano and saxophone to rework the San narrative as a jazz song; this again conflates time frames and, in the haunting notes of the saxophone, suggests how stories lost in time continue to haunt South Africa and live on in contemporary forms. The song makes the point clearly that this performance is not the original text or representation of the San culture, but a reworking of it. Neo Muyanga sings about how, when someone dies, the rain comes and 'washes away traces, the hollows of a dead man's footsteps, even before we have settled in our graves' (48.54–49.50 mins). Here, ironically, water is both the source of life and something that highlights humanity's ephemerality. Fire and rain are important elements for survival in the desert, both bringing destruction and new life. The dance that accompanies the song draws both on Martha Graham's style of contraction and release (worked through breathing and spirals) alongside contemporary South African dance styles: what Jazzart Dance Theatre call 'Afro-Fusion' (drawing on *isicathamiya*, *kwasa-kwasa*, *pantsula*, *kwaito* and hip-hop dance forms) and jazz styles that have developed in particular ways in Cape Town. In the latter, for example, couples 'use complicated "dips" (where the male holds his partner in a backwards or sideways dip semi-suspended above the floor), multiple spins, turns, lifts and dramatic poses' (Gibson 2013: 38). The final dance in *Rain in a Dead Man's Footprints* communicates both a sense of pain and loss, and a desire to let go. The figures have white paint on their faces and bodies, signalling engagement with the spirit realm. The various times and spaces encountered through *Rain* are brought together in this final celebratory ritual, which appropriately ends with the front of the stage bursting into flame and the evocative sound of the rain-sticks trickling their seeds against the beat of the dancers' feet on the earth. Finally, the song invites //Kabbo to 'dream of home,' and thus acknowledges the place of dreams in San cosmology, affirming that 'you still can change the world by dreaming the world' (57.50–59.56 mins) as the therianthrope figure with whom he dances leaves the stage. //Kabbo watches as a girl dances alone to this refrain, while a cameraman circles them, filming – a visual reminder to us of the role framing and perspective play in the reception of any narrative.

This final scene suggests the limits of cultural or historic recovery and contemporary nostalgia, which Svetlana Boym (200: xiii) defines as 'a longing for home that no longer exists or has never existed. Nostalgia is a sentiment of loss and displacement.' Many people in South Africa are now looking to the past to try and recover identities and cultural heritage lost during colonial and apartheid rule. This physical theatre piece engages with what remains, albeit in a reflective way, critiquing those who claim to find absolute truth, particularly through written texts that record only aspects of San culture, and not 'that which is most characteristic of their humanity, and therefore most valuable – their mind, their thoughts and their ideas' (Bleek 1873, cited in Skotnes 1999: 31). *Rain* engages with reflective nostalgia, which 'is more concerned with historical and individual time, and the irrevocability of the past; which we engage with through our imagination' (Boym 2001: 50), taking and reworking what is relevant from the past in the present. Magnet's production effectively juxtaposes image, movement and music against fragmented oral narratives so as to trouble the dominance of the written text and linear narrative, in favour of something more fragmented, more somatically and emotively layered, than the original Bleek–Lloyd transcriptions.

It is one thing to conceptualize an innovative process of creating a multi-layered, metaphoric theatrical work; audience reception is another thing. Measuring affect is difficult, whether in neuroscience (Blakeslee & Blakeslee 2008), social science (Wetherell 2012) or theatre studies (Thompson 2009). Although Miki Flockemann (2011) has offered an important reading of how 'thick theatre' highlights notions of complicity in and through cultural production, I would like to bring together James Thompson's approach to affect in theatre with theories on how sequential art, graphic novels and comics work in order to suggest another way of evaluating the significance of Magnet's innovative dramaturgy.

Scholars have acknowledged that 'the primary literacy of the twenty-first century will be visual' (Burmark 2002: 1), and have increasingly paid attention to the role of images as more than supplementary carriers of meaning in children's literature. Scholars like Lynell Burmark (2002), Lawrence Sipe and Anne Brightman (2009) and David Low (2012) have explored how readers close 'gaps' or 'spots of indeterminacy' in 'an active and continual communication with the text' (Low 2012: 369).

Scott McCloud's *Understanding Comics* (1993) has provided ways of analysing synchronous texts that deal in visuality and spatiality alongside textuality. In addition, Low (2012: 372) explains that because comics are 'a medium of conjunction' between a number of elements, parameters and procedures, '[e]ach panel is dependent upon the reader linking it and its semiotic space – through her or his interpretive imagination – to the panels around it.' This process involves the reader (and for my purposes, the audience member) actively making meaning in the 'gutters,' gaps or blank space between individual panels (or in our case, scenarios). McCloud (1993: 63) argues that we do this by means of closure, a process whereby we 'observ[e] the parts but perceiv[e] the whole.' This process involves collaboration between the artist and reader/audience member who uses his or her imagination to take two separate images and transform them into a single idea (1993: 66). McCloud (1993: 68) goes further to suggest that the reader is not only a collaborator, but also a silent accomplice, 'an equal partner in crime,' who 'join[s] in a *silent dance* of the *seen* and *unseen*. The *visible* and *invisible*' (1993: 92, emphasis in original).

Closure here involves interpreting connections between disparate parts based on previous experience. In applying this idea to Magnet Theatre's dramaturgy, memory becomes a key factor. Verne Harris (2012: 149) has argued that '[the] trouble with memory is that it is ubiquitous. It folds into every human discourse, transaction, record, conversation [...]. Memory of previous experience is a filter and feeler for present experience.' However, memory is only ever a trace, and Harris (2012: 153) argues that the trace 'never speaks for itself,' it is always 'narrativised, wrapped in a story, patterned by a narrative.' This means that, 'Always already, there is also *story*, there is *imagination* and there is *future*' (2012: 153, emphasis in original).

I suggest that productions like Magnet's *Rain in a Dead Man's Footprints* highlight these aspects of memory, narratives and traces by inviting audiences to critically engage with past narratives, and to insert themselves imaginatively into the gaps, absences and silences invoked by the core images, music and movement. By placing the audience in the role of active interpreter, we are provoked to re-evaluate what we think we 'know' historically via our somatic responses to alternative, embodied knowledge.

In the case of *Rain in a Dead Man's Footprints*, any single version of San historiography and representation is inherently troubled, and revealed as a partial, interpreted construction because of the fragmentary nature of the archives themselves, as well as the difficulty/impossibility/fraught nature of translating cross-culturally between ways of knowing and producing knowledge. By conflating different perceptions of time and space, the audience member is asked to imaginatively engage with narratives, experiences and world-views beyond their 'known' experience. As a result, an audience is asked to work across what Brown (2006:34) calls 'the so-called epistomological and cognitive divisions of tradition and modernity, the spiritual and scientific, the spoken and written to measure off a Songline on a map,' and thereby trouble contemporary terms of identity and belonging.

Two of Magnet's later productions, *Onnest'bo* (2002–06) and *Cargo* (2007), engage with similar challenges, drawing on written and oral archives related to forced removals during apartheid and slave history (which until recently has been a relatively under-researched aspect of South Africa's disavowed past).[14] However, I now turn to consider *Every Year, Every Day, I Am Walking* (2011), which was inspired by Glynis Clacherty's Suitcase Project, a psychosocial support programme for refugee children in Hillbrow in 2001, which resulted in the book *The Suitcase Stories: Refugee Children Reclaim Their Identities* (2006). Unlike *Rain in a Dead Man's Footprints*, *Onnest'bo* [Upside Down/Topsy Turvy] or *Cargo*, this piece was not based on a specific historical moment or archival sources; rather, it resonates with contemporary issues of migration and xenophobia.

Reznek and Yisa are displaced by violence in a Francophone African country in *Every Year, Every Day, I Am Walking* (2006). Photo credit: © Mark Wessels.

Every Year, Every Day, I Am Walking was originally commissioned for the African Festival of Children and Youth Theatre in Yaounde, Cameroon in November 2006, although it has been performed in many other African countries, as well as India, Brazil, Japan, the United Kingdom, France, Argentina, Sweden, Germany and the United States.[15] It traces the journey of young Aggie and her mother, who come to Cape Town as refugees from an unspecified Francophone country. Although immigration is a very real issue in contemporary South Africa,[16] Fleishman insists that this play is 'about displacement, a sense of loss of place, not just refugees' (Magnet Theatre 2011: 2.08–2.38 mins).

The spoken languages of the play are English and French, but Magnet resident performers Jennie Reznek and Faniswa Yisa characteristically use 'core' images to communicate the key emotions and experiences of the various characters they perform (for example, pairs of shoes come to represent refugees, violent acts and flying birds).

This strategy dramatizes the reality of refugees and immigrants, who often do not tell their stories for many reasons. Some cannot speak the local language; others (particularly those who have been sexually abused) are often 'afraid that their secret will be passed on, resulting in accusation or rejection' (Tankink & Richters 2007: 191), or they develop carefully selected strategies of silence or muted voice as conscious forms of agency (Thomson 2013).

In her analysis of this play, Emma Cox (2012: 121) situates it against other asylum narratives, particularly in Britain, where 'the verbatim theatre form, with its tendency towards a certain narrative rationality' has predominated. She critically 'investigates how, and for whom, victimhood and hope work in and through [this] production' (2013: 119), emphasizing the centrality of performance context and the expectations of different audiences of this transnational production. Cox (2013: 124) convincingly argues that the real efficacy of this production lies in the way in which it 'works outside of the limits of the verbatim "truth paradigm" that formalizes and privileges precise modes of bearing witness to suffering,' which 'fails to problematize or at least reflect carefully enough on the relationship between the imaginative and the historical,' and thereby 'maintains an innocent listening.'[17] Alternatively, I want to focus here on how this production pursues what Cox (2013:124) calls 'a non-factual truthfulness,' insofar as it 'eschews the literal/literate personal account for the immediate specificity of the body.'

In order to analyse how this works in *Every Year, Every Day, I Am Walking*, I would like to invoke both McCloud's (1993) process of closure between the various elements of the play (i.e. narrative, embodied images and soundscape) and Thompson's (2009) argument on the place of aesthetics for shifting theatre for social change from *effect* to *affect*. Thompson (2009: 117 & 140) argues for invoking 'the terrain of sensation: of the aesthetic concerns for beauty, joy, pleasure, awe and astonishment [as] the very point of departure for this type of performative work.' The resultant 'play or process not only communicates information about issues or ideas but is also understood to *show* something of the truth of the lives of those involved' (Thompson 2009: 116, emphasis in original).

Every Year, Every Day, I Am Walking begins with an image that is repeated through the play: young Aggie (Yisa) walks and runs around the perimeter of a circular floor cloth, changing direction and losing her way. This signals the title: the sense of walking, 'every year, every day,' without a sense of belonging. The play explores many reasons for this displacement: violence and civil conflict are the main reasons for Aggie and her mother's displacement, but the play also explores economic and psychic displacement.

Much of the play's affect works through empathetic engagement as the performers 'us[e] the shoes and gestures to reflect their emotional experiences.' From the start of the play, Aggie is drawn back into the past by her memories of her sister Ernestine (Reznek), who 'tempt[s] her back' (Reznek, Fleishman, Yisa & Marek 2012: 17) by manipulating Aggie's shoes that are on a metal table in the centre of the floor cloth. Aggie's little, pink shoes and her mother's worn, cream court shoes are used as hand-held puppets, which the actors animate, walking across the table or over their own bodies to evoke their experiences and feelings. In the scene entitled 'The Journey,' Mama (Reznek) and Aggie (Yisa) make the two pairs of shoes walk, endlessly crunching across the sand they have spread on the table. The movements suggest that they are walking in a huge landscape over a long distance. When Aggie's shoes falter and slide in the sand, Mama's shoes lift Aggie's onto her own, and they continue, one set of shoes carrying the other (2012: 33). This transforms into Mama literally lifting Aggie and carrying her, while Aggie lovingly wipes sweat from her mother's brow (2012: 33). Later, when riding a train, the actresses walk their shoes down their bodies and then scoop them up to beat like a heart against their breasts (2012: 36). These images are both beautiful and somatically moving, as they evoke both being trampled on and how people often hold or beat their chests when upset.

Later, in a refugee camp where the two women seek shelter, Mama is sexually abused; the violent act is performed by Reznek, who mimes walking a pair of heavy black men's shoes all over her prostrate body. While she tries to shift herself from under their weight, she is 'crying and her shoes are shaking with sobs' (Reznek et al. 2012: 35). The shoes here create just enough distance from the violence this scene depicts so that an audience can take in and witness rape, an abuse that is a ubiquitous experience for many migrant women.

As multifaceted symbols, the shoes not only invoke sadness and loss, but also previous joy. One of the first games Aggie (Yisa) recalls is that of a magical, blue origami bird that emerges from her pink shoe, and which her sister (Reznek) animates and flies with her hands into the sky (Reznek et al. 2012: 18–19). She loses the bird, along with her sister, when she and her mother are displaced by a brutal attack on their home (2012: 37). Later, toward the end of the piece, Aggie rediscovers 'a little blue bird nestling in the toe' (2012: 52) of the new shoes her mother gives her, accepting finally that her sister Ernestine is indeed gone forever. This image of the bird may evoke different associations for different audience members. In African folktales, for example, birds often give advice on finding happiness, overcoming poverty or fulfilling a dream (see, for example, McCall Theal 1886). In European fairy tales, bluebirds are associated with happiness. Thus, a single image is evocative, general and beautiful, with potential to evoke diverse associations, while clearly suggesting the power of memory and the fragility of happiness.

Yisa (Magnet Theatre 2011: 5.26–5.35 mins) suggests that 'music both enhances the performance and is also a character' in *Every Year, Every Day, I Am Walking*. The music soundscape, designed by composer Neo Muyanga, was created alongside the workshopped improvisations for this piece, and plays as effective a role as the core images. The play begins with 'a post apocalyptic soundscape,' that briefly gives way to joyous *mapantsula*[18] sounds, which are associated with joy and home. The apocalyptic soundscape then returns and intensifies, as people narrate stories of women and children being killed and houses being burned down. In a scene titled 'The Burning,' this soundscape frames the image of a man in a balaclava (Reznek) sharpening a machete behind a clothes line, and then coming through the cloth at the same time as Aggie (Yisa). The machete 'dances across his body, slowly moving the blade across his arms and neck' (Reznek et al. 2012: 31) before he sets fire to the paper house that suggests their home. The looter cuts the washing-line with his machete and the clothes fall, further suggesting the crumbling security of their home. These images are more indicative than detailed, and together with the soundscape, communicate something of the fear, horror and violence of such an attack.

Having survived the attack and fled their home country, Aggie and her mother arrive in Cape Town. On their arrival, the music is upbeat, in the style of the Cape Carnival (Reznek et al. 2012: 38),[19] but as their bewilderment grows, Mama's movement reverts to the physical gestures she used during The Burning (Reznek et al. 2012: 39). They are shunned instead of welcomed as foreigners in Cape Town. People around them become more hostile, calling them *amakwerekweres* (a derogatory term used to describe black Africans who are not South African nationals),[20] and the music becomes more soulful and evocative of their homelessness.

The official processes of trying to navigate an unknown and at times hostile city have a strong psychic effect that can be compared to the dehumanization of Ruyter in *Rain in a Dead Man's Footprints*. Here, such dehumanization is conveyed by Aggie and her Mama being finger-printed and questioned in English, Afrikaans and Xhosa over and over again. They respond to these experiences by using two plastic bags to create the rhythm of the ocean with them, 'tossing and lifting them like flotsam and jetsam' (Reznek et al. 2012: 41). Then:

> Mama climbs slowly and ceremoniously into the black bag and sweeps the second bag over her head as if she is making a blessing. She covers her head with the second bag so that she has completely disappeared. She sweeps up her shoes into the bag and collapses on to the floor. She rolls slowly on the floor as if she is a bag of human rubbish being blown around by the wind. She climbs out holding her shoes to her chest and looks at the audience.
>
> (Reznek et al. 2012: 42)

The image is beautiful and intensely sad. For Thompson (2009: 144, emphasis in original), beauty 'can be located in the object or experience [...] but these qualities are felt individually and provoke the desire to convince others of their validity.' The physical images before us invite us to engage empathetically with the theme of the play and the plight of migrants on a somatic and aesthetic level (in that we recognize Mama as being as human as we are, with the same hopes, fears and feelings as ourselves), rather than only on a rational level (where we may question the authenticity of a narrative, or assume a definite moral or political position relative to migrancy or refugees). This, I would argue, is an example of a 'dramaturgy of displacement,' where the company have communicated a strong emotion related to a specific experience without speaking for the subject. The audience is then left with the choice as to what to make or do with the residue of this affective experience, ranging from audience members rethinking their own assumptions regarding immigrants as Other, to engaging more critically with discourses on refugees and immigrants, to actively seeking to change the experiences of millions of immigrants.

It is important that the performers are aware – and make us aware – of the space between themselves and the characters they represent. This space is created in the way the actors play multiple roles and use physical theatre. When asked about the efficacy of physical theatre in a 2011 video interview, Magnet resident performer Faniswa Yisa suggests that a positive aspect of the form is that 'everyone can read the body, so they do not have rely on language.' However, her co-performer in the play, Reznek, acknowledged that a potential limitation of physical theatre is that:

> [...] not a lot of people are used to reading the body, so they are used to being told exactly what the story is about verbally. Physical theatre asks people to engage imaginatively with the images that they see in the space.
>
> (Magnet Theatre 2011: 3.53–4.26 mins)

Reznek suggests how the collaborators at Magnet Theatre have consciously engaged with various gaps, what McCloud (1993) terms the 'blank space between,' including their own experiences and those of their characters:

> Magnet has always made work try to find a conversation between an internal and personal landscape and an external social or political landscape. So, the piece, although on the outside is about refugees, Faniswa [Yisa] and I are not refugees, and in a way can only imagine into the refugee experience through empathy and through our own imaginations. But also through connecting with certain losses that we personally might have experienced. So, we feel that even though the piece is particular to refugees, it is also particular to every human being because the story is about loss and recovery and it's something that everybody's experienced, and us as well. We connect into the story through a particular, personal pathway.
>
> (Magnet Theatre 2011: 5.34–6.27 mins)

Every Year, Every Day, I Am Walking demonstrates the inadequacy of words to make meaning in the face of trauma, despite language being key to understanding others. Throughout the piece, Aggie (Yisa) writes her name in the sand with her shoe in English and French (Reznek et al. 2012: 34); she writes her lost sister Ernestine endless letters, often asking, 'Ernestine, where are you?' (2012: 35 & 41); and Aggie and Mama name various parts of their faces in English (2012: 43) in an attempt to create a new subjectivity for themselves. Narration is intrinsic to plot and storytelling, even the way in which we make meaning from our lives. Yet the extent of its inadequacy is illustrated in the story Ernestine tells Aggie about the elephants 'a long, long time ago,' who were free to walk 'anywhere and everywhere in Africa,' and who could find friends when they were lonely or their mother when they were afraid (2012: 28–29). This is a story of an 'ideal' world without frontiers, but throughout Ernestine's narration, machetes are being sharpened; and as Ernestine relates how one of the youngest elephants strays to eat from a delicious tree and is separated from the elephant family, she disappears forever (2012: 29). The rest of the play shows us what this disappearance means for Aggie, thereby demonstrating the inadequacy of words in the context of intense or traumatic experiences.

It is here that Magnet has contributed most profoundly to South African theatre over the past three decades: in experimenting with a truly affective theatre form that creates a space 'that allows people to deal with personal, social, and communal issues on a more intimate level' (Fleishman, cited in Magnet Theatre 2011: 7.43–8:00 mins), and through creating synchronous texts that are visual, aural, spatial and textual. Magnet Theatre invites us to enter the spaces between the 'fields of possibility' in performance, and thus we become co-creators of meaning. We imaginatively engage with the diverse audio, visual, intellectual and emotional registers of the performance, and create something greater when we perceive and synthesize the whole. At the same time, Magnet's work asks us to consider – and trouble – contemporary narratives of South African identity, history and memory. For Thompson (2009), affect is heightened when beauty is evoked alongside critical engagement with complex issues. And it is perhaps here that Magnet's dramaturgy makes the most impact, as it involves an audience's imagination, and thereby provides ways to imagine anew both the past and future in relation to present concerns.

References

Blakeslee, S. and Blakeslee, M. (2008), *The Body Has a Mind of It's Own: How Body Maps in Your Brain Help You Do (Almost) Everything Better*, New York: Random House.

Boym, S. (2001), *The Future of Nostalgia*, New York: Basic Books.

Brown, D. (1998), *Voicing the Text: South African Oral Poetry and Performance*, Cape Town: Oxford University Press.

—— —— (2006), *To Speak of this Land: Identity and Belonging in South Africa and Beyond*, Durban: University of KwaZulu-Natal Press.

Burmark, L. (2002), *Visual Literacy: Learning to See, See to Learn*, Alexandria, VA: ASCD.

Clacherty, G. (2006), *The Suitcase Stories: Refugee Children Reclaim Their Identities*, Cape Town: Double Storey Books.

Cox, E. (2012), 'Victimhood, Hope and the Refugee Narrative: Affective Dialectics in Magnet Theatre's *Every Year, Every Day, I Am Walking*,' *Theatre Research International*, 37: 2, pp. 118–33.

Deacon, J. and Dowson, T. A. (eds) (2001), *Voices from the Past*, Johannesburg: Witwatersrand University Press.

Fleishman, M. (1990), 'Workshop Theatre's Oppositional Form,' *South African Theatre Journal*, 4: 1, pp. 88–118.

—— —— (1997), 'Physical Images in the South African Theatre,' *South African Theatre Journal*, 11: 1/2, pp. 199–214.

——— (2005), '"Stories like the wind": Recontextualising /Xam narratives for Contemporary Audiences,' *South African Theatre Journal*, 19: 1, pp. 43–57.

——— (2011), '*Cargo*: Staging Slavery at the Cape,' *Contemporary Theatre Review*, 21: 1, pp. 8–19.

——— (2012), 'Remembering in the Postcolony: Refiguring the Past with Theatre,' Ph.D. thesis, University of Cape Town.

Flockemann, M. (2011), 'Facing the Stranger in the Mirror: Staged Complicities in Recent South African Performances,' *South African Theatre Journal*, 25: 2, pp. 129–41.

Foster, D., Haupt, P. and De Beer, M. (2005), *The Theatre of Violence: Narratives of Protagonists in the South African Conflict*, Cape Town: HSRC Press.

Gibson, J. N. (2013), 'Moving Bodies, Shifting Selves: Integration and Incorporation Through "Jazzing" and "Salsa" Dance in Cape Town,' *Journal of the Musical Arts in Africa*, 10: 1, pp. 33–52.

Halligey, A. (2005), 'Re-inventing Mythologies: Arguments Towards Cultural Identity in *Medea* and *Rain in a Dead Man's Footprints*,' *South African Theatre Journal*, 19, pp. 208–22.

Harris, Verne (2012), 'Genres of the Trace: Memory, Archives and Trouble,' *Archives and Manuscripts*, 4: 3, http://www.tandfonline.com/doi/abs/10.1080/01576895.2012.735825. Accessed 25 March 2015.

Hitchcock, R. H. and Biesele, M. (2002) 'San, Khwe, Basarwa, or Bushmen?: Terminology, Identity, and Empowerment in Southern Africa,' http://www.khoisanpeoples.org/indepth/ind-identity.htm. Accessed 1 October 2010.

Homann, G. (2009). 'Landscape and Body.' *South African Theatre Journal*, 23, pp. 146–75.

Hutchison, Y. (2004) 'South African Theatre,' in Martin Banham (ed.), *A History of Theatre in Africa*, Cambridge University Press, pp. 312-379.

——— (2005), 'Truth or Bust: Consensualising a historic narrative or provoking through theatre – the place of the personal narrative in the Truth and Reconciliation Commission,' *Contemporary Theatre Review*, 15:3, pp. 34-362.

——— (2009), 'Verbatim Theatre in South Africa: "Living Theatre in a Person's Performance,"' in Alison Forsyth and Chris Megson (eds), *Get Real: Documentary Theatre Past and Present*, Basingstoke and New York: Palgrave Macmillan, pp. 209–23.

——— (2013), *South African Performance and Archives of Memory*, Manchester and New York: Manchester University Press.

——— (2010), 'Post-1990s Verbatim Theatre in South Africa: Exploring an African Concept of "Truth",' in Carol Martin (ed.), *Dramaturgy of the Real on the World Stage*, Basingstoke and New York: Palgrave Macmillan, pp. 61–71.

Knowles, R. (2010), *Theatre & Interculturalism*, Basingstoke: Palgrave Macmillan.

Lewis-Williams, J. D. (1996), *Discovering Southern African Rock Art*, Cape Town and Johannesburg: David Phillip.

Loos, J. (1997) 'Portraits in Specimens of Bushman Folklore by Bleek and Lloyd,' *Quarterly Bulletin of the South African Library*, 52: 1, p. 13.

Low, D. E. (2012), '"Spaces Invested with Content:" Crossing the "Gaps" in Comics with Readers in Schools,' *Children's Literature in Education*, 43, pp. 368–85.

Magnet Theatre (2011), *Every Year, Every Day, I Am Walking* (filmed by ejcmedia, Caracois Voadores for Vox Africa), London: The Oval House Theatre, https://vimeo.com/19299079. Accessed 22 March 2013.

Magnet Theatre and Jazzart Dance Companies (2004), *Rain in a Dead Man's Footprints*, Stellenbosch: Oude Libertas Amphitheatre.

Mail & Guardian (2007), 'San, Bushmen or Basarwa: What's in a name?' 5 September, http://mg.co.za/article/2007-09-05-san-bushmen-or-basarwa-whats-in-a-name. Accessed 1 October 2010.

Mbeki, T. (2001), 'I am an African,' *Quest – An African Journal of Philosophy*, 15: 1/2, pp. 9–15.

Mbembe, Achille (2001), *On the Postcolony*, Berkeley, CA: University of California Press.

McCall Theal, George (1886), *Kaffir (Xhosa) Folk-Lore*, http://www.sacred-texts.com/afr/xft/. Accessed 25 March 2013.

McCloud, Scott (1993), *Understanding Comics*, New York: Harper Perennial/Harper Collins Publishers.

Mngxitama, Andile (2011), 'Blacks are Kwerekweres Whites are Tourists,' http://kaganof.com/kagablog/2011/07/18/andile-mngxitama-blacks-are-kwerekweres-whites-are-tourists/. Accessed 25 March 2013.

Reznek, J., Fleishman, M., Yisa, F. and Marek, F. (2012), 'Every Year, Every Day, I Am Walking,' in *The Magnet Theatre 'Migration' Plays*, Cape Town: Junkets Publisher, pp. 9–53.

Rudakoff, J. (2004), 'Somewhere, Over the Rainbow: White-Female-Canadian Dramaturge in Cape Town,' *TDR*, 48: 1, pp. 126–63.

Sichel, Adrienne (2010), 'Grappling with South African Physical Theatre,' *South African Theatre Journal*, 24, pp. 41–50.

Sipe, L. R. and Brightman, A. E. (2009), 'Young Children's Interpretations of Page Breaks in Contemporary Picture Storybooks,' *Journal of Literary Research*, 41, pp. 68–103.

Skotnes, P. (1999), *Heaven's Things – A Story of the /Xam*, Cape Town: UCT Press.

Skotnes, P. and Fleishman, M. (2002), *A Story is the Wind: Representing Time and Space in San Narratives*, Cape Town: LLAREC – The Museum Workshop at UCT.

Tankink, M. and Richters A. (2007), 'Silence as a Coping Strategy: The Case of Refugee Women in the Netherlands from South-Sudan Who Experienced Sexual Violence in the Context of War,' in Boris Droµzek and John P. Wilson (eds), *Voices of Trauma: Treating Psychological Trauma Across Cultures*, New York: Springer, pp. 191–210.

Thompson, J. (2009), *Performance Affects*, Basingstoke and New York: Palgrave Macmillan.

Thomson, S. (2013), 'Agency as Silence and Muted Voice: The Problem-Solving Networks of Unaccompanied Young Somali Refugee Women in Eastleigh, Nairobi,' *Conflict, Security & Development*, 13: 5, pp. 589–609.

Truth and Reconcilitaion Commission of South Africa (TRC) (1998), *Final Report* (vols 1–5), London: Macmillan.

The UN Refugee Agency (UNHCR) (2010), 'UNHCR Global Report of 2009 – South Africa,' 1 June, http://www.unhcr.org/cgi-bin/texis/vtx/home/opendocPDFViewer.html?docid=4c08f2c19&query=south africa asylum applications. Accessed 24 March 2012.

Vilakazi, B. W. (1993), 'The Conception and Development of Poetry in Zulu,' in R. H. Kaschula (ed.), *Foundations in Southern African Oral Poetry*, Witwatersrand: Witwatersrand University Press.

Wetherell, M. (2012) *Affect and Emotion: A New Social Science Understanding*, Los Angeles and London: Sage.

Notes

1. To read key extracts of this speech, see http://www.anc.org.za/show.php?id=4322. Accessed 27 April 2015.
2. Nguni praise poetry is oral poetry performed with strong emotion, with a strong rhythm that is established by a particular pace and style of delivery. It uses repetition, parallelism and personal nouns to evoke an image of a person symbolically (Vilakazi 1993: 61–67). For detail see Hutchison (2004: 326–30).
3. See Fleishman's (1997: 210–13) own analysis of how he achieves this in *Medea*, as well as Rudakoff (2004: 133–34) and Halligey's (2005) analyses of Magnet productions.
4. See Hutchison (2005; 2013) for more detail.
5. The /Xam represent one particular San group living in the southernmost area of Southern Africa. There has been extensive debate about these terms, which have been used to refer to the first hunter-gatherer peoples of Southern Africa, who speak related languages and today live in South Africa, Botswana, Namibia and Angola. Robert Hitchcock and Megan Biesele (2002) have traced 'the complex and problematic history' of using the terms 'San,' 'Bushmen,' or 'Basarwa' as possible appellations for the general group, because they have different meanings to different cultural and linguistic groups. Some people living in Botswana believe it 'pejorative because it did not signify the status of being a person.' Although 'representatives of various San groups met in Namibia and agreed to allow the general term "San" to designate them as a group externally [and] [t]his decision was reaffirmed at a meeting on "Khoisan Identities and Cultural Heritage" held in Cape Town […] in July, 1997.' See, for example, *Mail & Guardian* (2007).
6. When Wilhelm Bleek died in 1875, his work on Bushman [San] folklore and language was not complete, and another 36 years were to pass before Lloyd was able to publish the results of their joint research, *Specimens of Bushman Folklore* (1911) (in Loos 1997).

7. Fleishman (2005: 50) analyses his use of this mode in his first production, *The Sun, The Moon and The Knife* (1995), based on Stephen Watson's poem *Return of the Moon*, which presented space, time and narrative as linear and chronological.
8. These included 'Early Time,' when there was no difference between humans and animals; 'After Time,' when animals became wild and lost their humanity and humans developed laws, beliefs and their human form; 'Colonial Time,' the vantage from which we perceive the San and their stories; and [as Fleishman adds] 'Contemporary Time,' from which we perceive the performance (Fleishman 2005: 52).
9. All future references to this production refer to the March 2004 recording.
10. All roles not specified were performed by Jazzart Dance Theatre and members of the Jazzart Dance Theatre Young Adult Training and Job Creation Programme.
11. See Lewis ('Performance Labours') for a similar analysis of a shard of pottery in *Cargo* (2007).
12. See Lewis-Williams' (1996: 44–51) explanation of these figures in relation to // Kabbo and /Han#kass'o's narratives.
13. *Isicathamiya* refers to a Zulu style of a cappella singing, as well as the tightly-choreographed dance moves that accompany the singing.
14. See Lewis ('Performance Labours') for a detailed analysis of *Cargo*.
15. See Flockemann ('Being There') for another analysis of *Every Year, Every Day, I Am Walking*.
16. According to a UNHCR Global Report for 2009 (2010), South Africa continued to be the country that received the largest number of asylum applications in the world, with some 222,000 submitted in 2009.
17. The South African Truth and Reconciliation Commission attempted to acknowledge the complexities of verbatim testimony in its outlined four modalities of 'truth' for the hearings: factual or forensic truth; personal or narrative truth; social or 'dialogue' truth; and healing or restorative truth (TRC 1998 vol. 1: 110–14). Foster, Haupt and De Beer (2005) outlined and analysed in detail the significance of these modalities for the ways in which narratives of violence were framed in the commission. However, verbatim text has long been incorporated into South African theatre in ways different to the European or American models. Hutchison (2009; 2010) has analysed this particular approach to verbatim, and Homann (2009) shows how these four modalities of truth are useful in offering a structure to investigate pre- and post-apartheid theatre's engagements with narrative and violence.
18. A flat-footed African tap-and-glide style of dance that developed in the South African urban context with Kwaito as the accompanying music.
19. This is a minstrel festival that takes place annually on the 2nd of January in Cape Town. Originally involving slaves from Africa and Asia, it is now a celebration of Cape Malay and coloured cultures that have survived slavery and apartheid. The music, characterized by the *ghoema* beat, is a fusion of styles, and influenced by jazz.
20. See Mngxitama (2011) for more on the dynamics of xenophobia in South Africa.

Chapter 13

Magnet's Recipe for Considered, Conscious Theatre-Making: A Conversation with Frances Marek[1]

Frances Marek was a project manager at Magnet from 2009 to 2011. As a student studying theatre and performance at the University of Cape Town (UCT), Frances was taught by Mark Fleishman, Jennie Reznek and Mandla Mbothwe. She has collaborated on scripts for Magnet, most notably Die Vreemdeling [The Stranger] *(2010) and* Kragbox [Power Box] *(2011) with Dann-Jacques Mouton and Ephraim Gordon. She also co-directed* The Children and the Bees *(2011), a companion piece to the opera* Brundibar *at Artscape. Frances also worked on the Clanwilliam project over a number of years.*

When she saw her first Magnet show, *Onnest'bo* [Upside Down/Topsy Turvy] (2002), while at UCT, performed on UCT's Hiddingh Campus in what was formerly the Ping Pong Palace and now a car park, Marek describes being 'totally transported by it.' She adds, 'What I remember most about that production was just the sheer joyfulness of it. It was infectious. It was so bold, so sure of itself. That was my first experience of Magnet.'

'What I admire so much about Magnet as a company,' says Marek, is 'their sense of artistic integrity' and 'how they have evolved in such a considered, conscious way. They have done what every theatre company dreams of doing which is to be around long enough to try things, and then learn and grow and build on what came before, rather than starting from scratch every time [...]. What Mark and Jennie knew they wanted – and where I think they succeeded – was in creating something sustainable that allowed them a framework for there to be support; a base for that next production to build on so that next time they could implement what they had learned from the ones before.' Describing her experience with Magnet over the years, Marek says it has been 'a process that had a lot of space, a lot of room in it for development and growth and creativity. Magnet's process is the product of many years of work, of consideration, of respect and of dedication to the creation of work, rather than simply the performance of it.'

As someone who was trained by Fleishman and Reznek at UCT, Marek says, 'Mark was my theatre-making lecturer, and I think his teaching played a big role in my starting to think that I might be a writer and a director as well as a performer. Jennie taught me movement in the first year, which was also a total revelation. I had always danced while at school, but she introduced us to ways of using the body that I had never imagined.' Marek believes the inclusivity of Fleishman and Reznek's process is a central asset of the company. Because Jennie and Mark are teachers as well as artists, she says, 'They recognize that all performers are always in a state of learning and development, and so they know that what happens in the rehearsal room is almost more important than what happens out there on the stage. It's more lasting; it matters more and for longer to the people involved; and it feeds directly into the final product, even if it's not finally seen onstage.'

Marek contends that 'every theatre practitioner has a guru, one particular person that they look to or think about when they need help. Mark often speaks about Barney Simon in that way. I think, for me, Mark's been my theatre guru. I'm so inspired by him; not just by his work, but by the way he works. I have never met a director who is more considered, who allows themselves time to investigate and analyse and discover. He never loses his cool, and his cool is made up of an enormous amount of intelligence and integrity.'

Marek believes Magnet's greatest value resides in its way of working: 'Rather than working slowly, I would say that what Magnet does, is allow themselves the luxury of time. Within that time frame, they work incredibly fast. But they have planned and structured their creative process so that the time they need *is there*, which I think is very important and also quite rare.'

Marek reminisces about working on the Clanwilliam project and the spirit of playful, collective creation that Magnet espouses and encourages:

> It was late at night after a very full day and we were a group of students, dancers and musicians in an old kitchen at the back of this warehouse, surrounded by paint pots and glitter and the artworks the children had made that day. We were all perched on tables and chairs and sinks, and Mark wanted to look at all the different elements we had musically and start working with some of the dancers. Everyone was very tired and there was very little space. But Mark was quite patient and he treated everyone as equals; he wasn't deliberately making space for the students – we were all just artists collaborating. And one of the musicians began improvising and then someone else came in. We had two French horns and a violin and a drum, and something started to happen in the room; people were dancing in the space between the desks and the kitchen just filled up with music as one by one each person found a place to come in. It was just the most generous, supportive space for creativity and improvisation. What we created that night was magic and partly unrepeatable, and I was worried that we'd never manage to do it again just like that. And then I realized it didn't matter because what we had made there, just between us, was as important as the final performance and would inform whatever that final performance became. That's when I realized that the process, the germination; the stuff that you make in the small space of the rehearsal room is just as important as what you perform on the stage in front of a crowd of strangers.

On the collaborative process of making *Die Vreemdeling*, Marek describes how the process was a layering of several elements: Marek's short story that she developed after travelling up the West Coast with fieldworker Lavona de Bruyn;[2] Mark's prompts around themes, elements and structure; and the process of improvising and developing the play with actors.

Marek has a strong sense of Magnet's recipe for success. She remembers one particular rehearsal of *Die Vreemdeling* 'where things were just flowing really well, and we were improvising and writing music and dialogue and blocking all at the same time.' They needed to find some text, an articulation of 'a wild accusation from one character to another.' Someone in the room suggested trying a translation of a Shakespeare quote into Afrikaans. 'So we found this incredible quote,' says Marek, '"Temptation is the fire that brings up the scum of the heart," which we translated into the voice of the character and which came out as: "*Versoeking is die vuur wat die etter van die hart ontbloot.*"' She describes 'the look of excitement on Mark's face when we found it because it was such a perfect line for that character to say,' and she got the sense that he 'just loved being able to run with people's ideas in the moment and draw on all these different influences; to put all these separate ideas and songs and quotes and gestures into one very rich stew. He often uses cooking metaphors when he teaches directing. He speaks about all the separate ingredients becoming greater than the sum of their parts when they've been heated and simmered and mixed together for a while, and changed and added to one another. Mark creates a space for all that. That's what gets him going where directing is concerned; the bringing together and mixing and development of all the separate elements. It's a beautiful thing to watch and be involved in.'

References

Marek, F. (2013), e-mail interview with A. Krueger, 22 June–18 July.

Notes

1. Interview quotes in this chapter are taken from Marek (2013).
2. See De Bruyn ('Catalysing a Community').

Chapter 14

The Performance Labours of Magnet and Jazzart's *Cargo* (2007)[1]

Megan Lewis

Megan Lewis (co-editor) is an assistant professor of theatre at the University of Massachusetts Amherst. Her research and teaching interests include African film and cinema, as well as theatrical and public performances of race, gender and nation in South Africa. She has published on South African performance in the Theatre Journal, *the* Performing Arts Journal, Text & Performance, Theatre Topics, Modern Drama *and the* Journal of Dramatic Theory and Criticism. *In addition to co-editing this collection with Anton Krueger, Dr Lewis is also currently working on a monograph about whiteness and Afrikaner performance.*

Adding to the shame-filled history of colonialism and apartheid in South Africa is the oft-hidden history of slavery and human trafficking at the Cape Colony. Slavery endured for the first 186 years of white settlement in Southern Africa. However, the slave past is for the most part pushed out of the country's collective memory. In this chapter, I will examine the performance labours of Magnet Theatre's 2007 production of *Cargo*,[2] their seventh and final collaboration with Jazzart Dance Theatre, where they 'put theatre to work on the past' (Fleishman 2011: 12) to (re)member – to recall and to embody – the invisible and silenced bodies, shattered fragments and incoherent ghosts of the slave archive. *Cargo* brought the fragmentary and palimpsest slave archive to life onstage in the postcolony (Mbembe 2011),[3] using live performance and dancing bodies that infused life into the archive. Staged in 2007, this powerful dance-theatre piece performed the vital cultural intervention of engaging contemporary South Africans with their shameful and shaming past, and asked them to reflect on exploitative practices in their own moment in history as well.[4]

Emptying the secret contents of its container into the twenty-first century, *Cargo* was developed in honour of the bicentennial commemoration of Britain's abolition of slavery across her territories in 1807. The production, which featured Jennie Reznek and Faniswa Yisa as the piece's main narrators, was staged to rave reviews and critical acclaim in March 2007 at the Spier wine estate in Stellenbosch (a former slave plantation); at the National Arts Festival in Grahamstown in July; and at the Baxter Theatre in Cape Town in August of that year (Brommert 2007; Jordan & Mackie 2007; Lewis 2008).

As Reznek has deftly articulated in her chapter in this collection, Magnet Theatre foregrounds the language of the body in their physical theatre work. In collaboration with partners like Jazzart, Magnet uses the language of movement as a means of overcoming vast linguistic diversities in South Africa. Their physical theatre productions set out to engage with the complexities of South African culture, as well as the new multicultural democracy attempting to move beyond its apartheid past. As Reznek affirms, over the past three decades Magnet has striven to be a 'moving force' – physically, intellectually and politically – in South African culture. Magnet's partner on this project, Jazzart Dance Theatre (1973–present), is the oldest contemporary dance company in the Cape, if not Africa. Described by arts critic Adrienne Sichel as a 'democratic dance collective' open to dancers 'across the racial spectrum,'[5] Jazzart – like Magnet – is committed to creating a vital, politically engaged body of bodywork.

In the opening scene of *Cargo*, a tiny illuminated ship sails out of the darkness over a giant cargo container that dominates the stage. We hear the deep chanting of voices as more ships emerge, carrying candles that light their paths. The voices grow louder, until suddenly the enormous container bursts open towards the audience, revealing its *roerende en oproerende* ['moving and unsettling'] human cargo.[6] In the 90 minutes in which *Cargo* takes to unload its story, the audience journeys across the seventeenth to the twenty-first centuries, marking the 186 years (between 1652, when the Dutch first settled the Cape, and 1838, when the slaves were finally emancipated) that slavery was a part of Cape colonial society.[7] *Cargo's* story ends in 2007, over 170 years after the official end of slavery, with reference to the human trafficking and labour exploitation that plague South Africa today – distressing reminders of the troubles of both colonialism and neocolonialism.

Fleishman (2011: 12) explains that the goal of *Cargo* was 'to make the archive speak in unspeakable ways.' Working through the body as a primary site of theatrical exploration, the 16 performing bodies in *Cargo* were able to 'express a language beyond words' (2011: 12). Using mostly movement punctuated with scripted scenes, *Cargo* brought to life the shame-filled silences around the history of slavery in South Africa. It told the story of the thousands of slave bodies upon whose bloodied backs the Cape Colony was founded and at whose expense it profited. In essence, the live dancing bodies testified for those anonymous and buried in history; they embodied a witnessing, they spoke for the silent.[8]

Cargo was organized around two symbolic and physical principles that Fleishman and his collaborators (Fleishman 2011:15) found in their year-long research in the slave archive: 'listing or inventorizing' and performing social relations in the 'colonial household and its environs.' The slave archive includes documentary and archaeological collections at various institutions in Cape Town, heritage sites around the city, and the living bodies and stories of those contemporary South Africans descended from slaves. Thus, the enormous cargo container which provided the principle set served both as a 'double volume cargo crate' or slave ship and, once open, 'simulate[d] the layout of a Cape Dutch household without walls, as if turned inside out but also turned around so that the audience's entry point is from behind, as was that of the slaves' (2011: 15). By foregrounding the backside of history, *Cargo* evoked the sexual and labour exploitations of slave life at the Cape; and by framing its narrative from the point of view of those whom history has often forgotten or erased, the play asked the predominantly white audience to confront the taboo subject of South African slavery.

As the cargo ship opened, the company of 16 dancers – an array of men, women, black, brown and white performers – formed a tableau, as if a photographic snapshot of the past. Dressed in white muslin pants and skirts, pinstriped tops with scarlet accents and buttons, their heads wrapped in muslin *doeke* [head scarves], the ensemble was placed amidst mattresses, crates and other cargo, and they locked eyes with the audience, gazing resolutely at us from the present across the unreachable past. As our gazes locked, *Cargo*'s larger cultural labour became clear: to overcome the dilemma of a postcolony that simultaneously demanded remembering, but in which remembering was also highly fraught, if not impossible.[9]

Suddenly, one of the performers, Thembeka Zondi, began calling out the 'inventory of the ship, *Waalvis*, from Malacca,'[10] and the frozen bodies in the tableau sprang into motion, carrying cargo out of the ship's hull. One performer listed the ship's contents, 'Tamarind, cardamom, cinnamon, saffron;' another tried to sell a pair of shoes; a third auctioned off the ship's animate cargo: 'Item: Rachel van de Caap, from Bengal.' Reznek then read from an archival letter dated 26 May 1652 to the Dutch East India Company and signed by Jan van Riebeeck,[11] requesting the use of slaves at the new colony he had formed at the Cape of Good Hope. This archival moment was bookended with another at the end of the piece, in which a woman (Jackie Manyaapelo) slowly emerged from a big black steamer trunk filled to the brim with papers: a live body materializing out of an inanimate container; the slave body emerging from the archive. This complex image resonated on multiple levels: the woman-as-trunk (i.e. a body as an object) indexed how human beings were historically treated as chattel or property of their masters. Correspondingly, the trunk-turned-woman (i.e. an object become human) evoked for audiences the living, breathing bodies of slaves of the past, come to life through performance. Another woman, with a large bundle of cloth on her head, walked across the ship's stern, deliberately protruding her posterior in an image evocative of Sara Baartman.[12] This familiar and iconic posture, and her measured movement across the stage that beckoned us to follow her posterior with our gaze, sutured the audience in 2007 to the seventeenth-century colonial moment. Her posture alluded to the historic consumption of brown female bodies by white men, epitomized by the French anatomist Georges Cuvier's obsession with Baartman before and after her death.[13] The sexual consumption of slave women by white *burghers* [citizens] was commonplace in the Cape colony; according to a study by Van den Berghe, an estimated 75 per cent of children born to female slaves at the Cape had white fathers.[14]

The focus on the Baartman figure's posterior, paired with *Cargo*'s perspective from the back door (backside) of the farmstead, made visible the complex historical matrix of sexual exploitation, gender and slavery that defined Cape colonial society. The lengthy and careful process of making *Cargo* took the artists into the archive. *Cargo*'s text, content and emplotment were assembled from both material and documentary traces: the artists consulted materials such as shards of pottery, clothing or architectural remains;

Reznek and Yisa embrace the spirit of play in rehearsal for *Cargo* (2007).
Photo credit: © Garth Stead.

meanwhile, the documentary traces they worked with included archival documents, letters, slave ship records, trial records and accounts of slave life. After a research process of over a year, including visits to slave sites in Cape Town, the company began an intensive process of physical rehearsal. Because, as Fleishman claims, 'the memory of the past comes to us in fragments,' the performers worked with 'fragments' drawn from the research process, which they in turn responded to with their bodies, voices and intellects through improvisations, movement work and scripting based on prompts, as is Magnet's devising practice. In his role as director, Fleishman (2011: 13 & 19) then sought out and pieced together these fragments of performance material into an 'assemblage' movement piece that offered 'mnemonic provocations' to audiences. Thus the evocation of Sara Baartman acted as a mnemonic provocation for the audience; a reminder of the history of the exploitation of black and brown women and of the objectification of human

Bodies and/as objects in *Cargo* (2007).
Photo credit: © Garth Stead.

beings in the service of empire. As an assemblage, *Cargo* was structured as an inventory of objects, organized into several scenarios: *koekje van seep* [cake of soap], *'n hoopje sout* [a pinch of salt], *drie oude wielen* [three old wheels], *dertien grawe* [13 spades/graves], *acht beesten* [eight cattle], *een partij oude schoenen* [one pair of old shoes]. Throughout the performance, objects and live bodies intermingled and blurred, strategically making visible the historic practice of treating human beings as objects or consumable products.

In keeping with this sense of hybridity and mixing, *Cargo* was performed in both English and Afrikaans, the mother tongue of the 4.5 million coloureds who live mainly in the Eastern and Western Cape provinces. By focusing on and celebrating coloured bodies that occupy an in-between-ness – between black and white, past and present, secrecy and exposure, shame and pride – *Cargo* asked South African audiences in 2007 to face up to these contradictions; to see, hear and engage with the practice of slavery at the Cape, and the lasting scars and shame this practice etched into South African culture, particularly around coloured identity.[15]

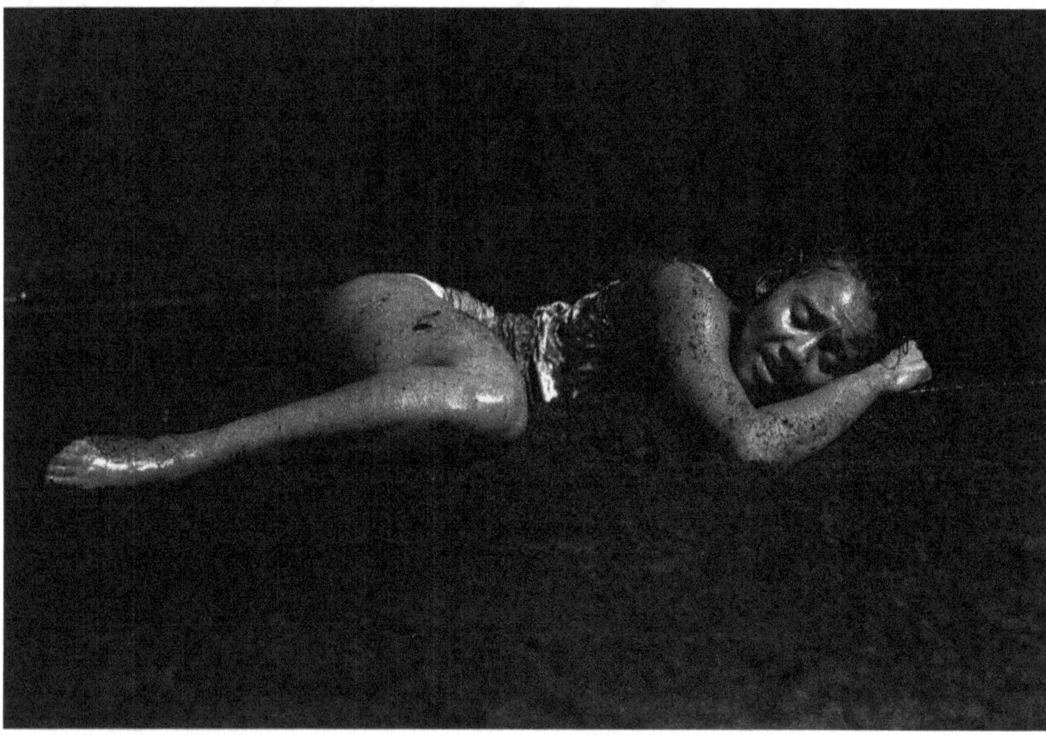

Levern de Villiers fights for her life in *Cargo* (2007).
Photo credit: © Garth Stead.

The shame and historic exploitation of black and coloured women (a prevalent theme in *Cargo*) manifests most clearly in two scenarios: one regarding the drowning of children by slave mothers; and the other concerning the story of Katie, a slave wet nurse, inspired by the life of Katie Jacobs, a slave woman interviewed at age 96 in 1910. Much like the Baartman scenario described earlier, these stories creatively explored the physical and psychic pressures placed on female slaves in the Cape Colony. As Yisa and Reznek tell us, 'A woman slave first hurled her four children into the water and then also herself and drowned together with three of her children.' Later, 'An officer in the ninety-third regiment said he had seen no fewer than 13 infants washed up by the tides on the Cape Town beach,' as the brave, yet vulnerable Levern de Villiers flails in the moat of water that surrounds the cargo container. In this scenario, the archive's secrets – the pressures placed on slave women's bodies as bearers of children (some of whom were the products of rape by their masters) and as nursing mothers to children of their own, as well as wet nurses to their mistresses' offspring – spill into the present, and are made to 'speak in unspeakable ways' (Fleishman 2011: 12) through de Villiers's dancing body. As she tries to drown herself, her brown body mixing with the muddy water, Katie struggles for gasps of air, and seems to fight against her own gravity, as if the water was pushing her downwards. As de Villiers dances this emotionally charged piece, it is uncertain whether she is fighting to die or fighting to stay alive. And as we watch her struggle, we as audience members are asked to respond empathetically; to contemplate what life must have been like for this woman, whose body did not belong to her, whose breasts and uterus were in non-stop reproductive mode, and for whom life became so unbearable that she drowned her children and then tried to drown herself. And to ponder: if women suffered like this in the colonial past, were there women in contemporary South Africa suffering similarly?

Fragments such as the mysteries of Katie's life and her attempted suicide are central to *Cargo's* dramaturgy, which is focused on the (im)possibilities of staging the past in the postcolony. A literal fragment is foregrounded in a scene in which narrator Jennie Reznek walks along a 'beach' of sand that surrounds the central cargo container, and discovers a small piece of porcelain, 'a small part of something else,' that she tells us came 'from somewhere else, another time, another place.' She struggles to find a matching piece to her fragment, which has thin blue and grey lines on it (echoing the pinstripes in the costumes and mattresses from the cargo container). She longs to connect the tiny grey lines to something whole – 'something that fitted, some other part that might connect' – but to no avail. All that remains is a fragment. With this gesture, *Cargo* recognized its own impossible position in relation to history: while re-membering the slaves of the past using live dancing bodies, it also marked the past as fragmentary and illusive, impossible to assemble completely. Peace that comes from satisfactorily piecing the past together is impossible; rather, *Cargo* reminds us that we must confront that impossibility and work through the fragments that remain if we are to engage in the tenuousness and impossibility of (re)membering in the postcolony.

Another scenario of tension and multiple significations, entitled *koekje van seep* [cake of soap], took place in the moat of water that surrounded the central cargo container. The Afrikaans word *koekie* [Dutch: *koekje*] is the diminutive of cake – here a little cake of soap – but *koekie* is also a word for female genitalia. This homophone articulated both the gendered politics of objects (soap, associated with laundry, a traditionally female form of labour) and the objectification of gendered bodies (slave women whose work often included sexually servicing their white masters). In *koekje van seep*, the dancers wash their laundry rhythmically in the water. They drape the strips of cloth back and forth like the tides of the ocean. Water and sand from the moat's beach mix and become muddy, and the crisp white fabric takes on a brown hue, referencing again the brownness of coloured identity, racial mixing and miscegenation. The dancers then throw their balls of wet fabric into the air, extending them skywards and then snapping them back towards their bodies, sending sprays of moisture into the hot lights and darkness of the theatre. The scene simultaneously conveyed the repetitive manual labour of indentured washerwomen, as well as liberatory gestures of freedom. As the dancers played with the fabric, shouting out gleefully, the scene also celebrated the coloured community's vitality today. The live moving bodies articulated, beyond language, the complex legacy of slavery; its forced, repetitive, dehumanizing labour, as well as the moments of community born of common oppression. And the audience could not remain passive or immune in this scene; we were physically moved by the action, reacting as the moisture of their wet fabric sprayed across the fourth wall and covered us with droplets of muddy water, the smell of wet earth visceral in our nostrils.[16]

Now, a line of women, wearing head *doeke* and pinstriped bodices laced up with thick scarlet cord, dance under and around sheets of white fabric. Between these material sheets of fabric, they explore the dirty little secrets that happened to slave women between the sheets in the colonial Cape. As each dancer kneads and pummels her fabric, the audience feels the metaphoric violence of aggressive hands on unwilling bodies. The dancers face upstage, showing the audience their rhythmically moving buttocks as they scrub the floor, revealing scarlet laces on their costumes that look like bloodied scars across their backs. The dancers' movements once again suggest (white) desire for (brown) bodies. By framing the audience's gaze and the women's gyrating rumps in this relation, the scene positions the predominantly white, middle-class audience as the consumers of this spectacle, asking us to experience and reflect upon a colonially-charged scene of labour and desire. And the dancers are conscious of the audience's gaze on their bodies; they display themselves for our viewing pleasure, turning their heads ever so slightly to watch us watching them – a consciousness that also suggests that not all slaves in the Cape Colony were passive victims of sexual exploitations. Within their limited range of agency, some slave women engaged in a system of exchange in which they strategically bartered their bodies for comforts, access to resources or other privileges.

Just as the red laces on the backs of the costumes reference the gruesome punishments wrought on the bodies of slaves for disobedience or resistance, so too do later scenes draw attention to this violence.[17] In another scenario, *drie oude wielen* [three old wheels], Yisa describes the violence perpetrated on slave bodies, speaking the words of a slave who was brutally punished: 'my master flogged me with the quince twigs, with which I was punished five at a time.' With the potential of such punishments looming over them, the washerwomen slowly smuggle a cake of soap between them, passing it from woman to woman in downturned palms. They pass the soap behind their backs, but, because they are facing upstage, the audience is made witness to this secret act. The women secret the bar of soap – with its slippery connotations as a lubricant, a cleansing agent and as a slang term for female genitals – between themselves and beneath the controlling gaze of their masters (in this case, we, the audience). By forcing us to gaze upon their undulating buttocks and their subversive act of smuggling, this powerful, multi-layered scene not only evoked the practice of miscegenation at the Cape and the apartheid regime's shaming of interracial sexuality,[18] but also simultaneously marked the agency of these women, who operated beneath the radar of those in power, despite the potential of violent retribution. In the present performance, the women protect their *koekies*, those private anatomical places that were historically invaded by their masters. As the scene progresses, and the dancers flip their fabric more and more aggressively, the women now express a fierce agency of their own, resisting oppressive power with each whip of their wet sheets, metaphorically 'flipping off' their overlords with their soaked linens.

Cargo also addressed the gendered experience for male slaves. In the scenario entitled *acht beesten* [eight cattle], the cargo container's lid is hoisted into an upright position, creating a wall against which eight men – the cattle of the scenario – are auctioned off with business-like efficiency. The men begin to kick up sand and lock into battle, shoulders pressured together as if in a rugby scrum or yoked in a harness. Sound designer Neo Muyanga's soundscape[19] augments the masculine struggle of the performing male bodies with growls, distorted wails, guttural grunts and the deep gurgle of a lion's roar. The men then take to the cargo container's front surface, scrambling up the side of the container, defying gravity as they lift and invert one another in full body presses against it. In their fierce displays of physical strength, one man literally supporting another in an inverted lift (a signature Jazzart move), the male dancers escaped and defied the system of enslavement that yoked them, as *beesten*, to the ground. The physical gestures of this scenario articulated, beyond words, the double bind that male slaves were caught in: they were at once aggressive and enslaved, asserting their raw manly strength as they were yoked together and treated as *beesten*.

Cargo engaged in simultaneous acts of exposing the harsh realities and trauma of slavery (the past) and celebrating the rich ethnic heritage of Cape culture (the present and future). In one scene in the Dutch household kitchen, dancers build a subversive rhythm with drums, penny whistles and a tambourine, exploding into a full out *ghoema* song.[20] Women flip their skirts and the men gyrate behind them. This display of sexuality, between equal and consenting adults, is markedly distinct from the sordid colonial consumption of brown bodies by white masters referenced earlier. The men and women

Jazzart Dancers defy the gravity of slavery in *Cargo* (2007).
Photo credit: © Garth Stead.

dance both in defiance of the power structure that enslaves them and in homage to the vibrant present-day coloured culture in the Cape.

Cargo ended where it began, with lists of inventory. This time, however, in *een partij oude schoenen*, each dancer comes forward, wrapping arms around his or her own body, presenting the audience with their own pair of shoes: 'Jenny, from Pietermaritzburg,' says Reznek, as she places her small running shoes centre stage. Two male dancers offer their shoes up with 'Luvuyo, from Langa…Owen, from Alex.'[21] A pair of shoes – the simple yet poignant symbol of a single human being, and a recurring motif in Magnet's work[22] – works metaphorically to mark the place in which we stand, literally and figuratively. In *Cargo,* shoes become reminders of absence – of the slave bodies silenced by history – as well as reminders of present realities – the circulation of branded products within slave and contemporary market economies. Presenting the audience with their individual shoes, and stating aloud their proper names, each of the dancers conjure up and reassemble the lost bodies of those who came before them. Mark Fleishman explains:

> Slaves were not allowed to wear shoes, and a mark of manumission was the wearing of shoes by ex-slaves. In the beginning each cast member removes his/her shoes and takes on the name of a slave from the archive, and at the end each cast member puts their shoes back on again and retakes their own name.
>
> (Fleishman 2015)

The shoes map the journey from bodies as objects (slaves, chattel, items on a shipping log) to subjects (real people who live, breathe, suffer and love, and whose descendants are a vital part of South Africa's modern human tapestry).

According to Fleishman (2011: 19), 'If *Cargo* is a history, it is not the history of the past as much as it is the history of the present.' In its coda, *Cargo* offers a biting indictment of our contemporary forms of slavery. '*Ek sê, ek sê*' ['I say, I say'], a clowning performer (Yisa) calls, as she holds up for sale one of the pairs of sneakers lined up at the front of the stage. 'These are not made in America,' she boasts; indicting our contemporary global economic trade into this charge, she shouts, 'these are authentic Converse® products, made in China!' She then proceeds to tell the audience that Chinese children, who make 'amaT-shirts, amaPorcelain, hush-hush, under the carpet,'[23] manufactured the shoes she is holding. And then the cargo container begins to open yet again, this time revealing, as our wise fool has just told us, another shipment of cargo. But this one is for the twenty-first century, and is laden with 'amaCheapgoods, amaDrugs, amaWomen…' In this moment, the words of the wise fool unite the absent slave bodies of the past, represented by the shoes, to the contemporary trafficking of live human beings. Indeed, human trafficking started at the Cape Colony in 1652 and continues to be a serious problem in democratic South Africa, where, according to a 2010 study by the National Prosecuting Authority Conference on Human Trafficking, significant numbers of women, girls and boys are trafficked for a variety of purposes, 'including prostitution, pornography, domestic servitude, forced labour, begging, criminal activity (including drug trafficking), and trafficking for the removal of body parts (or *muti*)' (Mokwena 2010).[24]

Citing contemporary forms of exploited labour, cheaply manufactured products and the global market economy, *Cargo* exposed the oppressive practices of the past that ghost through and persist in our own time. *Cargo* moved its audiences to contemplate the parallels of the then and the now, as we witness live bodies bringing the spirits of those long dead to life onstage as they sweat and bend, labour before us, stand rigid and fight tall. We watch Levern de Villers struggle in the muddy waters surrounding the cargo container in colonial Cape Town, and then imagine what struggles the next boatload of trafficked women unloaded at the Cape's docks today will face as they are forced into labour or prostitution in South Africa's neo-liberal democracy.[25]

The labours that *Cargo* performed were multi-layered and visible in degrees. On one level, by offering 'mnemonic provocations' to both the dancers in rehearsal and the audience watching the final piece, *Cargo* brought to life stories of invisible indentured labourers: men and women whose bodies were put to work in the fields, households, battlefields and bedrooms of the Cape Colony. On another level, the physical labours of the dancing bodies, sweating and lifting, moving and emoting, linking past and present through embodiment, were an immediate and visible part of Fleishman's goal to 'put the theatre to work on the past.' And in the larger social context of the postcolony, *Cargo* performed the important labours of making visible and making present a shamed past; a past that is at once unrepresented and unrepresentable. As it laboured – physically and intellectually – to 'put together the fractured body' of the past, *Cargo* evinced the fluidity and instability of both performance and history, which, for Fleishman (2011: 8 & 19), 'must be worked at, brought into being, creatively imagined, reinvented, collectively sustained, argued over each and every time.' As an emotionally moving, movement intervention, *Cargo* brought the issue of slavery in the colonial and neocolonial contexts vividly and creatively to life onstage. In the dialogue between the performers and their audiences, between past and present, between theatre and history, *Cargo* made visible the complexities of re-membering in the postcolony. With her words – 'We carry you now, but by and by, it will be your turn to carry us' – Reznek offers the audience a challenge: to consider where we stand in time, the power dynamics and burdens of the past, and our responsibility for – and to – history.

References

Bhabha, H. (1990), *Nation and Narration*, London: Routledge.

Brommert, B. (2007), 'Slaves to Nothing But the Rhythms,' *Cape Argus: Tonight Edition*, 27 February.

Crais, C. and Scully, P. (2009), *Sara Baartman and the Hottentot Venus: A Ghost Story and a Biography*, Princeton: Princeton University Press.

Farred, G. (1999), personal conversation, 27 January.

Faul, M. (2013), 'South Africa Violence Against Women Rated Highest in the World,' *Huffington Post*, 8 March, http://www.huffingtonpost.com/2013/03/08/south-africa-violence-against-women_n_2837804.html. Accessed 8 March 2013.

Fleishman, M. (2007), 'Director's Note,' *National Arts Festival Programme*, p. 41.

—— —— (2011), 'Cargo: Staging Slavery at the Cape,' *Contemporary Theatre Review*, 21: 1, pp. 8–19.

—— —— (2015), personal communication, 11 March.

Giliomee, H. and Mbenga, B. (2007), *New History of South Africa*, Cape Town: Tafelberg.

Jordan, M. and Mackie, H. (2007), 'Theatre – Cargo,' *Business Day*, 27 February.

Lewis, M. (2008), 'Past, Present, and Future: A Tense South Africa Performs,' *PAJ: A Journal of Performance & Art*, 30: 2, pp. 93–101.

Mbembe, A. (2001), *On the Postcolony*, Berkeley: University of California Press.

Mokwena, D. (2010), 'Study Reveals Human Trafficking as a Serious Problem in South Africa,' *Human Sciences Research Council*, http://www.hsrc.ac.za/en/media-briefs/democracy-goverance-and-service-delivery/study-reveals-human-trafficking-as-a-serious-problem-in-south-africa. Accessed 24 March 2010.

Sichel, A. (n.d.), 'Jazzart website,' http://www.Jazzart.co.za. Accessed 20 February 2012.

Skinner, E. B. (2010), 'South Africa's New Slave Trade and the Campaign to Stop It,' *Time*, 18 January, http://www.time.com/time/magazine/article/0,9171,1952335,00.html#ixzz1lL12rWY3. Accessed 18 January 2010.

Sylvester, W. (2012), 'Shocking Reality of SA Human Trafficking,' *Independent Online*, 31 January, http://www.iol.co.za/news/crime-courts/shocking-reality-of-sa-human-trafficking-1.1224202#.UZt_ZeszKeY. Accessed 31 January 2012.

Van den Berghe, P. (1960), 'Miscegenation in South Africa,' *Cahiers d'études africaines*, 1: 4, pp. 68–84.

Wicomb, Z. (1998), 'Shame and Identity: The Case of the Coloured in South Africa,' in Derek Attridge and Rosemary Jolly (eds), *Writing South Africa: Literature, Apartheid and Democracy, 1970–1995*, Cambridge: Cambridge University Press, pp. 92–93.

Notes

1. My gratitude to Christine Woodworth and Beth Osborne for casting their editorial eyes over a previous version of this chapter.
2. All references and citations refer to the production of *Cargo* I saw at the National Arts Festival in July 2007. They are drawn from my personal notations and an early, unpublished script from Mark Fleishman.
3. Fleishman (2011:12), citing Mbembe, defines the 'postcolony' as the 'multiple, contradictory moments in everyday life in Africa read against the persistent accretions of slavery, colonialism, apartheid, and neoliberal forms of democracy.'
4. I refer here to a very specific population: white, English-speaking South Africans (WESSAs), who usually attend the annual National Arts Festival in Grahamstown (I am a South African-born, American-educated scholar and thus consider myself an informed insider/outsider.) It is my contention that *Cargo* specifically educated this population about slavery's legacy at a time when public discussions about inclusive cultural citizenship, memory and remembering were circulating in the new democratic dispensation. The night I saw *Cargo*, the house was about three quarters full (capacity: 939), and the audience was comprised of predominantly white, middle-class theatre-goers. But, importantly, *Cargo* also educated the company itself, which was predominantly black and coloured, about South Africa's slave history. It should also be noted that audiences outside of Grahamstown were less uniformally white.

5. Described by arts critic Adrienne Sichel as a 'democratic dance collective' (Sichel nd), Jazzart today continues the politically committed performance work upon which it was founded. During the apartheid era, 'when professional dance theatre was the virtually exclusive domain of the ruling white elite,' choreographer Alfred Hinkel fostered a 'teaching and performance ethos' based in the 'populist thinking of the South African political struggle.' Jazzart's style has always been focused on 'trust and spatial risk,' robust and acrobatic physical prowess, and exceptionally high quality professional dance that fills performance spaces with dynamic, politically engaged human bodies in motion (www.jazzart.co.za).
6. The first slaves arrived at the Cape on 28 March 1658, on board the *Amersfoort* from Angola. Slaves were imported from Madagascar, Mozambique, the East African coast, India and the East Indies (Sumatra, Java, the Celebes, Ternate and Timor).
7. Despite the Abolition of Slave Trade Act of 1807, which made trade in human beings across the British Empire (which controlled the Cape after the Dutch) illegal, slavery was still widely practiced within the colony until 1 December 1838, when slaves at the Cape were finally emancipated.
8. In his Director's Note to the *Cargo* programme, Fleishman (2007) writes, 'Our *Cargo* is [...] an attempt to use performance to get at what has been left out. [...] One needs to be open to listening in the silences. One needs to be crafty, to know where to look for the shards. How to provoke the body to express itself from under the mass of the official, the academic and the documentary? How to remember?'
9 Fleishman cites the disparate desires and interests of the many stakeholders around Prestwich Place, the central Cape Town site where, in 2003, over 3000 human skeletons were discovered in what amounted to a mass slave graveyard. For Fleishman (2011: 9), the question became: 'Are the bones artifacts, units of information, of cold, hard data, or are they ancestors, to be awakened, recalled, honoured, recognized and remembered?'
10. From 1641 to 1824, the Dutch controlled the slave port of Malacca in the southern region of the Malay Peninsula.
11. Jan van Riebeeck (1619–77) was a Dutch colonial administrator of the Dutch East India Company, who founded the Cape Colony on 6 April 1652.
12. Sara Baartman was a Gonaqua woman displayed as a curiosity in Europe during the eighteenth century as the 'Hottentot Venus.' For Crais and Scully (2009: 6), 'Sara entered Europe's psyche, modernity's psyche, not as a woman, a living breathing person with emotions and memories and longings, but as a metaphor, a figment, a person reduced to a simulacrum.'
13. Baron Georges Cuvier, who established the field of comparative anatomy, sketched from Sara Baartman's live body in his laboratory at the Museum of Anatomy in Paris. After her death, Cuvier made a body cast of her and then dissected her. He preserved her brain and her genitals in jars, which were on display at the Musée de l'Homme (in Cabinet Number 33) until 1982.

14. For Pierre van den Berghe (1960: 69), 'The history of miscegenation [institutionalized concubinage between white men and non-white women] in South Africa is as old as the first permanent Dutch settlement at the Cape in 1652.'
15. Grant Farred suggests that the future of South Africa lies in the metaphor that coloureds represent: the space of mixedness, of complexity, an interstitial space of 'partial affiliations' (personal conversation with the author). As the offspring of Malaysian slaves and Dutch *burghers* [citizens], whose very existence points to the taboo practice of miscegenation, South African coloureds offer to the race-obsessed archons of apartheid what Homi Bhabha (1990: 300) might call a 'counter-narrative' of the nation that 'continually evoke[s] and erase[s]' the nation's totalizing boundaries by 'disturb[ing] those ideological manoeuvres through which "imagined communities" are given essentialist identities.' Zoë Wicomb (1998: 92–93) suggests that there is a 'pervasive shame' carried on the bodies of coloureds, especially coloured women, that is a product of a history of 'nasty, unspoken' miscegenation, 'the origins of which lie within a discourse on "race", concupiscence, and degeneracy.'
16. While I found this liquid breaking of the fourth wall to be exhilarating and provocative, not all my fellow audience members enjoyed the experience. There were audible gasps and flinching bodies all around me. A gentleman in the row in front of me offered his handkerchief to his wife to calm her distress at being moistened by the performance.
17. Historians Hermann Giliomee and Bernard Mbenga (2007: 56) detail such punishments: 'Convicted slaves were broken alive on the wheel, their flesh was pulled off with red-hot tongs; slaves were mutilated, impaled, and slowly strangled.'
18. See the Immorality Acts of 1927 and 1950, as well as the Prohibition of Mixed Marriages Act (1949), listed on: http://www.sahistory.org.za/politics-and-society/apartheid-legislation-1850s-1970s.
19. Neo Muyanga's soundscape, *Fire Famine Plague & Earthquake*, which underscored the live action onstage, includes the following tracks: 'The Sea of Many Names,' 'In The Belly of the Ship,' 'The Washer Women,' 'Acht Beesten,' 'There are Children in the Water,' 'Ballad of a Mutiny,' 'Out the Dark Must Come Forth Light,' 'Kitchen Amok,' 'Drie Oude Wielen, Qho!' 'With My Shoes' and 'On Met Die March.'
20. Songs, named after the barrel-shaped drum, or *ghoema*, that are a signature element of Cape coloured musical and carnival culture.
21. Luvuyo Mabuto is from Langa, a historically black suburb of Cape Town. Owen Manamela is from Alex, short for Alexandria, a township north of Johannesburg.
22. Shoes feature prominently, for example, in Magnet's 2007 two-woman play about forced migration and xenophobia, *Every Year, Every Day, I Am Walking*. One moment a pair of flip-flops are imagined as the wings of a bird in flight; the next, heavy black boots become the perpetrator of a violent rape.

23. The Zulu prefix *ama-* indicates a plural. Note how the cheap porcelain goods from China echo the fragment of porcelain Jennie and Faniswa attempt to piece together on the beach.
24. The Centre for International Policy (Sylvester 2012) claims that global human trafficking accounts for R230 million ($2.5 million) of illicit trade annually, only one third behind drugs and counterfeit goods. A recent *Time* magazine article stated that, 'Despite more than a dozen international conventions banning slavery in the past 150 years, there are more slaves today than at any point in human history' (Skinner 2010).
25. Despite paying lip service to the issue, Presidents Thabo Mbeki (1999–2008) and Jacob Zuma (2008–present) have done little to stem the rising tide of crime, particularly against women, in contemporary South Africa (Faul 2013).

PART THREE

Community: Making Space for Cultural Interventions

Chapter 15

Making Space for Community: Magnet Theatre 'Intervenes' in Khayelitsha

Gay Morris

Until her recent retirement, Gay Morris was associate professor in the Department of Drama at the University of Cape Town. Her research and teaching focuses on applied theatre and educational drama, and she is an executive committee member of the International Federation of Theatre Research (IFTR). She also serves on the editorial review panel of the South African Theatre Journal *and the editorial advisory board of* RIDE: The Journal of Applied Theatre and Performance.

When a child grows up, you see, they grow and grow! There is a central pole [supporting the rondavel roof] when we grew up, that you would hold onto. But in the location there are beds and stools that the child uses to support him/her as the child grows – which is Magnet. Right? Magnet was like that central pole, right? Magnet was like those chairs to that child – to crawl around up until that child can be able to stand.

(Mluleki Sam, 10 November 2007)[1]

This book coheres around a spatial metaphor, and in this chapter I would like to examine Magnet's theatrical practice in the townships, with particular emphasis on spatial aspects. Because Magnet's work in the location of Khayelitsha was indeed a 'central pole' supporting theatre activities, I shall recruit Lefebvre's theorization of space to examine Magnet's contribution in spatial terms. I introduce the reader to how Magnet began to work in the townships of Cape Town.[2] Examining common characteristics of many township plays staged at Magnet events provides a lens through which to scrutinize Khayelitsha as a township, highlighting the challenges arising within a township environment. My account of how Magnet has endeavoured to address these challenges will be illustrated with examples from a single play staged at a Magnet festival.

In *The Production of Space* (1991), Henri Lefebvre approaches the study of space neither as a subject nor as an object but 'rather as a social reality – that is to say, a set of relations and forms' (1991: 116). Here, he defines space in three ways: he identifies *physical space* as nature that entirely surrounds us when not interfered with by human endeavour; he posits that *mental space* is the sphere conceptualized for logico-mathematical categories; yet Lefebvre's chief interest lies in *social space*, or space as it is socially produced, which implies that human agency and intention are integral to spatial practices. He writes:

'theoretical thought [...] has re-embraced the body along with space, and as a generator (or producer) of space' (1991: 407). Lefebvre proposes that we humans actively engage with space in three ways: as perceived, conceived and lived. We *use* space, which has a determining effect on its shape and character; we *represent* it, for example in our maps and planning, which organizes space for the purposes of exerting power and control; and we *experience* it, so space also has a representational character (1991: 33).

There are many senses in which Magnet's work engages with space, with space-time and with spatial practices. First, Magnet's physical theatre performances incarnate, transform, dissect, traverse, rewrite, reinvent, re-mythologize and represent the symbolic and physical space of theatrical production. Second, Magnet also engages thematically with pathways, journeying and routes in Africa and Southern African in productions such as *ingcwaba lendoda lise cankwe ndlela* [the grave of the man lies next to the road] (2009), *Inxeba Lomphilisi – The Wound of a Healer* (2010–14) and *Every Year, Every Day, I Am Walking* (2006–present). Thirdly, between 1987 and 2007, Magnet did not have a specific theatrical home; rather, the company obtained space for rehearsals, workshops, administration and performance by renting, squatting, organizing, inhabiting and representing spaces – both indoors and outdoors – in custom-built theatres, as well as streets, containers, school halls and sports fields, prisons, museums, disused warehouses and public open spaces in the city. Magnet was continually in the business of making spaces into rehearsal venues, sites and theatres.

So, how might Magnet's work in the townships of Cape Town operate spatially, and why is it exceptional? My answer, based upon research I have conducted since 2005,[3] rests on two key considerations. The first is the consideration of how economic and political power continues to affect urban planning in Cape Town, South Africa's oldest city. The second is the impact on the city's townships, particularly those far from business precincts and more established suburbs. Town planning affects townships both as social spaces and as contexts for producing theatre, since there is a dire shortage of spaces for any cultural or recreational activity.

From the start, colonialist urban planning has favoured European settlers, who dwelled along the mountain chain running south from Table Bay to Cape Point, and who spread along the arterial route to the north east through Paarl during the apartheid years. The townships, conceived after the 1923 Urban Areas Act, were specifically situated between these two legs of development. The intention was to house so-called 'natives' (i.e. Africans) who might unavoidably be found in the Cape – first in Langa, established in 1927, then Nyanga in 1946, Gugulethu in 1958, and after 1985, Khayelitsha and Delft; each township penetrating ever further from the city centre, deep into the inhospitable, low-lying, wind-swept reaches of the Cape Flats:

> These are enormously unappealing locations aesthetically [...]. Defined by highways, railway tracks, industrial zones, sewage treatment plants, refuse dumps and the like, the vast majority of new housing developments in Cape Town are on the Cape Flats,

> a low-lying sandy area prone to stifling heat in summer and cold and floods in winter, with the highest incidence of tuberculosis in the country.
>
> (McDonald 2008: 148)

This essay examines Magnet's strategies and tactics for theatre-making and education in the context of a township environment, as well as Magnet's responses not only to social and cultural needs, but also to infrastructural incapacity with respect to physical space. Magnet Theatre's mission and output is deeply imbricated in the South African context. Although inescapably trapped between the rock of our bleak and violent South African past and the hard place of desperate longing for a brighter, kinder future, Magnet's work is politically and ideologically rooted in Cape Town in the contemporary moment, which is part of the reason why Magnet first went to these townships.

Mandla Mbothwe was invited to join Magnet as director and trustee in 2000, after ten years of association with the company as a collaborating artist. Mbothwe's theatrical career originated with a township theatre group, and he went on to study acting at the University of Cape Town Drama Department.[4] Upon graduating in 1994, Mbothwe worked both as a freelance actor (frequently with Magnet Theatre) and developed theatre with his group in the Nyanga East township. At the same time, he fostered theatre in the townships generally, such as in Delft, where he worked with unemployed women,[5] and in Clanwilliam (240km north of Cape Town) on Magnet's Arts Project. Not long after his appointment as a director, Mbothwe suggested that Magnet take theatre into Cape Town's black townships.

Magnet Goes to Khayelitsha

In 2002, under the Magnet umbrella, Mbothwe and Lulama Masimini, another UCT graduate, identified four theatre groups that were already functional in their respective neighbourhoods within Khayelitsha, initiating a three-month interaction with those groups that culminated in a shared performance event. This experience was so enthusiastically received that the engagement was lengthened from three to six months in 2003. More groups were included and theatre skills workshops were regularly offered to all groups, as well as visits to play performances. The interaction culminated in a day of performances in Khayelitsha. By 2004, with seven groups involved, Magnet committed to an annual Intervention, and in 2005, at a planning workshop held with all the groups, consensus resolved that the work would remain exclusively in Khayelitsha until the end of 2007. So, between 2002 and 2007, Magnet evolved a strategy for engaging with theatre in Cape Town's black townships, the core features of which are still being sustained at the time of writing in spite of changes in personnel and financial circumstances. In 2008, Magnet found resources to initiate a formal training programme at their newly acquired premises in Observatory, an inner-city Cape Town suburb, specifically for township/

Members of Magnet's Full Time Training and Job Creation Program (2010).
Photo credit: © Mark Wessels.

disadvantaged youth who demonstrate exceptional talent, but who would otherwise have no access to formal tertiary education because they have not qualified, cannot afford, or are not psychologically prepared for it. And so Magnet withdrew from working in the townships until 2010, when UCT graduate Noluvuyo Sam resumed Magnet's field work in the informal settlement of Dunoon.

Magnet Theatre's commitment to sustained engagement with township communities is unusual, in part because of practical difficulties. The landscape of Cape Town's black townships is a random one: disordered and disorderly; overcrowded and massively under-resourced in terms of infrastructure. Khayelitsha is Cape Town's youngest, largest and poorest black township. It has many active theatre groups, but there are no coordinating bodies, no playhouses, and pitifully few events that might inspire or actually assist young play-makers. Identifying an enormous need in this location, Magnet elected to begin their township work in Khayelitsha.

When I went in to see the work that was being made, I was interested in identifying the subject matter and theatrical form of these plays, and finding out more about the relationship between the nature of the plays and the world of Khayelitsha in which the theatre-makers live and work. Of the 40 plays I saw created by township groups, 35 had located action in the township. The overarching impression is of the vitality of players engaged in a world alive with possibility, promise and danger. The fragility of sustained social order in the township is mirrored by the scant attention to moveable objects in performance. Stage representations of litter and disorderliness suggested a place of abandonment or destruction, whilst wielding guns and knives represented having power. In this world, tables, chairs and dustbins serve a multitude of purposes beyond their everyday uses: as shelter in *'Street Peoples' Stories'* (Mathew 2006);[6] and as seating, barricades or profound physical obstacles such as illness in *'Mzantsi'* [Our Country] (Iqhude 2006). The objects themselves are insignificant, but not the precision and inventiveness with which the actors use them. Considerable care is expended on costuming, perhaps because it is easier to signify social status, for example, by means of a smart church guild (or school) uniform, or even your brand of sneakers that always travels with you, than by means of a run-down shack several circuitous alleys away.

The improvisational style of this theatre mirrors the unstable locus of township streets, in which people trade, court affection or respect, or where they exercise power over those weaker than themselves. In contrast, the domestic sphere – in which characters sometimes seek but seldom achieve refuge – is easily disrupted by neighbours, gangsters or police. Characters are depicted in relation to what they do: making a living and sustaining the home are regularly part of a play's background. Characters engage in cleaning and cooking, petty trading, building, hawking or occasionally office work. Those sustaining, honest livelihoods are frequently juxtaposed against those who are lying, bullying, blackmailing or peddling drugs or sex. For instance, *To Whom it May Concern* (Manyanani 2005) ends with the chorus claiming in unison: 'Let's work together and destroy crime!' In these plays, recreational pastimes such as playing games, 'hanging out,' sports, dancing or choral singing testify to the liveliness of local, performance-based cultural practices. Protagonists are often intent on accruing social capital: seeking a wife, consulting a *sangoma* [traditional healer], getting married, having sex and making a baby. However, the plays also present accounts of the abuse of power through gambling, drunkenness, street brawls, shootings, rape and murder. They are replete with the fatal consequences of actions that range from stigma to loss of innocence, exile, HIV/AIDS, disability and death. Positive consequences depicted in the plays are few, although many include characters who learn lessons the hard way. Single characters who seek to exercise power are often juxtaposed against the greater power and influence of social collectives. For example, in *Old Brown Joe* (Iselwa 2005), citizens honour those who died in the struggle but stigmatize their teacher because he survived the struggle. In *'Mzantsi'* (Iqhude 2006), a chain gang – representative of South Africa's entire population – works cohesively to build the country through its joint efforts, but in *'144 Months into the New SA'* (Manyanani 2006), citizens question whether their votes indeed count. In *'The Drunk Priest'* (Masimbambisane 2006), a choir and other church officials support their priest even when he goes seriously off the rails; whereas in *'Murder in the Family'* (Isibane 2007), the court of public opinion convicts local perpetrators on the basis of rumour. In *'Traditions vs Christianity'* (Masimbambisane 2007), a clan supports coming-of-age rituals for its nubile adolescents, but in *'Thobeka Dreams too Much'* (Iselwa 2006), a child is exiled by the pressure of family elders. All of these works testify to how concerned youth in the townships are about power, order and the law.

Khayelitsha, Cape Town's Newest and Largest Township

Essentially, the picture of Khayelitsha obtained from these plays mirrors the township itself, which has always been conceived of as residual to the city:

> Since until the mid-1980s the primary purpose of African presence in the cities was defined as serving white-owned commerce and industry, physical and social linkages between African townships and the rest of the city were considered only in the crudest possible terms. These areas were never intended to sustain a rich and diverse internal life, and most are underserved in the context of an urban structure that distributes urban opportunity of every kind unequally.
>
> (Awotona et al. 1995b: 11)

Extensive research has shown that Cape Town's inequitable city planning has profoundly negative effects on the quality of life for township inhabitants.[7] Infrastructure is inadequate and consequently immiseration and environmental degradation continues apace, and industrial and commercial development cannot take hold. Commuter transport is essential, but costly and undermining of family time.

The divided city is further divided in the townships by political loyalties. Threatened by governmental regulation, local leadership exploit divisions and uncertainties within neighbourhoods to retain and extend their power:

> [H]igh unemployment and poverty generate intense competition for limited resources such as land, shelter and fuel. The pressures are intensified by the inflow of new rural migrants with even fewer resources and formal skills. Local gatekeepers (or 'warlords') take advantage of people's insecurity and the weak governance of the area. They allocate sites and other scarce resources in return for financial payments, loyalty and favours. Rivalry between them means an ongoing struggle for territory and power, which periodically breaks out into conflict and violence. This causes injury, trauma

> and social dislocation among innocent bystanders. The police are far too stretched to cope, leading to their demoralisation and implication in crime.
>
> (Turok & Watson 2001: 127)

These challenges pertain especially to Khayelitsha, Cape Town's poorest metropolitan district. When the apartheid government dismantled the Coloured Labour Preference Policy and abolished the Pass Laws in 1985, black Africans began streaming into Cape Town from the impoverished rural Eastern Cape, swelling the black African population in Cape Town eightfold. Khayelitsha was established to address the dire need for urban accommodation. The original housing plan for the township was sorely inadequate, so spaces between formal housing and the major roads have rapidly filled with 'site and service' shacks and shanties that house the excess of migrants to the city. But the development of roads, drainage, refuse removal and electrification, as well as the establishment of schools, clinics, libraries and other community facilities, has lagged hopelessly behind population growth. Khayelitsha also has the highest level of HIV prevalence among Cape Town clinic attendees. Jelsma, Mkoka and Amosun (2008: 351) researched Khayelitsha residents' perceptions of their health-related quality of life in 2004. They discovered that environmental factors, including having food at home, owning a brick house with electricity, water and sanitation, protection from crime and killings, and being able to spend time with your family, outweighed all other factors.

Such statistics and research evidence how easy it could be to demonize township inhabitants along with their impoverished environment, as if township circumstances are the fault of the poor who dwell therein. But there are many researchers and urban planners who reject dystopian predictions, and return agency to township dwellers themselves (e.g. Robinson [2009], Van Donk et al. [2008] and Simone [2004]). Conceiving of the townships as intrinsically part of the Mother City, and as a key resource rather than an unfortunate detritus, foregrounds the townships as sites of possibility and change. In a meditative essay on his South African childhood from a contemporary perspective, Dlamini (2009: 112) emphasizes 'the role that townships must play in the constitution of the public sphere, the evolution of nationhood, citizenship and identity in post-apartheid South Africa.'

Theatre in Khayelitsha

Township theatre-making is exactly such an instance of the construction of the public sphere in contemporary South Africa. Capacitated by their training in, and involvement with, the performance-based repertoire of social and cultural practices alive in the townships – such as coming of age, wedding and funeral ceremonies, singing and worship practices, and socialization in dancing and storytelling – theatre-makers are always busy with the project of revisioning their world. This is where Magnet Theatre's work has had significant impact. But good intentions notwithstanding, the problem of space continues to beset Magnet's work in Khayelitsha, where purpose-built arts spaces are non-existent. Schools disallow after-hours use of their rooms for security reasons, and community halls are largely taken up by sports groups. When I held a symposium in 2008 for ten leading theatre-makers from the townships, they identified space as a huge issue. When I asked the delegates what spaces theatre groups use for meetings and rehearsals, they responded as follows:

> R4: Various different spaces, dining rooms, garages, fields, reception, hospitals…
> R: Crèches.
> R: Schools.
> R2: Anything that's a space.
> R: Ja, just if you find a space, just if you find a space…
> R: Container.[8] [Laughter]
> R: Funnily enough, some go there outside, to the backyard.
>
> (Morris 2008: 69)

Lefebvre maintains that space is not only physically but also socially produced. In the absence of purpose-built spaces, Magnet's solution is to shape social space with a particular pattern of use which serves the needs of arts practice. Lefebvre (1991: 175) maintains that space and time are always interactive: 'Time is distinguishable but not separable from space. The concentric rings of a tree trunk reveal the tree's age […]. Times, of necessity, are local and this goes too for the relations between places and their respective times.' Magnet generates a particular aesthetic space by, in De Certeau's (1984: 38) terms, a tactical use of time; tactics being 'procedures that gain validity in relation to the pertinence they lend to time.' Magnet's regular visitations to the groups in the townships opens the space of the crèche, the container and the community hall to theatre by instituting theatrical events and regularly audiencing their groups (Fiske 1998), while their encouragement of young theatre-makers generates representational spaces in acts of theatre. Between 2002 and 2007, Magnet's interaction in Khayelitsha culminated in the annual Community Groups Intervention (CGI) Showcase held each November. This event takes place on a Saturday morning to avoid any clash with funerals (which are customarily held in the afternoon) in a community hall hired for the day (to avoid transport difficulties). Community halls in Khayelitsha are not enticing buildings. Lefebvre maintains that social space not only has a physical dimension that is specific in terms of its materiality, structure and locality, but it always already embodies its own history; a history produced by the agents who conceived of the space, as well as those who currently perceive, use and experience it. Spaces generate their own rhythms of usage, and the Andile Msizi community hall in Khayelitsha, in which the 2007 Showcase was held, is no exception. It was a vast, cavernous space with a concrete floor, cream and orange painted walls with small windows near the roof, and echoing acoustics. There was no curtaining or lighting on the concrete-floored stage – a challenge indeed to anybody endeavouring to generate a space for representation or subjective experience. So Magnet's Showcase sought to eventify the occasion so that the community hall becomes a site for theatre.

Theatrical event theory suggests that considering theatre as a 'thing' is missing the point; theatre is in fact something that occurs. A train arriving at a railway station is also an occurrence, but not in the sense in which such an event is out of the ordinary; however, a theatrical event is lifted out of its surroundings so that it is noticed, and becomes wholly theatrical when it is 'eventified' (Hauptfleisch 2004). Eventification is what distinguishes theatre from performance in everyday life and is something that is clearly evident in Magnet's management of the annual Showcase.

Magnet Theatre's Community Groups Intervention (CGI) Showcase

Magnet's Showcase is advertised by word of mouth and a handful of posters, and attracts an audience comprised of the participating groups, their friends and families, as well as a smattering of interested outsiders such as myself. As we, the audience, show up at the venue – which is vibrating with *kwaito* music broadcast over the specially hired sound system – a throng of excited 'insiders' welcome us and show us to our seats, the plastic chairs filling the hall. At the 2007 Showcase, on which this account is based, respondents observed to my research assistant Cindy Mkaza:

> R1: We don't just come to perform. Here they give us things to do: maybe they give a duty to be at the door or catering or to tell the audience to keep quiet.
>
> Mkaza: Oh, so you want to be involved when there is an event, you don't only want to perform?
>
> R2: Yes, we don't only want to perform, but to be involved as well.[9]

As we enter the space, a slide show depicting the participating theatre groups in rehearsals and at workshops is projected onto the rear wall of the curtainless stage. Captions read: 'We learn from watching each other' and 'Circle of stories.' These foster a common understanding of this event by illustrating the process that leads to it. Performers and audience gleefully identify their friends, their group or themselves in the images. At around 10 a.m., the Magnet facilitators gather all the participants from the six theatre groups into a large circle in full view of the expectant audience for a last-minute team talk, which raises the stakes for both performers and audience. One respondent explained: 'We are here to celebrate the beauty of arts and the cooperation we have had with Magnet Theatre for the last five years. So we are here to showcase all the things we have learnt from Magnet.' Another pointed out that Magnet's purpose is 'obviously to help talented young stars to actually realize that they have talent, that they can do things, such as acting and being involved in theatre-making,' while another argued that the purpose of the event was also 'educating the youth and empowering them [convincing them] that there is more to life than sitting on the corner of the street doing drugs, crime and teenage pregnancy.' When the team talk with the performers is over, the Magnet facilitator announces the name of the first performance group over the loudspeakers, serving as an aural/oral 'programme' which accompanies images of the group projected onto the wall – a visual programme – as the performances begin.

I have discussed the contents of the plays, but just as important is the theatrical aspect of these stories and how they have been nurtured by Magnet's input. In a recent interview with Zwelakhe Khuse (2013b),[10] who since 2012 has run the Magnet Intervention in the townships of Dunoon, Delft and Phillipi, I was intrigued to hear Khuse testify to what he actually does with the groups for two reasons: first, his appraisal resonates with what Mbothwe and others achieved from 2002 onwards;[11] and secondly it testifies to how doing theatre organizes space in its own interests. Khuse says he watches the groups whom he mentors. He is their first audience and thereby creates a theatre environment for them: 'I look at the plays. I am trying to encourage the groups to break out of the ghetto. Although their work is mostly about their community, I want them to reach a broader audience: to feel they are performing on stage, through doing theatre.' At the same time, there is no specific style or convention which he foregrounds: 'I don't want [the performers] to be confined to a particular thing, which is anyway not the same in all groups. What do they need? What they are doing? I develop that.' Khuse says that when Mbothwe led the CGI, 'he was helping you with what you are doing [anyway].' And it is apparent to me that Khuse, who trained with Mbothwe, is taking the same approach with the groups he now mentors. Khuse is sponsored to visit the groups on a weekly basis for a year, rather than for three or six months and so, as he puts it, he is 'also teaching.' He specifically avoids directing the groups; rather, he formalizes the theatre space by providing the groups with a theatrical vocabulary, which strengthens and develops what they need. Re-examining the footage of the CGI Showcases in 2005, 2006 and 2007, it is evident that the CGI developed the theatre vocabulary of the groups over time, thereby opening up spaces of representation, particularly in two formative ways: by means of transformation and imagery. The explication that follows draws upon the 2007 Showcase and the work of Iqhude Theatre Group in their play, which I have titled *'Medical Ethics'*.

Transformation

The Community Groups Intervention Showcase works to overcome infrastructural disadvantages in under-resourcing by transforming the 'untheatrical space' of a community hall into a space for theatre. In the 2007 Showcase, theatre group members infused the space with performance energy, literally creating a theatrical event out of a bleak community hall. Since there are no curtains, when entry ways onto stage are poorly positioned or inadequate for a large cast to negotiate before the audience becomes bored, the performers use their bodies to create the stage convention. Standing onstage against the rear wall to indicate 'off stage,' they array their properties and costume changes on the sides and back of the stage, which serve as 'the wings.' In effect, the presence of performers, awaiting their cues to enter the action, charges the stage space with energy, and counters the dreariness of the dirty yellow walls of the community hall's stage. Similarly, rather than an empty silent pause signifying the passage from one scene to the next (with no lighting or set change to effect transitions), the groups use a number of devices, such as rhythm, mime, movement or clapping, to transition the action from where it is towards where it is going.

In spite of the unprepossessing stages on which they perform, theatre groups in the township generate the appropriate mood for a play because, in theatrical performances, imagination takes precedence over reality. The everyday context is transformed into a different world through disciplined cooperation in choral work, dance and song. By and large, group members work with extraordinary awareness of how the contribution of each member is part of a whole that is more than the sum of its parts. This is greatly to Magnet's credit, because discipline in terms of regular attendance, punctuality and concentration on the performative task at hand, rather than attention-seeking, is always a challenge with young people in voluntary pursuits. Magnet's expectations of accorded and required respect shore up the fragile intentions and minimal resources of the groups, and go a long way to ensuring that theatre is sustained in the township context.

Finally, Magnet's physical orientation provokes the youth into claiming the community hall as a performance space by its adept usage. Levels, diagonals, circles, spirals; moving on the stage and between stage and auditorium; using bodily shapes such as curl, twist or spread-eagled; floor patterns such as rectangles, diagonals, parallel lines, clustered groupings, symmetry and asymmetry; as well as gradual or marked shifts in energy – all these are enacted by individuals and groups in concert since they have been practiced.

The work is further dynamized by changes of oral accompaniment, rhythm, pace, pause, volume, pitch, movement and stillness. Emotions such as exhilaration, pain, grief or disdain find expression through collective movement, physical imagery, song and chant, perhaps more than via the spoken word. This multisensory approach transmits easily to the receptive audience at the Showcase (plastic chairs, crying babies and restless children notwithstanding.)

Image

Perhaps Magnet Theatre's most significant contribution to opening up spaces of representation is through image creation. In the physical theatre discipline, an image refers to an idea, a proposition or thematic motif within a play. Such images are rendered intelligible and accessible by means of performed, embodied metaphors, which become core units of theatrical meaning. Images provoke a response because they stand out as unusual in representations of everyday interaction onstage. The Iqhude Theatre group deployed these devices to great effect. Cleo, who is a long-standing member of the Iselwa Le Sizwe theatre group, with plenty of her own experience of theatre-making, had this to say about Iqhude at the Showcase:

> Iqhude is motivating me all the time. Every time I watch their play it is something different every time. It is not always the usual! I think the play is well researched. That is what is good. When you write a play, you have to research it. It takes a lot of time to research a play, you know. That is why I can say about the Showcase and other groups. They did very well; but personally, I love Iqhude because the energy – it's there. It's everything. It's like, wow!

In deploying rhythm, repetition, patterning, song or dance, as well as movement and word, images are open-ended and suggestive, appealing through the senses to the imagination, and inducing the imagination to move beyond the limits of the everyday. Images tend to interrupt narrative linearity at the same time as they dilate the stage action so that it is compelling. Iqhude's *'Medical Ethics'* begins with a prologue: the image of the working hospital and doctors depicted by means of a tableau of the performers, animated in slow motion. An intent doctor writes on the back of his suffering (bowed over) patient, whilst the doctor behind him practices his golf swing. In the upstage right and downstage left corners of the stage, doctors circle slowly in a ring like bloodhounds in search of prey, with a stealth that is both intriguing and disconcerting. We know they are doctors because of their immaculate white coats and caps and their red ties.

There are any number of ways of developing a theatrical image, such as the use of a prologue or epilogue in the form of an animated tableaux (as was the case with the prologue that I have just described); one could also use a ritualized or patterned movement sequence frequently accompanied by a soundscape, chant or song, as well as first person accounts, juxtaposition and layering of motifs in the onstage action. All of these devices focus the audience on particular concerns that permeate the entire performance. *'Medical Ethics'* revolves around the question of to whom a doctor is ultimately answerable: his patient or his medical colleagues? A woman, who is caring for a parentless child, falls ill from the stresses the youngster puts her through. Admitted to hospital, she requires a blood transfusion. Although no blood relative of his 'Auntie,' the boy offers his blood and the harried doctor accepts. The woman recovers but the doctor is scapegoated by his colleagues. The inference is that the 'medical profession' is more concerned with covering up their own malpractices and financial kickbacks than caring for the well-being of their patients. Cleo offered me her view of the significance of the play in light of township medical clinics:

> Ja, it's very important because people die – they actually die – because the other doctors […] want money – they don't care about other patients. Everything that is happening in the clinics, in the hospitals – we have to look at it with another eye, because people they are really dying.

Whilst this conundrum drives the play, what makes it enthralling is its theatrical form. The play develops around a core image of 'The Medical Profession.' Costumed in spotless white shirts, trousers and doctor's coats, with red ties and white caps, eight performers embody the motions of tending patients, having consultations and covering their tracks, as impressively as a well-oiled machine. And yet in their robotic motions there is little room for the feelings and needs of their patients.

In a series of scenes – each of which develops an image impelled forward rhythmically by movement, drumming, a capella singing or recorded music – the dehumanizing medical environment is depicted by the full company, who swing into mechanical motion. Communication between the child and his sick carer becomes impossible. First, there is a meeting between the accused doctor and the chorus of his colleagues, who admonish the accused in unison, striking rhetorical gestures, thumping on their briefcases and their knees, and crossing their legs in resignation as accompaniment to their prolonged, indignant and formal speechifying. The symmetry and hypocritical elegance of their display of professional concern is communicated powerfully, even though all the speech during the actual performance is virtually inaudible due to the powerful echo in Andile Msizi hall (which also became a problem when I reviewed my audio-visual recording of the show).

The boy's relationship with his Auntie is foreshadowed in the prologue when Auntie looks out for the boy but cannot find him. When the scene shifts to their home environment, their relationship is depicted by the boy's youthful obstreperousness and the aunt's consequent refusal to hand him his plate of food. The two performers play a game of 'catch,' stretching, grasping and evading one another, symmetrically depicting the oppositional strategies of child and adult. Their struggle, patterned into a dance, is further amplified by four of the other actors, who also stretch and grasp at plates in pairs, in the air, on each other's backs, through legs, over and underneath each other's efforts at grasp and evasion. Their precision had the audience bursting into spontaneous applause.

However, when the Auntie, having relented and fed her hungry boy, confesses that she is not actually his real mother, the upset child storms out of the house, pursued by his Auntie. The scenic transition to the hospital is effected in just 15 seconds. Calling after the boy, Auntie goes to her doorway, picks up the doorframe, and keeps moving upstage right and across left as drumming underscores her transition. Still calling the boy, she puts down the frame upstage left, stepping through it in frantic search. Her screams reduce to whimpers as she despairs of finding the boy. She sways, staggers and then collapses upstage centre onto the table, which now becomes the consulting bench in the hospital.

When the boy donates blood, the white-coated figures become a machine that draws the boy's 'blood' out of his chest in ribbons, created by the red ties, which 'circulate' the blood in streamer-like, rhythmic waves. A 'machine' (the cast) beeps at regular intervals, until finally the 'blood' enters the inert woman; Auntie slowly revives on the table and falls into the arms of the boy.

A Time for Celebration

Enthusiastic cheering from the audience followed the closing performance, enhanced by spontaneous praises from Mandisile Maseti, a local *imbongi* (praise singer) and ardent theatre-maker. Then Mbothwe introduced a mother of one of the involved youth to the audience. She paid her own tribute to the young performers, the theatre work and to Magnet, without whom, she told the audience, she didn't know where her son would be. Certificates and DVDs were then presented to each of the group leaders by Jennie Reznek and Mandla Mbothwe, and every member of each group who performed was given a Magnet T-shirt as a parting memento.

Then the freestanding plastic chairs were rearranged in a huge circle and, a beast having been slaughtered in celebration the previous night, a delicious hot lunch with a cold drink was served to all attending, both audience and performers. Food is a conventional part of township celebrations and it heightens the value of the event in the eyes of all those who participate. As we munched our meal with relish, Mbothwe offered the microphone to anyone who wanted to pay a special tribute, ending with Mark Fleishman, who said:

> Drama is about change. Things change, they don't stay the same [...]. And in some sense the whole Intervention for the past six years has been about change; about changing you as people, about changing us as an organization. It has been about changing the kind of theatre that we make, the stories that we tell. And I think this year was a really good culmination of the six years. We saw a very wide range of content, a very wide range of stories being told, that were important to the community [and] that were important to you as people. What was very impressive was the physical language: the use of the body to tell stories, the images that were created were of a very high standard.[12]

Theatre groups in this Showcase demonstrated a precise use of rhythm, image, transformation and heightened performance. Self-taught skills were enhanced by the theatrical vocabulary developed during Magnet's Intervention field work, which transformed the community hall (in lieu of a formal theatre) into an imaginative space through the power of performance. The entire Showcase event became a social space of aesthetic and cultural celebration, effected through Magnet Theatre's Intervention and the abilities and enthusiasms of young people in Khayelitsha. One young woman, asked how she felt about the end of the CGI responded:

> It's sad, really sad. But we can't be sad that much because Magnet Theatre brought us lots of skills; they took us from the ground and put us at the standard where we [are] at right now. So I mean that we are crying for the fact that this is the end, we are losing them. But we are not crying that much, simply because.. it's like Magnet Theatre was breastfeeding us for the last five years, you see. So we [are] the toddlers who are still stumbling and trying to stand. We can be able to do things for ourselves, just because our mother has been there for us, breastfeeding us all this time…

References

Awotona, A. et al. (1995a), *Integration and Urbanisation of South African Townships: Conceptual, Theoretical and Methodological Issues*, Newcastle upon Tyne and South Africa: Centre for Architectural Research and Development Overseas (CARDO), University of Newcastle upon Tyne and University of Cape Town, School of Architecture and Planning.

—— (1995b), 'Townships in Cape Town: Case Study Area Profiles,' in *The Integration and Urbanisation of Existing Townships in the Republic of South Africa* (ODA Research Scheme Number R6266), Newcastle upon Tyne and Cape Town: University of Newcastle and University of Cape Town.

De Certeau, M. (1984), *The Practice of Everyday Life*, Berkeley: University of California Press.

Dlamini, J. (2009), *Native Nostalgia*, Auckland Park, South Africa: Jacana.

Fiske, J. (1998), 'Audiencing: Cultural Practice and Cultural Studies,' in N. K. Denzin and Y. S. Lincoln (eds), *The Landscape of Qualitative Research: Theories and Issues*, Thousand Oaks, CA: Sage, pp. 359–78.

Hauptfleisch, T. (2004), 'Eventification: Utilising the Theatrical System to Frame the Event,' in V. A. Cremona et al. (eds), *Theatrical Events: Borders, Dynamics, Frames*, Amsterdam and New York: Rodopi, pp. 279–302.

Iqhude Theatre Group (2006), *'Mzantsi,'* Khayelitsha, Cape Town: Magnet Theatre Community Groups Intervention Showcase.

—— (2007), *'Medical Ethics,'* Khayelitsha, Cape Town: Magnet Theatre Community Groups Intervention Showcase.

Iselwa le Sizwe (2005), *Old Brown Joe*, Khayelitsha, Cape Town: Magnet Theatre Community Groups Intervention Showcase.

—— (2006), *'Thobeka Dreams Too Much,'* Khayelitsha, Cape Town: Magnet Theatre Community Groups Intervention Showcase.

Isibane (2007), *'Murder in the Family,'* Khayelitsha, Cape Town: Magnet Theatre Community Groups Intervention Showcase.

Jelsma, J., Mkoka, S. and Amosun, S. L. (2008), 'Health Related Quality of Life (HRQoL) Domains Most Valued by Urban IsiXhosa-speaking People,' *Quality of Life Research*, 17: 2, pp. 347–55.

Lefebvre, H. (1991), *The Production of Space* (trans. Donald Nicholson-Smith), Malden, MA: Blackwell. First published 1974.

Manyanani Entertainers (2005), *To Whom it May Concern*, Khayelitsha, Cape Town: Magnet Theatre Community Groups Intervention Showcase.

——— (2006), *'144 Months into the New SA,'* Khayelitsha, Cape Town: Magnet Theatre Community Groups Intervention Showcase.

Masimbambisane (2006), *'The Drunk Priest,'* Khayelitsha, Cape Town: Magnet Theatre Community Groups Intervention Showcase.

——— (2007), *'Traditions vs Christianity,'* Khayelitsha, Cape Town: Magnet Theatre Community Groups Intervention Showcase.

Mathew Goniwe High School theatre group, (2006), *'Street Peoples' Stories,'* Khayelitsha, Cape Town: Magnet Theatre Community Groups Intervention Showcase

McDonald, D. A. (2008), *World City Syndrome: Neoliberalism and Inequality in Cape Town*, New York and London: Routledge/Taylor and Francis.

Morris, Gay (2008), *Symposium on Township Theatre*, 7 June, University of Cape Town Department of Drama, Cape Town.

——— (2010), 'Own-Made in the (Post-)New South Africa: A Study of Theatre Originating from Selected Townships in the Vicinity of Cape Town,' Ph.D. thesis, University of Cape Town.

——— (2013a), 'Flexible Weaving: Investigating the Teaching and Learning Opportunities in the Practices of Theatre-Makers and Performers from Selected Townships in Cape Town,' *RiDE: The Journal of Applied Theatre and Performance*, 18: 1, pp. 4–24.

——— (2013b), personal interview with Zwelakhe Khuse, 22 February.

——— (2014), 'Playing with Change: Repetition and Innovation in Township Performance,' in V. A. Cremona et al. (eds), *Playing Culture: Conventions and Extensions of Performance*, Amsterdam and New York: Rodopi, pp. 201–22.

——— (2015), 'Ubizo – *Voices of elok'shini:* Listening Afresh to Theatre Voices from Cape Town's Townships,' in G. Homann and M. Maufort (eds), *New Territories: Theatre, Drama, and Performance in Post-apartheid South Africa,* Bruxelles: P.I.E. Peter Lang, pp. 23-56.

Ndegwa, D., Horner, D. and Esau, F. (2007), 'The Links Between Migration, Poverty and Health: Evidence from Khayelitsha and Mitchell's Plain,' *Social Indicators Research*, 81: 2, pp. 223–34.

Pillay, U. (2004), 'Are Globally Competitive "City Regions" Developing in South Africa?: Formulaic Aspirations or New Imaginations,' *Urban Forum*, 15: 4, pp. 340–64.

Robinson, J. (2009), 'Living in Dystopia: Past, Present and Future in Contemporary African Cities,' April, University of Cape Town, Centre for African Studies Seminar.

Sam, M. (2007), 'Tribute to Magnet Theatre,' Khayelitsha: Magnet Theatre Community Groups Intervention Showcase, 10 November 2007. [video and audio recordings of the showcase and speeches delivered in the possession of the writer, this tribute transcribed and Xhosa words translated].

Simone, A. (2004), 'People as Infrastructure: Intersecting Fragments in Johannesburg,' *Public Culture*, 16: 3, pp. 407–29.

Swilling, M. (ed.) (2010), *Sustaining Cape Town: Imagining a Livable City*, Stellenbosch, South Africa: SUN MeDIA.

Turok, I. and Watson, V. (2001), 'Divergent Development in South African Cities: Strategic Challenges Facing Cape Town,' *Urban Forum*, 12: 2, pp. 119–38.

Van Donk, M. et al. (eds) (2008), *Consolidating Developmental Local Government: Lessons from the South African Experience*, Cape Town: UCT Press.

Notes

1. Mluleki Sam is the leader of Masimbambisane, a group that participated in the CGI (Community Groups Intervention) from 2002 until 2007. Sam became a fieldworker for Magnet, and delivered this speech at the 2007 Showcase. In it, he exhorts the theatre-makers of Khayelitsha to use the space and capacities created with Magnet's assistance to go forward independently. Sam remains active in Khayelitsha. On 19 April 2013, I attended the Masimbambisane Festival at the Baxter Theatre. When I refer to Magnet's fieldworkers in 2007, these were Mluleki Sam and Ntokozo Madlala, who now teaches at the University of Kwa-Zulu-Natal. A *rondavel* is a round African hut; the 'location' is another word for township.
2. This chapter only deals with Magnet's work in Cape Town's black townships; i.e. those largely inhabited by Xhosa-speaking Africans. There are townships in Cape Town (such as Bonteheuwel) in which the population, by and large, comprises of so-called 'coloured' people (in South African parlance), but those townships are not covered in this account.
3. My doctoral research (2005–09) involved watching some 40 plays made by local township groups in performance, interviewing groups, individual theatre-makers and audience members (in groups and as individuals) at theatrical events. I also held a symposium on theatre in the township with ten leading township theatre-makers, at least half of whom had been mentored by Magnet. The participants were Thando Doni, Mfundo Hashe, Xola Honono, Zimasa May, Mandla Mbothwe, Thembile Nazo, Andile Nebulane, Mzimasi Nongwe, Khaya Sihamba, Mfundo Tshazibane, myself and my colleague Heather Jacklin. I have continued with this research until the present (see Morris 2010; 2013a; 2014; 2015).

4. See interview with Mandla Mbothwe ('Theatre That Can Organize, Mobilize, Conscientize').
5. Mbothwe was invited by DELTA (Development, Education & Leadership Teams in Action) to facilitate the Delft Drama Group. In 2004, the group produced *Beyond Silence*, a performance about the voices of women, directed by Mbothwe and Ntokozo Madlala.
6. I saw all of the plays referenced here in Magnet's Community Groups Intervention Showcases. When the plays are untitled I have ascribed *'a title'* for reference purposes, which encapsulates what the play is about.
7. See, for instance, Awotona et al. (1995a), Jelsma, Mkoka & Amosun (2008), McDonald (2008), Ndegwa, Horner & Esau (2007), Pillay (2004), Swilling (2010) and Turok & Watson (2001).
8 The speaker is referring to transport containers, frequently used in the townships as small retail outlets and even for day care centres. It is usually the latter which are 'borrowed' in the late afternoon for the purposes of theatre rehearsals.
9. All quotations in this account of the 2007 Showcase are from audio recordings of interviews with young people in the body of the hall, before, during and after the performances, conducted either by myself or Cindy Mkaza. The audio tapes were transcribed and translated where necessary, and are stored in my archive.
10. See interview with Zwelakhe Khuse ('Keeping Theatre Alive in the Community').
11. Unsurprisingly, there is a similarity in the practices of Mbothwe and Khuse. Khuse was part of the Iselwa le Sizwe theatre group in Khayelitsha from 2003–07, and hence part of the Magnet Theatre Community Groups Intervention. In 2008, Khuse attended the New Africa Theatre Association training programme, before completing his Performer's Diploma in Community Theatre at UCT (2009–11), which was led by Mandla Mbothwe.
12. The audio of Fleishman's address was recorded by Mkaza.

Chapter 16

Vividly Feeling the Extremes of Being in the World: A Conversation with Margie Pankhurst[1]

Margie Pankhurst, Magnet's administrator, graduated from UCT with a performer's diploma in 1983. She worked as an actress both in Cape Town and Johannesburg, and also as an actor's agent, running her own casting director's agency for nine years. Margie worked for Artscape from 2005–09, after which she joined Magnet Theatre, where she still serves as administrative officer. She also oversees the Full Time Training and Job Creation Programme and has been very involved with various community development programmes run by Magnet.

'In a small company like Magnet,' says Margie Pankhurst, 'titles become really redundant.' She has witnessed Magnet weather funding crises while both developing the next generation of theatre-makers through their community interventions in Khayelitsha and Clanwilliam, and also while making their own work. Typically, work on a Magnet production takes time: 'They have the safety to make a first draft and a second draft and a third draft. They're not tied in like other companies that have a three-week rehearsal process and then have to have a product. They know they're developing their work, and it can change.'

'One of the greatest challenges Magnet faces, like any other arts organization in contemporary South Africa, is funding,' says Pankhurst. Over its lifetime, Magnet has been funded by the National Arts Council (NAC), as well as many corporate funders and the National Lottery. Having their own space – The Old Match Factory in Observatory – since 2008 has allowed Magnet to develop their own work in a permanent home, but also to 'make space for' community organizations. 'An added bonus of Magnet having their own theatre [is that we] can become a home for young emerging artists, who can't find space anywhere else,' says Pankhurst. 'Space in Cape Town is difficult to find,' she remarks, 'It's great that we can be a little bit of a hub in that.'

For Pankhurst, part of the way that Magnet 'makes space' is by developing young theatre-makers: 'A lot of township youth are clearly very talented,' she says, 'but they do not have access to university for whatever reason, and there was the need for a bridging programme between the university and the community. That's where the Training Programme came from.' The Full Time Training and Job Creation Programme, a two-year full-time certificate programme, with travel bursaries to help students get from the townships into Cape Town each day, 'really fills a huge gap,' she asserts, 'there's really nothing like it available in Cape Town, in terms of drama. [We] could probably run four streams of training and not fulfil the need that's out there.' And she describes the quality of the training, which benefits from Mark, Jennie and Mandla's collective talent and expertise, as 'extraordinary.'

Although Magnet put the Community Groups Intervention (CGI) on hiatus while they developed the Full Time Training and Job Creation Programme, Pankhurst is encouraged by the next generation of young talent who have taken the helm once again. 'Both Nolovuyo Sam[2] and Zwelakhe Khuse,[3] who's running it now, came from the original programme. They met Jennie and Mark through the Community Groups Intervention. Jennie and Mark facilitated their entrance into UCT Drama School. They have both now graduated and are back working in their community groups. It's a really lovely story.'

Not everything about the Training Programme is rosy, Pankhurst cautions. There are challenges accompanying this population of developing artists: 'As soon as you start working with underprivileged youth, you're working with all their issues, and also with their whole community and its problems and difficulties as well,' she says. 'For instance, in winter in Cape Town it gets light very late, and we start class at 9:00 and we have very stringent late coming rules,' she explains. 'But from May onwards I think there are a goodly number of students who come late simply because it's dangerous for them to walk from home to a taxi rank when it's still dark [...] they're maybe having to risk their life.'

She explains how 'Brink Scholz[4] directed a production with them in the middle of 2012. It was a beautiful production, really drawing on their personal experiences, and a lot of stuff came up for a lot of them. I think about 50 per cent of them started really struggling through that production. And you have to accept that that's part of it. You have to accept that the value of the work is in what the young performers themselves are going through. A lot of past experience tends to go in, and it takes a lot of responsibility to take them there.' For Pankhurst, this vital work means 'you kind of feel the extremes of being in the world very vividly.' The work is, however, definitely worthwhile, she claims, as she gets to witness young South Africans 'blossoming.'

Magnet's long-term investments in local communities include a commitment to leadership succession. For example, describing the growth of the project in Clanwilliam,[5] Pankhurst traces how it began 'from their annual lantern festival. A little community grew up from this festival and Magnet became involved with that, and they actually are just about an NGO in their own right now. They're in a very good position currently; they're getting lots of support from the Clanwilliam community itself.' Still, it's also vital to grow new leaders who are qualified to facilitate it in future: 'At the moment we have a young man in Clanwilliam who's amazing – Angelo Cloete. He's very responsible [but] he still needs a lot of training, so Magnet's still sending mentors and training to Clanwilliam on a regular basis.'

For Pankhurst, this long-term investment mirrors Magnet's slow and deliberate devising process, and their deep commitment to the people they collaborate with. 'Part of the family aspect of Magnet is that even when people are no longer permanently employed, Magnet is incredibly loyal and will work with them again as much as possible.'

References

Pankhurst, M. (2013), personal interview with A. Krueger, 7 June.

Notes

1. Interview quotes in this chapter are taken from Pankhurst (2013).
2. See interview with Nolovuyo Sam ('Magnet Never Forgets its People').
3. See interview with Zwelakhe Khuse ('Keeping Theatre Alive in the Community').
4. Brink Scholtz was the resident director of the Grahamstown-based theatre company UBom from 2006–11. She directed Magnet Theatre's *running with goldfish and gift wrapping the sea* (2012), and is currently completing her Ph.D. at UCT under Fleishman's supervision.
5. The Clanwilliam Arts Project is in its 15th year since its inception in 2001. It is an annual project coordinated by Magnet Theatre, and includes student facilitators from UCT Drama School, the Michaelis School of Art, UCT Music School, ComNet and other independent practitioners (namely, Jazzart, Namjive and The Living Landscapes Project), who all use the project as a site for community arts training. Workshops in art, drama, dance, lantern-making, storytelling, drumming, stilt-walking and fire performance are run with 700 learners from the schools in Clanwillliam over the period of a week in early September. The project culminates in a lantern parade and performance of a /Xam narrative (chosen from the Bleek and LLoyd collection) by the children and the facilitators, and is attended by between 2500 and 3000 audience members from the town (http://magnettheatre.co.za/project/clanwilliam-arts-project/). See also De Bruyn ('Catalysing a Community') and Leffler ('Bursting the Bubble').

Storytelling In Pictures: The Clanwilliam Arts Project

By photojournalist Mark Wessels

www.markwesselsphoto.com

Every year in the first week of Spring, I travel north, up the West Coast of South Africa, to join other like-minded people as we partake in the annual Clanwilliam Arts Project run by Magnet Theatre and the University of Cape Town (UCT). I always feel as if I'm embarking on an assignment of great importance and I treasure the unique opportunity I have as a photojournalist to capture the valuable work being done through visual impression and pictorial storytelling.

I enjoy seeing how the mixed band of creative theatre folk, artists, musicians and volunteers make it all happen together. The tick-tock of time turns dreams into ingenious artworks. Working day and night, they bend and bind cane, making magical shapes with papier mâché and turning fabled fantasy into reality with mystical, ancestral beings and mythical creatures that come to life through carrying hand and flickering flame.

The depth of delight and energized excitement experienced by the local children is for me one of the most worthwhile reasons to be a witness to all that is the Clanwilliam Arts Project. The remarkable and marvelous all culminate in happy chaos. It is something special to see through the eyes of children how the impact of positive theatre, music and song brings powerful change to socially challenged communities.

By celebrating the rich cultural heritage of a Khoisan past, this festival continues to be beautiful and wonder-filled. Despite the continued pressures of raising awareness, finding funding and the direct social needs of disadvantaged people, the show still goes on year after year, and this sort of fortitude and perseverance is a typical Magnet Theatre trait that always amazes me.

I love photographing Magnet's work because of what it is and what it does. It is not just about seeing but more so about the believing that happens when theatre comes to life! I become one with the story played out in the rhythm of souls so deeply intertwined in the veridical meaning of this event. The images in this photoessay capture one part of Magnet's hope-filled vision of transforming lives after the candlelit creations have gone and the danced dust has settled.

But some stories are best told in pictures…

Mark Wessels is a freelance photojournalist who is based in Cape Town but works wherever assignments take him. Focused on social issues, he firmly believes that pictures can influence positive and powerful change in our world and its people. He is passionate about storytelling with images. Mark has worked with Magnet Theatre for more than 10 years and since 2010 has covered the Clanwilliam Arts Project with them. Recently Wessels created a Photo Life Workshop to teach students how to take pictures to tell their stories and life skills as part of the Clanwilliam Arts Project.

A face-painted boy watches the final performance.

A sea of children with glowing lanterns before the parade begins its yearly journey through the community.

Young performers rehearse choreography together.

With enthusiasm and energy, Magneteers create fantastic beings.

A young girl applies the finishing touches to a lovely lantern.

Magnet's Jennie Reznek rehearses the puppet show.

A giant praying mantis, glowing from within, comes to life and is carried through the town.

A child shows off his feathered mask as he waits to participate.

A young boy watches while he sits with others amidst lanterns.

A boy calls out excitedly as the moon rises and night falls.

Magnet volunteers paint slip clay on their own faces along with the children.

Mystical creatures light up the night.

Illuminated by lantern light, a child watches the show in wonder.

A Magnet volunteer stands with a giant rhinoceros before the parade.

A giant bird flies through the night as it is carried during the parade.

An enthralled crowd watch Khoisan stories come to life.

Children watch fire-spinners whirl spinning poi and twirl batons to the rhythm of the music in the firey finale.

Chapter 17

By Telling Stories We Can Learn Something from Life: A Conversation with Thando Doni[1]

Thando Doni is a multi-talented theatre-maker and graduate of Magnet Theatre's training programme, who now teaches in the same programme. He is a resident actor at Bonfire Theatre Company, and was nominated as Best Director at the Baxter's Zabalaza Theatre Festival in 2011 and 2012. Doni also won GIPCA's prestigious director's bursary in 2012 with a show entitled Utopia, *which deals with the perpetual striving for happiness. He has been nominated for the Fleur Du Cap Best New Director Award for the Magnet Theatre/ Baxter production of* Passage *(2014). Doni has performed in a number of Magnet productions, including* incwaba lendoda lise cankwe ndlela *[the grave of the man lies next to the road] (2009);* Inxeba Lomphilisi — The Wound of a Healer *(2010–14) and* Voices Made Night *(2010–14). More recently, he was assistant director with Mark Fleishman on* Heart of Redness *(2015).*

For Thando Doni, 'Performing, directing, just being in the theatre world, the adrenalin – it makes me so happy!' He smiles broadly as he shares his enthusiasm for making 'work that will actually move people.' Doni believes that theatre plays a vital role in society. 'Theatre gives you energy,' he exclaims, 'Just being on stage and performing and making work, and having people coming to see what you have created and having conversations about the work and about life – ja…the entire theatre energy is just beautiful to me. Especially if you work for Magnet Theatre.' Citing Magnet's training, care and use of the body as his major artistic inspiration, he explains: 'We get to tell stories and we get to live other people's lives through characters that we play. By telling people's stories, we can learn something from life. That goes way back to the days when we used to sit with our grandmothers and they used to tell us stories. There's always something of moral value in that.'

Reflecting on his training through the Magnet Full Time Training and Job Creation Programme, Doni says, 'I understand a lot of things differently now than how I understood them before.' He believes that Magnet's physical approach to theatre, the devising process and 'the quality of work that it brings to people' are what makes the company unique. 'There's something about the workshop process Magnet uses which is very special,' he explains, 'How to look at detail and also the language of the body, and how on its own the body speaks a language, and how you can use that to say what you need to say. Sometimes you don't even need to speak about things with words. When people use bodies, we all understand what they mean,' he says, 'There's no need to translate each and every word.'

Doni admits, 'For me, Magnet is a family and they do beautiful work. It's something that is very important for the theatre industry at large here. Because it's a physical theatre company – which you don't get a lot, especially in Cape Town. It's the only one I know that does physical theatre. There's something special about the language they're using; there's something special about the work – it's worth seeing, it's worth experiencing.'

Doni, at age 27, describes himself as 'a work in progress,' who is still figuring out his own style and developing his craft. But he is certain of one thing: 'Collaboration is the future. There's so much you can learn from other people. When you work with other people, you learn to see how they're feeling and what they're thinking and how they do things; and somehow it does enhance or change how you do things. It's important for us to link to other people and for artists to understand each other. Together we stand, divided we fall…'

Reference

Doni, T. (2013), personal interview with A. Krueger, 10 June.

Notes

1. Interview quotes in this chapter are taken from Doni (2013).

Chapter 18

Catalysing a Community: Magnet's Clanwilliam Community Intervention Project

Lavona de Bruyn

Lavona de Bruyn taught high school learners for 26 years before she returned to study drama full-time at the University of Cape Town (UCT), graduating with an MA in Applied Drama and Theatre Studies in 2009. She first met Mark Fleishman and Jennie Reznek at UCT, and worked with Magnet Theatre from 2007 until 2012, helping them to develop theatre activities in the Cederberg region of the Western Cape.

I would like to begin by introducing the drama of my own identity as a coloured woman in South Africa, mentioning the forces which have shaped me. Then, I would like to provide a brief overview of the community of Clanwilliam, and my work there with Magnet Theatre and the Community Networking Creative Arts Group (ComNet) between 2007–12. After that, I will discuss two case studies of work we made in Clanwilliam: *Jingle Dreams* (2007) and *Vastrap Van Jan Dissel Tot Tra Tra* [Stand Firm from Jan Dissel to Tra Tra] (2011).[1] Following this, I will talk about this work's impact on my ongoing development as a community catalyst, and reflexive interventionist and activist.

Introduction – The Drama of My Own Identity

In 2007, I was a student in the Drama Department at the University of Cape Town, reading for my honours degree. My interrogation of my identity as a coloured[2] South African woman propelled my desire for investigating, and perhaps affected the way I see myself in the context of the post-apartheid era. Little did I know at the time that I was embarking on the journey of social transformation which would lead to a profound shift in my identity as a woman born in District Six in Cape Town in 1952. When I first became involved with Magnet Theatre's Clanwilliam Arts Project in 2007, my life took a new direction. My studies in Drama at UCT coincided with my search for a personal, social and political identity in contemporary South Africa. I was inspired by Magnet's vision to 'celebrate a spirit of theatrical research and to challenge participants [...] through experiences that shift bodies, assumptions, feelings, beliefs and understandings' (Magnet Theatre 2007–08). This spoke to me very clearly, because my life has always been compelled by a desire and vision for social transformation. I have always been driven by a strong sociopolitical impetus.

In 1968, I chose teaching as a career, because I believed that I could make a difference with regard to the coloured identity of young people who were defined by the ideals of the apartheid government. During the 1970s and 1980s, I was involved in the political struggle against apartheid, and I believe that I was able to contribute to the anti-apartheid movement from my position within the education system. For example, I encouraged students to deconstruct their identity as 'coloured,' to interrogate what the textbooks said about their history and to examine the ways in which they viewed themselves. In this way, I was able to subvert apartheid ideology. I taught history and English, and devised techniques, methods and strategies to reinforce the identity of young people as equal before the law. In every lesson and extracurricular activity I taught, I set out to raise awareness of the unjust laws of apartheid.[3]

The issue of race has long been a fundamental point of departure for social identity in South Africa. During the period of imperialism and colonialism, hybridity was seen as a shameful consequence of the sexual relations between European settlers and others. Nicholson (2005: 65) postulates that individual identity is shaped by the historical remnants of events and experiences in life. Social identity is shaped through the assimilation of lived experiences of the past that have become an integral part of individuals within their communities. Social identity focuses on process, and consists of negotiations between the individual and the collective. On the other hand, Bogad (2006) argues that individuals 'make up collectives,' and are thus also agents of social change. To establish social transformation, changes are required not only collectively, but also at an individual level, in the very habitual processes of interaction that affect how individuals negotiate with the world. While choices made today do not change the past of a community, they may have a direct impact on the responses to past events when reconstructing them. In the same way, the reconstruction of past events through theatre has the potential to reshape individual and community identities.

Magnet Theatre not only creates theatre for entertainment, but also makes theatre for transformation. This aspect of Fleishman and Reznek's vision is evident in the meetings, conversations and (more significantly) the actions undertaken by them. This became evident to me when I worked with them on the Clanwilliam Arts Project. Their probing into the work I was doing as a fieldworker in Clanwilliam, and their feedback on the monthly reports I submitted to them, brought my impetus and actions in Clanwilliam into perspective. This symbiotic relationship reinforced the interconnectedness of my personal goals with Magnet Theatre's vision.

The Clanwilliam Arts Project

Clanwilliam lies on an important transport axis about 240km northwest of Cape Town, in the Cederberg Municipality. Agriculture drives the local economy, and the town is dominated by citrus, vegetable and grape farming. It is also the centre of the rooibos tea industry in South Africa, and is currently the only place in the world where rooibos can be cultivated. Clanwilliam's central location close to the Olifants River Valley makes it an ideal site for secondary industries related to citrus, such as the processing of fruit juices. The town also accommodates storage and cooling facilities, as well as supplying packaging for factories producing chemicals for farming activities in the region. Light industries include cement and engineering services, and the Strassbergers Shoe Factory, where a variety of *veldskoene* are handmade. This town is one of the ten oldest in South Africa (Wesgro 1999). Many tourists are attracted by the San rock paintings and the Clanwilliam Dam. Annual events include the Cederberg Festival in April, the Spring Wild Flower Show and the Clanwilliam Arts Project in September.

According to historical and archaeological sources, the three indigenous groups who inhabited this area in the seventeenth century were the /Xam, the Namas and the Griquas (*Olifantsrivierontwikkelingsvereniging* 1987: 3). Land alienation began in the Clanwilliam district around 1712 when white colonists first entered the Oliphants River Region (Penn 1995: 38–40). The period between 1770 and 1800 was characterized by a desperate struggle for survival, as the advancing *trekboers* [migrant Afrikaans farmers][4] vied for land and water.

Coloured identity in Clanwilliam is rooted in tensions between the /Xam, the English settlers and *trekboers*. Some of the local people also trace their origins to slaves who escaped from the Cape of Good Hope and other outlying areas. The coloured people in the region originated from interactions between these groups, particularly by those groups who were dominant at particular times. The different racial groups in the town still live in the separate areas demarcated by the Group Areas Act of 1950, even though this Act was repealed in 1991. A process of interior decolonization has affected ethnic minorities who possessed reserves of memory but little or no historical capital. In Clanwilliam, for example, archaeological sites record the tangible history and cultural heritage of the / Xam in the form of rock paintings; however, the impact of colonization and apartheid caused the collapse of historical memory and the loss of a sense of the significance of these paintings for the coloured community.

In order to contribute towards rectifying this situation, Magnet Theatre (in conjunction with the UCT Drama Department, the Michaelis School of Fine Art, Jazzart and Namjive Dance Companies and, for the past three years, the UCT Music Department) have been running a series of workshops since 2000 for the Clanwilliam Arts Project as part of their community outreach programme.

Each year around 500 local schoolchildren workshop a story selected from an archive of /Xam narratives recorded by linguists Lucy Llyod and Wilhelm Bleek over 130 years ago. The workshops are conducted over a period of five days, and they involve dance, storytelling, shadow puppetry and art, culminating in a lantern-lit procession and performance based on /Xam storytelling elements, including fire dancing, music and illuminated objects made by the learners (De Bruyn 2007–08). This project was the forerunner to Magnet Theatre's Community Outreach in Clanwilliam.

The Community Networking Creative Arts Group (ComNet)

In 2007, actress Riana Alfreds, director Mandla Mbothwe and I facilitated a group of high school learners in Clanwilliam as part of the Community Networking Creative Arts Group (ComNet). The 14 participants were young people from the Clanwilliam coloured community, aged between 15 and 19, some of whom had participated before in the Clanwilliam Arts Project. The aim of our first meeting in 2007 was to build a creative arts group comprised of community members. The vision was that ComNet would continue to function with Magnet Theatre's support until they could become self-supporting within five years, which was one of the original goals.

The convergence of my personal vision with Magnet Theatre's objectives provided the impetus for a pioneering creative adventure. The objectives provided a guide to the work I was doing in Clanwilliam, regularly evaluating whether I was still maintaining the spirit of the vision first set up by Fleishman and Reznek. I worked with them for five years and learnt an enormous amount. In their day-to-day lives, they embody the mission, vision and objectives of the organization which they created. Their experience as directors was invaluable, as they offered their advice and assistance in the formation of the community theatre group. Their years of experience in theatre, their depth of knowledge of drama, and their commitment to social transformation guided me through the unchartered territory of my search for identity as a coloured woman in post-apartheid South Africa. They assisted me in my investigations into alternative ways of impacting young people from previously disadvantaged communities in South Africa through drama.

Magnet Theatre financed my trips to Clanwilliam, paying for my accommodation, as well as food for the participants and workshop materials. They provided the audio-visual equipment, technical assistance and artistic advice for productions during all of the five years that I was involved in Clanwilliam (2007–12). Their support was central when I became involved in conducting drama workshops at schools in Clanwilliam and neighbouring towns in the area. Magnet subsidized the group when we had to attend arts festivals and participate in drama competitions in other towns; they also sponsored the accommodation of members of ComNet when they attended workshops in Cape Town, and when they made theatre visits to Cape Town and Oudtshoorn. Throughout the process of organizational support, however, Magnet Theatre made it clear that these contributions were not designed to make the group dependent on them, but that they were rather hoping to facilitate a gradual move towards self-reliance.

Magnet Theatre supported my work with ComNet through funding from various sources, which suggests a redistribution of resources that were not easily accessible and available to those disadvantaged under the apartheid government. Magnet's intervention in Clanwilliam can be seen as an example of a transformative and affirmative strategy; a remedy for the cultural injustices of the past and a dismantling of social identity based on race; a counter to what Fraser (1995: 70-71) has called 'cultural injustices [...] rooted in social patterns of representation, interpretation and communication [which] require redistributive, affirmative, transformative action to redress the injustices of the past.' Social identity reconstructed from past injustices can be remedied through the intervention of drama and theatre organizations like Magnet Theatre, and their involvement in Clanwilliam addresses both historical and contemporary socioeconomic injustices.

Case Study 1: *Jingle Dreams*

While reading for my MA in Applied Drama at UCT, I worked as a Magnet Theatre fieldworker in Clanwilliam. The production on which the research for my master's was based, *Jingle Dreams*,[5] was the first collaborative theatre piece created by ComNet, and it was performed in December 2007. After completing my master's, I continued to conduct drama workshops and to create productions in Clanwilliam with ComNet and with the schools in the area. My involvement in the schools was aimed at providing a foundation from which to inspire and empower youth in the area using theatre skills. My involvement in the schools and in the community located my research in the ambit of community theatre, which seeks to provide 'a catalyst for social change, and to give voice to those silenced and marginalised by mainstream public culture through the efficacy of drama to present and explore reality through fiction' (Mattingly 2001: 450). Theatre created in, and by, the community depends on some level of shared understanding and experience, consequently allowing the imaginative space offered by performance-making accessible to the audience because it contains elements of recognizable characters, symbols and places. The introduction of drama was challenging, and I found that my teaching style had to become more collaborative, with a greater awareness of participant involvement.

Set in the town of Kleinwillem, *Jingle Dreams* reveals familial, communal and intergenerational relationships. The play revolves around the September family, consisting of the father, Mr September (played by Angelo Cloete), his daughter, Jennie (Candice Jephta), and his son, Bennie (Sergio Fortuin). Bennie, Matak (Jacquis Witbooi) and Poen (Gilroy Fortuin) are members of a gang who also want to perform their song 'Iensy Wiensy Spider' at the talent competition. Jennie and her friends, Anna (Merryl September) and Spikes (Howard Kotze), have rehearsed a song and dance routine called '*Superstêr*' ['Superstar']. Two other groups enter the talent competition, namely the Hip Hop Girls and the DYC Dance group.

Bennie and Matak, however, experiment with crystal methamphetamine, which affects Bennie's relationship with his father, especially since the father practices the same behaviour from which he wants to protect his son. Jennie, on the other hand, is a hard worker and wants to be a professional dancer, but her father finds it difficult to accept her choice. In this way, although there is scope for a lot of humour in the play, it also touches on real issues such as gangs, drugs and life choices – the same issues faced by the young people who participated in the production. The final dance is a triumphant celebration of a revitalized and renewed spirit of community that developed among participants during the processes of drama.

The community was able to celebrate their success as negotiators of a reconstructed future for young people in Kleinwillem, and successfully performed a play that they had devised in collaboration with Professors Gay Morris and Mark Fleishman, and myself as theatre practitioner interventionists. Feedback from participants revealed Fleishman and Reznek's capacity to apply and translate scholarly proficiency into experiential skill in a language that could easily be understood. Often they were speaking to Afrikaans-speaking young people who understood and implemented the notes given when they attended rehearsals in Clanwilliam.

The processes of devising *Jingle Dreams* ensured that the local community could relate to the play, since participants were members of the community for which they wanted to perform. From the beginning, they wished to perform a play that would portray social and economic problems in their community. The rehearsal processes and the performances also presented an opportunity for the participants to explore where they stood in relation to these issues.

Fleishman and Reznek have a keen understanding and intuitive insight of community dynamics grounded in academic research. As theatre practitioners, they gave me the opportunity and the freedom to explore my role as a reflexive community interventionist and activist. I was conscious of how I positioned myself in relation to the group with whom I was working and the community in which I was operating, and I had to navigate my way through community politics and relationships. In this way, I brought the totality of my sense of who I am to the project – my identity, my values, my experience as an individual, as well as my knowledge as a teaching artist.

My positionality affected both the exploratory nature of the dramatic process and the safe space that I endeavoured to create. It integrated my self-knowledge, my practitioner skills, and my understanding of the social, cultural, economic and political circumstances of the community. Respect for the values, stories and history of participants and the community itself was vital to the process, as was my ability to contextualize what the participants wanted to express. From a repertoire of resources that included listening, observing, critical questioning and encouragement, I selected strategies and theatre modes suited to my interaction with the group. These enabled me to be a catalyst in the small community. Zakes Mda describes catalysts as:

> [...] those outsiders with specialist skills in theatre and in community development who work with organised groups in communities [...]. They must have a higher level of social consciousness than the (local community) based on their education and general social experience [...]. They should increasingly involve the participants both in creating and performing the play. To reach its ideal, a catalyst should not only be able to raise the consciousness of the target group, but also to impart theatre skills, and an understanding of the relation between drama and problem exploration [...]. They should also have a higher level of critical awareness in terms of political and social issues.
>
> (Mda 1993: 20)

In addition to this, 'catalysts should involve themselves in the practical lives of the target group for a period of time [...] and participate in the [...] social and economic lives of the participants [...] as sympathetic observers of their daily lives and problems' (Mda 1993: 20). In light of this context, the question did arise as to how effective I could be as a catalyst for change in Clanwilliam. Firstly, in relation to ComNet, I was an 'outsider' for various reasons. Clanwilliam is situated in a rural area and I come from the city of Cape Town; however, I spent 16 years in Stellenbosch, which is also a semi-rural community. Therefore, although I was an outsider, I had had experience of living in a rural community, which helped me to understand the social dynamics of a small town. Secondly, I was working with a group of young people ranging from 14 to 20 years of age, while I was 54 years old at the time. This difference in age located me as an outsider, and yet it was balanced by my professional experience with young people as a high school educator for 26 years, as well as my experience of being a single mother of two sons in their early 20s. In both of these capacities, I was able to deepen my understanding of the group's language and the issues that young people face. On the other hand, my age also positioned me as an insider, since they started seeing me as a mother figure once trust had been established between the participants and myself. It was especially helpful that I speak Afrikaans fluently, since this is the mother tongue of the participants.

The varied roles of the applied theatre practitioner as catalyst, facilitator and interventionist were all employed in my work in Clanwilliam. Fleishman and Reznek modelled a way of personal, professional and relational behaviour as I negotiated these roles, and their integrity added significance and value to the purpose of drama and theatre in Clanwilliam. Their insights, questions, recommendations and support at meetings and informal discussions provided a strong base from which I could interface with community institutions, and in negotiating communication between divided and sometimes suspicious community leaders. Their involvement in my work with ComNet – at the school, with community leaders and with the community at large – added weight to the purpose of drama and theatre in Clanwilliam. I have a high regard for Fleishman and Reznek, whose encouragement and persistence provided me with a tenacity to continue working in Clanwilliam through gruelling times and life-changing experiences. They were always able to keep their mission in sight.

Case Study 2: *Vastrap Van Jan Dissel Tot Tra Tra* [Stand Firm from Jan Dissel to Tra Tra]

I would now like to consider another case study of my work in Clanwilliam. For five years, the members of ComNet wanted to create theatre around social issues, and in 2011 the group was invited to do a production for the Cederberg Arts Festival.[6] The young people in the drama group with whom I worked wanted to represent the history of their place, as well as to interpret the historic sites through their own eyes, and reawaken an awareness of the beauty and historic significance of the Cederberg, where they live. This encapsulates the vision of Magnet Theatre which aspires 'through explorations of our historical, contemporary and stylistic contexts [to] dedicate ourselves to raising levels of resources and energizing audiences and theatre practitioners in the community at large' (Magnet Theatre 2007–08). The production included drama, dance and song, creating theatre based on the journey along the R364 road from Clanwilliam (previously known as Jan Dissel) to Wupperthal (previously known as Tra Tra), highlighting the historic places and people along the route.

I regarded this production as a milestone for Clanwilliam. *Vastrap* was the first of a series of productions that ComNet devised based on historical figures and places in Clanwilliam and the Cederberg. This has started a journey in which the coloured community have begun to fill the 'empty (w)hole of [historical] memory in an attempt to summon the past and seek identity,' as suggested by Suzan-Lori Parks (cited in Malkin 2002: 153). Since 2011, the group has continued to research and contribute to performing the /Xam, slave, coloured and white history of the town.

Lasting Impacts

Magnet Theatre made it possible for me to become part of the community of Clanwilliam for five years. During that time, a dialogical encounter took place in the process of making theatre which changed my life. My understanding of social identity shifted my focus from the historical factors shaping identity to more contemporary influences; a realization which coincided with my own personal search for identity. I left Clanwilliam in 2012 with the insight that I am not defined by my race as a 'coloured' woman. My social identity is continually being shaped in community with others with whom I share a common goal, a common vision, and shared experiences of belonging.

When I initially scrutinized the processes and script of *Jingle Dreams*, I looked for evidence of social identity strongly rooted in race. Based on my experience, I was of the opinion that the racial connotations of the past still defined social identity. For decades, race has played an enormously significant factor in defining social identity for individuals and families. An analysis of the processes and the performance led me to conclude that ComNet (as representative of the coloured youth in Clanwilliam) may be suggesting a new mode of thinking about social identity, one which is not attached to race (even though it is not devoid of racial connotations). This proposed identity is based on a collective identity of an 'imagined community' (Benedict Anderson) with whom they are working towards a common goal.

In 2012, ComNet became an independent non-profit organization, with some of the original members managing the work alongside role players from Clanwilliam. Magnet Theatre still plays a supportive role in the ongoing projects. Their objective is being realized, and they are contributing to 'job creation by empowering people to become employable and by employing recent graduates from University Drama Departments who originate from the previously disadvantaged communities of the city, and giving them valuable work experience under the supervision of highly skilled practitioners' (Magnet Theatre 2007–08).

Sustaining ongoing development in the arts also involves engaging primary school learners. Magnet Theatre's vision is vital to the Community Intervention Programme. Their hope is:

> [...] to help restore the culture of learning and teaching in our schools through sustained and focused arts interventions, providing learners and teachers with a new sense of self-awareness and focus, and a new range of skills and capacities, combined with personal development.
>
> (Magnet Theatre 2007–08)

I would like to propose that in contrast to the divisive grand narrative promulgated by the apartheid government, the inclusivity of the community into the exploration of the communal past of their town by means of drama has resulted in a lasting reverberation throughout the community – both for actors and audiences – and has led to the reshaping of history and the transformation of social identity. The impact of the work done by Magnet Theatre continues to resonate through many individuals and communities both locally and abroad, leaving a lasting heritage of healing and transformation.

References

Bogad, L. (2006), 'Tactical Carnival: Social Movements, Demonstrations, and Dialogical Performance,' in J. Cohen-Cruz and M. Schutzman (eds), *A Boal Companion: Dialogues on Theatre and Cultural Politics*, New York: Routledge.

De Bruyn, L. (2007–08), 'Monthly Reports sent to Magnet Theatre Educational Trust as the Field Worker,' Clanwilliam: unpublished.

—— (2008), 'Exploring Social Identity through Theatre: An Examination of the Process of Creating Jingle Dreams with Youth in the Coloured Community of Clanwilliam,' MA thesis, University of Cape Town.

Fraser, N. (1995), 'From Redistribution to Recognition? Dilemmas of Justice in a "Post-Socialist" Age,' *New Left Review*, 212, pp. 68–93.

Magnet Theatre (2007–08), *Annual Report 2008*, www.magnettheatre.co.za/.../Magnet_Annual_Report08_spreads.pdf. Accessed 12 April 2014.

Malkin, J. (2002), *Memory – Theatre and Postmodern Drama*, Michigan: The University of Michigan Press.

Mattingly, D. (2001), 'Place, Teenagers and Representations: Lessons from a Community Theatre Project,' *Social and Cultural Geography*, 2: 4, pp. 445–59.

Mda, Z. (1993), *When People Play People: Developmental Communication Through Theatre*, Johannesburg: Witwatersrand University Press.

Olifantsrivierontwikkelingsvereniging (1987), *Beplanningstreek 2: sosio-ekonomise streekstudie.*

Nicholson, H. (2005), *Applied Drama: The Gift of Theatre*, New York: Palgrave Macmillan.

Penn, N. (1995), 'The Northern Cape Frontier Zone – 1700–1815,' Ph.D. thesis, University of Cape Town.

South African Police Service (2012), *Crime in Clanwilliam (WC) for April to March 2003/2004 - 2011/2012.* http://www.westerncape.gov.za/assets/departments/community-safety/clanwilliam.pdf. Accessed 1 April 2014.

Wesgro (1999), *Clanwilliam – Investment and Development Opportunities*, Cape Town: WESGRO.

Wetherell, M. (2012), *Affect and Emotion: A New Social Science Understanding*, London: Sage.

Notes

1. A script of *Jingle Dreams* is reproduced in my master's thesis (De Bruyn 2008: 62–80).
2. In South Africa, the term 'coloured' is applied to people of mixed race and does not carry the pejorative meaning it has in the United States.
3. In my fight for a free, non-racial and democratic South Africa, I saw being 'black' as a means of uniting us in our struggle against apartheid. I regarded myself as a black woman, and 'coloured' was a label I rejected with contempt. However, the use of the term 'coloured' became acceptable during the process of my research and work in Clanwilliam, as my focus shifted from the apartheid political ideologies that shaped my identity, to seeing myself as a woman whose identity has also been influenced by individual and collective heritage.
4. The *trekboers* were a group of Afrikaans farmers who moved away from the Cape to escape colonial control (Penn 1995: 158).
5. My work with Magnet Theatre afforded me the opportunity to base the field work component of my master's in the town of Clanwilliam. My thesis, 'Exploring Social Identity through Theatre: An Examination of the Process of Creating Jingle Dreams with Youth in the Coloured Community of Clanwilliam,' was the culmination of the creative work of the group based on Magnet Theatre's mission, vision and objectives: 'to create exciting, innovative and sophisticated African theatre which engages with our present condition in South Africa; to radically shift access to performance and arts activities by taking theatre and arts education to communities' (Magnet Theatre 2007–08).
6. See www.cederbergfees.co.za.

Chapter 19

Bursting the Bubble of Play: Making Space for Intercultural Dialogue

Elliot Leffler

Elliot Leffler holds a Ph.D. in Theatre Historiography from the University of Minnesota, a BS in Theatre from Northwestern University and an MA in Applied Theatre from the University of Cape Town. His academic and community-engaged work focuses primarily on the use of theatre in framing and fostering intercultural dialogue. He has worked as an actor, director and playwright, and has led theatre programmes with young people in the United States, South Africa and Israel/Palestine. He is currently a visiting assistant professor of theatre at Reed College.

Introduction: A Story About a Cell Phone

In the early 1990s, when Magnet Theatre was still in its infancy, co-founder Mark Fleishman wrote an MA thesis (1991) and a South African Theatre Journal (1990)[1] article in which he interrogated the intercultural dynamics of workshop theatre. In this scholarship, he described this collaborative, improvisation-based approach to devising original performances as essentially dialogic and democratic, as it frees ensemble members from the authoritarianism of the traditional playwright and nurtures an environment in which participants' cultural differences can inform and challenge each other (Fleishman 1990: 103; 1991: 60–62). He articulated the value of recognizing and negotiating fundamental cultural differences, and suggested that theatrical ensembles were an important site for this negotiation. Fleishman profiled the Serpent Players and Workshop '71 as prominent South African ensembles whose processes testified to this intercultural negotiation. In the time that has passed since he wrote these early essays, his own professional casts have become another prominent example of these dynamics. Yet the number of people that Magnet engages in intercultural dialogue within its professional ensembles is relatively small. Through its community-based programmes, Magnet (and others) may have the possibility to engage many more of South Africa's citizens in the complex intercultural dialogue that Fleishman has argued is intrinsic to workshop theatre. This chapter examines one of Magnet's community-based projects to analyse how Magnet's theatre processes make space for intercultural dialogue among amateur artists.

Like the preceding chapter of this volume, this chapter focuses on work that Magnet Theatre has produced in Clanwilliam, a small community about 200km north of Cape Town. While Magnet Theatre's work in Clanwilliam began with the Clanwilliam Arts Project,[2] the company developed a momentum and a following there that has led to more sustained involvement in the town, spawning a number of other projects. One of these projects is a community theatre ensemble of teenagers and preteens known as the Community Networking Creative Arts Group, or ComNet. ComNet has been devising and performing original plays since 2007, and for the first five years, these plays were largely under the direction of fieldworker Lavona de Bruyn. At De Bruyn's invitation, I joined ComNet in 2010 as an assistant director for their workshop theatre production of *Soek 'Os 'It Soe?* [Is This What We Want?]. My personal friendship with De Bruyn dated back to 2007, when we were MA students together at the University of Cape Town. But I was particularly interested in this project because she told me that it was going to mark their first attempt to recruit an interracial cast.[3] As a scholar of intercultural theatre, and an enthusiast for Fleishman's own early scholarship on intercultural dialogue in workshop theatre, I was fascinated to observe how this ensemble (which had always been exclusively coloured) would attempt to welcome, and to function with, black and white participants. The opportunity to participate in – and to learn from – that process was irresistible.

As an ethnographic study of the process that produced *Soek 'Os 'It Soe?*, this chapter documents and interrogates the project in order to contribute to a growing body of theory on collaborative theatre-making as a site for intercultural dialogue. This chapter is therefore the analysis of a *process* – not of a text, nor a performance – and I have attempted to write it with a self-reflexive awareness of my own partiality and my influence on the events which I have documented and analysed. As such, I have employed a subjective, first-person style that relies on – and reminds the reader of – my own presence on site, despite the fact that doing so breaks from the style of many chapters within this volume.

My first introduction to the challenges of intercultural dialogue in Clanwilliam came several days before rehearsals started. I was at a short meeting on the front *stoep* [veranda] of the house that Magnet co-founders Mark Fleishman and Jennie Reznek had almost finished building in Clanwilliam. To my right sat Jesmory, a 20-year-old coloured woman who had been participating in ComNet shows for the past three years, and who was now both an actor in the productions and the administrative leader of the group.[4] To my left sat Lavona de Bruyn, a coloured woman in her early 50s, who in addition to directing ComNet's shows, was also mentoring Jesmory as a leader. And then there was me: a 30-year-old white American, having travelled across the world to observe and assist with this production.

Jesmory gave us some bad news. She had been recruiting teenagers within the black and white communities, and while she hadn't been entirely sure that the black participants would show up, she had been more confident that the white participants would. She had recruited them through her friend Werner, a 17-year-old white, Afrikaans-speaking boy whose mother employed Jesmory's own mother as a domestic worker. But now Jesmory explained that Werner and his friends might not show up for the first few days, because they were surfing in a nearby beach town. When I heard this, I immediately began to worry about the ensemble's dynamics. I explained that I thought the first few days of this process were crucial, and that if the white participants were absent, it would present a lot of problems.

Jesmory responded, 'Well, I will tell him [Werner] to come. If I tell him to come, he will come.'

I asked: 'Really? Just like that? You think so?'

She responded, 'Yes, I know he will. Werner is like my brother.'

I said, 'Alright, then – let's call him now!'

She said, 'I can't call him, because I don't have his cell phone number.'

I responded playfully, 'You don't have his number? Jessy, I thought he was like your brother! I have *my* sister's phone number!'

There was a moment's pause, when I realized that I had said too much. When she responded, her words were stark and her voice thick with tension. 'I don't have his number,' she said, 'because he's white and I'm black' (Leffler 2010).[5]

Her words rang with the omnipresent racial divisions that still criss-cross the social landscape of South Africa. Even Jesmory and Werner, who were too young to remember apartheid (Jesmory was born in 1990, and Werner in 1993) and who described each other as being like siblings, were separated by taboos, social norms, historical oppression and socio-economic divisions that sustained separations and rendered the constructed categories of 'white,' 'black' and 'coloured' concrete. Jesmory and Werner may both harbour nostalgic memories of playing together as small children, but she didn't have access to his personal phone number.

Based on this introduction to Werner, I imagined that integrating him into the ensemble would be nearly impossible. I envisioned him as elitist and entitled – but I could hardly have been more wrong. Not only did he show up for rehearsal the following morning, but he proved to be a gracious, friendly and humble young man. His family was among the most affluent and powerful in town, but that didn't impede his ability to make friends with the other teens, or to treat the project's leaders with respect and deference.

Weeks later, just before I left Clanwilliam, I reminded Jesmory of our discussion about Werner from that first Sunday afternoon, and I asked her to reflect on her relationship with him. I wondered if a coloured woman and a white man in Clanwilliam could really maintain the sibling-like relationship that she had initially claimed to have with him. She breathed heavily, eyes downcast. When she spoke, she said that it was difficult to sustain the close, playful relationship that they had as small children; and yet, she noted, she now had his number in her phone – a testament, she seemed to suggest, to the fact that change was possible, and that a theatre project could contribute to such change. 'We are getting closer, like when we were smaller,' she told me, 'but it will take time' (Jesmory 2010).

Werner, too, noted a modest change in his intercultural relationships with cast members. He turned out to be the only white cast member, and he said that many of the participants didn't go to his school, so he hadn't known them before, 'but over the past two weeks, I […] actually got to get to know them. It's weird to see how they reacted to me. At first they were like 'shhhhhh' [Werner's sound and gesture indicated scepticism of him and a desire to keep distance]. And then later they got more closer to me.' Closer, but still somewhat distant: 'The rejection is always there,' he said. While he felt that certain behaviours had changed, he wasn't sure that they genuinely accepted him: 'I hope it was an internal change, but I don't think so' (Werner 2010a).

Both Werner and Jesmory expressed ambivalence about the impact of the project on their intercultural relationships. Their hope for change was cautious and sceptical. ComNet created space for intercultural dialogue, but that dialogue has not proven to be transformational – at least not yet.

In the pages that follow, I interrogate three moments in ComNet's process that illustrate both the potential and limitations of using workshop theatre to make space for intercultural dialogue. But first, to define 'dialogue,' and to explore what kinds of dialogue might be meaningful, I appeal to Paolo Freire (2000: 88), who defines dialogue as 'the encounter between men, mediated by the world, to name the world.' For Freire, *naming the world* is a radical act: when we 'name' the world, we articulate how its power structures operate; we arrive at a richer, fuller understanding of how our society functions. Moreover, *naming the world* anticipates an intervention to change the world, to make it more just (2000: 88–89 & 129). For dialogue to be *mediated by the world* means that dialogic relationships are not formed in an artificial bubble. We engage each other not by shutting out the complicated and potentially polarizing dynamics of the world around us, but by engaging with them (2000: 93). Freire (2000: 89–91) argues that we can begin to foster this dialogue – these messy encounters in which we explore the dynamics of the world around us, seeking to articulate them and ultimately to change them – only when we have established love, faith and humility. Therefore, in this analysis, I try to better understand: what processes within Magnet's initiative allowed that love, faith and humility to develop across the racial barrier that is so omnipresent within South African society? What processes allowed the participants to collectively articulate how the power structures of their world operate? What processes allowed them to glimpse their potential role in changing those dynamics? And what processes limited their ability to achieve these things?

As I document and analyse these three moments, I draw on, and attempt to contribute to, both the literature on dialogue and also the literature on play. I believe that scholars and practitioners of theatre can learn a lot from the scholarship on play – and contribute a lot to it – if we think about our art form as a form of play, a 'stepping out of real life into a temporary sphere of activity with a disposition all of its own' (Huizinga 1949: 8). This interpretation of play theory mirrors Fleishman's (2009: 124) and Reznek's (2012: 39–41) own scholarship.[6] They have each theorized play in different ways, building on various scholars in order to analyse the dynamics of their own performance methodology (Fleishman 2009:124, Reznek 2012: 39-41). While I turn to different play theorists than Fleishman and Reznek do, and leverage them to different ends, I share their conviction that play is essential to the devising process, and I am ultimately interested in thinking with *Soek 'Os 'It Soe?* about how play might contribute to – and limit – efforts to nurture intercultural dialogue.

Episode One: Contact

It was the third or fourth day of rehearsal. After two days of drama workshops, the two choreographers, Denise and Sandra,[7] had begun to teach dance and movement skills. One of the activities they led is a staple of Contact Improv workshops, in which actors work in pairs to preserve a single point of contact with each other, while continually rolling that point of contact so that their bodies touch in different places and ways. The goal is to move in a continuous flow from one bodily arrangement to the next.

This was not an easy activity for a mixed-gender, racially-heterogeneous group of South African teenagers. Most of the girls in the group were reluctant to make physical contact with the boys that might involve their chests or pelvic areas. These reservations resulted in a physical connection that seemed to be marked not by a sense of flow, but by hesitation and restraint. When dancing with Werner, the discomfort seemed heightened. In an interview, he tried to describe their reaction towards him, but was at a loss for words: 'They were like… ' and then he made a wincing facial expression (Werner 2010a).

The reluctance is unsurprising: though apartheid ended 16 years prior, and none of them were old enough to remember a time when physical intimacy between racial groups was outlawed, there are still implicit boundaries that preserve social segregation along racial lines. Keith, one of the participants who was in Werner's class at school, explained to me that Werner and his white friends were in one social circle, and that Keith and his coloured friends were in another. There was no animosity between them, but also no intimacy (Keith 2010). Moreover, Jesmory (2010) explained to me that 'some of his [Werner's] friends doesn't like coloured people.' Therefore, the reluctance of the coloured women to glide their bodies across Werner's is, in my mind, an understandable combination of adolescent gender anxieties compounded by insecurities associated with racial mixing.

More remarkable than the resistance itself was the ultimate softening of that resistance over the course of the rehearsal process. Werner (2010b) noted that the physical intimacy of Denise's dance exercises ultimately eased the social tension between them: 'I like it [the physical intimacy of the dance work] because the person opens up and I get to know them a lot better. When we talk, it's like… they *talk* to me.'

I want to propose that this exercise, and others like it, ultimately relaxed the social tension between participants of different racial, social and cultural backgrounds because it functioned as a form of play. This was particularly true for Jesmory and Werner, who shared a childhood history of playing together, as well as a love of – and aptitude for – dance. When the two of them were paired together, they synced up their bodily rhythms and leaned into each other with trust and grace. With Denise's music playing loudly in the background, they rolled that point of contact across their bodies, gliding from their wrists, elbows and forearms to their bellies, chests and thighs. Werner (2010b) later recalled: 'We got to know each other through the [physical intimacy of the dance activity]. She was at her ease in doing it with me.' Perhaps, I thought as I watched, they were not only 'at ease,' but actually delighting in their own agency to transgress societal norms, and to share this taboo sensual experience within the safety of the rehearsal hall and the clearly-defined boundaries of Denise's activity. As they pressed the weight of their bodies into each other, they implicitly dared each other: 'touch me,' 'catch me,' 'trust me.' As they accepted these dares, and gradually their dance became more sensual, more taboo, the game took on slightly higher stakes and became more exciting to play.

I don't mean to suggest that they experienced this game as erotic. I don't think they did. But as they played this game, they implicitly created a fiction that existed on the margins of eroticism. All play, according to Roger Caillois (2001: 8), relies on fiction. In this instance, Jesmory and Werner created a fiction that suggested a relationship that coloured and white people don't/can't have in Clanwilliam. This was possible precisely because it was 'only' a fiction. As Stuart Brown writes, 'We are safe precisely because we are just playing' (Brown with Vaughan 2010: 34). One night during the rehearsal process, I went out to a local bar with Sandra, the coloured choreographer who was approximately my age, and we received violent threats because we appeared to be an interracial couple. In contrast, Werner and Jesmory could simulate this physical intimacy because it was bounded by the framework of rules that Denise provided through a movement exercise. It was only a game.

The critical question is what this feeling of safety engenders. Shulamith Lev-Aladgem, a contemporary Israeli scholar, draws on ideas from Eugen Fink and N. Henri Atlan to suggest that play empowers players to reach beyond the realm of givens, to glimpse and then realize alternate realities. She calls these alternate realities 'possibles,' and argues that play has the 'capacity to reconnect human beings and the "possibles," and thus to facilitate the conversion of the "possible" to the substantial' (Fink & Atlan, cited in Lev-Aladgem 2010: 55). In other words, Lev-Aladgem proposes that the space of play is a laboratory, and that the alternate reality nurtured in the safety of that lab can outgrow the lab in which it was created. Werner's own analysis of the event supports this idea: when he said that the game enabled them to get to know each other better, and to really talk with each other, he seemed to suggest that the contact improv activity enabled them to not just imagine a more intimate relationship across racial lines, but also to nurture the relationship that they imagined.

And yet, Freire might argue, the feelings of safety (Brown 2010: 34) and possibility (Lev-Aladgem 2010: 55) that characterise play come at a price. The fiction that frames the world of play shuts out the non-fiction 'real world,' at least temporarily. In the fictional world that they created, Werner and Jesmory experienced what Victor Turner (1982: 47-48) calls *communitas*: 'a direct immediate and total confrontation of human identities,' freed from the 'culturally defined encumbrances of [...] role, status, reputation, class, caste, sex, or other structural niche [such as race].' That kind of *communitas* is addictive. Mihaly Csikszentmihalyi (2009: 20, 44 & 65), who studies 'optimal experiences' in which people feel so absorbed in the pleasure and challenge of an experience that they experience a sense of oneness with those around them, argues that once people have such an experience, they seek to recreate it.[8] But if Werner and Jesmory seek to recreate this experience of *communitas* in the same way, they will continually turn away from the material conditions and cultural patterns that structure their world. The circumstances that made this *communitas* possible did not involve wrestling with the complicated sociopolitical reality of Clanwilliam or South Africa; the encounter was not 'mediated by the world' (Freire 2000: 88). Having glimpsed the seduction of interconnectedness and equality, might Werner and Jesmory have emerged as even less likely to directly address the more thorny, difficult, cultural and historical realities that made their lives so different?

Some anecdotal evidence suggests that this might well be the case. At the conclusion of the process, Lavona approached Werner to thank him for his involvement in the process. Lavona and I were both moved by Werner's inclination to defy the social segregation within Clanwilliam. For three weeks, Werner had spent his days on the coloured side of town, nurturing relationships with a coloured peer group, humbly adjusting to the rhythms and material conditions of their lives. Lavona wanted to personally thank him, and to communicate what it meant to her to see young, privileged white children doing what he did. She told him that he gave her hope for the future of South Africa. He replied graciously, but deflected the compliment. 'I'm doing it to learn to dance,' he told her. Despite the intimacy he had shared with his coloured peers, many of whom were mired in extreme poverty, he didn't seem to emerge with an altered consciousness about their conditions or a commitment to social justice. He understood his involvement with ComNet primarily as an opportunity for self-betterment.

And yet, I believe that there were moments in the process where he and I both experienced play not only as a fleeting sense of interdependence, but also as an opportunity to mark our own privilege in the 'real world.' These playful encounters blossomed in the safety of 'just playing' (Brown 2010: 34), but they felt 'mediated by the world' (Freire 2000: 88), and they seemed to allow a naming of the world that might have brought the ensemble closer to an intercultural, transformational dialogue. I turn now to an investigation of these moments.

Episode Two: White Man Rapping

It was the last week of rehearsals. Sandra and Denise had left Clanwilliam, their work complete; Lavona and I were running daily eight-hour rehearsals with the full cast through the final stretch. We had developed about six or eight theatrical vignettes. We were now rearranging those vignettes and threading a narrative through the piece.

One of the vignettes was based on a real story that Werner had told the cast. Early in the process, when Denise had asked all the performers to share personal stories, Werner had talked about his frustration with people in Clanwilliam who dismiss his family's extensive charitable work as 'taking over the town.' 'They're not doing *anything*,' he had said, referring (he later clarified) to the other white families who criticize and dismiss his family's efforts, 'and yet, they look at what my family is doing and they say these things' (Leffler 2010). Based on Werner's sense of injustice and frustration, Denise and Sandra had scripted and choreographed a rap that we referred to, within the cast, as 'Werner's Story.' It featured Werner in a rhythmic 'duel' with about six or seven other men, representing the collectivity of the town. The problem was that the six or seven other men were all coloured. As we approached opening night, Lavona and I grew concerned that audiences might read the scene as juxtaposing white responsibility (represented by Werner) with coloured laziness. This was not what Werner had intended, and Lavona and I wanted to rectify the problem.

The solution we found required a second white body onstage: mine. We decided that if I were to go onstage as part of the collective, then the collective would not be read as 'coloured,' but rather, as racially heterogeneous. Thus, for several days, I took advantage of every spare moment to learn the steps and the words. I had to learn a choreography that was developed for the bodies of 15 to 18-year-old coloured South Africans. My white, middle-class, American, non-rapping habitus made this difficult, despite my years of training and experience as a performer. The young men in the scene coached me through the challenges, and with their help, I learned to execute most of the steps. However, there was one move that I just couldn't get. We called this 'the roll.' I recorded in my field notes:

> The roll is a quick eight counts of the rap, but I just can't get it right. It's a dancified version of a gangster walk. I think it's mostly associated with coloured gangsters. It involves swinging my right arm on the beat, extending my left arm in front of me, clapping on the fourth beat, and walking with a bent left knee. What's interesting is the kind, playful, laughter-infused attempts by the boys (Keith, Trevor, Werner, and Charles) to teach me how to do it. At one point, Werner said, and the others agreed, 'We know you're doing something wrong, but we're just not sure what.' I was also told, 'You're walking like a robot,' 'You're swinging your hands too much, like [and they mimicked me],' 'You must bend your knees,' 'You must be mad about something,' 'Can you lift one eyebrow?' and lots and lots of: 'Just do it like this [and then they show me how THEY do it].' These comments all feel to me in good fun. We're all enjoying the dynamics of youth expertise, and adult ignorance. I like to think that I'm modeling (performing?) humility. During all these times, I was very aware of my whiteness, and my adultness, and my foreignness, but not in a way that was awkward, uncomfortable, or even serious. It was playful.
>
> (Leffler 2010)

These rehearsals offered me a chance to play a rapper; but far more importantly, they allowed us to tepidly begin to play status games with each other. In general, my age and my title of assistant director made me an authority figure over them, but in these moments we created a playful alternate reality (Lev-Aladgem might call it a 'possible') that inverted those power dynamics. Within this alternate reality, they became firm but affectionate authority figures: they interrupted me with 'No, no, no, Elliot, it's right, *then* left!' – and they firmly chanted, 'Five, six, seven, eight!' to signify that I needed to try it again – but they also nodded, smiled, and offered enthusiastic exclamations of support in Afrikaans laced with teen slang. Within this alternate reality, I remained a pretty incompetent performer whose age, whiteness and Americanness contributed to his deficiency. As we worked out the steps and played this status game, my incompetence elicited fits of laughter, both from me and from the teenagers. Our collective laughter established that we were 'just playing' – that I needn't feel vulnerable or incompetent, that we were working in a spirit of camaraderie (Brown 2010: 34). It was a form of meta-communication in which we expressed a delight in our ability to playfully destabilize the power structures. Laughter, which Henri Bergson would argue is 'always the laughter of a group,' softened the starkness of the differences that my awkward body was articulating (Bergson 2008: 11). We worked together in implicit recognition of the cultural differences that my failed roll articulated – differences between Americans and South Africans, whites and coloureds, adults and teenagers – but as we did so, our laughter positioned us in a place of emotional unity and mutual appreciation. The dynamics of play enabled us to tacitly acknowledge some of the cultural differences that divided us while nurturing affective personal alliances that spanned those very chasms.

This process seems encouraging, and indeed it *was* a process in which participants' cultural differences informed and challenged each other. In that sense, it substantiates some of Fleishman's (1991: 60–62) claims about the intercultural value of workshop theatre. But it doesn't quite make space for 'dialogue' in a Freirian sense: the tacit acknowledgement of cultural differences is not quite a *naming of the world*. Our bodies articulated a cultural divide, and our focused effort in rehearsals acknowledged those divisions, but our failure to *name* them is significant. My botched roll marked me as a white American adult; but which of those three characteristics did my failure make most visible? My age? My race? Or my nationality? To what did the teens attribute the essential differences between me and them? I am still not sure, because within the space of play, we worked not to better understand the difference or to address it on a systemic level, but to mend it on a personal level. The laughter which marked me as different also made me feel acceptable. It could have offered us the opportunity to investigate the cultural dynamics further: I could have initiated a discussion, or even an Image Theatre workshop, based on an inquiry into why our work on the rap was so 'funny.' But I did not. Perhaps I failed to do so because the performance was days away, and we had a lot of work to do. But perhaps it also had to do with the addictive quality of play. As Csikszentmihalyi (2009: 44) suggests, once we experience *communitas* or social oneness, we seek to re-experience it from within, not to analyse it from without. Bursting the bubble of play feels like an act of violence.

Episode Three: Cleaning House

In those final few days of rehearsal, I could hardly keep up with all the changes we were making. In addition to the six to eight central vignettes that anchored the piece, there were suddenly four or five additional scenes and an increasing number of small changes: exits formerly stage-left now were stage-right; a character played by one actor was suddenly played by another; one scene, formerly in the middle of the play, suddenly became the opener; and so on. As all the dialogue of the play was in Afrikaans, it increased the challenge exponentially. Thus, on opening night, I found myself still discovering some of the subtleties that had emerged in the previous few days.

One of these new scenes involved about five actors, including both Werner and Jesmory. It was scripted as an altercation between an older lady (played by Jesmory) and a couple of young teenagers (one of which was played by Werner). This scene included fast-paced dialogue, so I was never sure exactly what was being said. In the rush of these final days, what was 'good enough' didn't demand my attention as assistant director; but on opening night, as I watched this scene, something about it seemed more charged, more aggressive than usual.

Lavona later explained to me that the scene grew tense at a moment when Werner's character insulted Jesmory's. In that night's performance, Jesmory had responded, 'Do I clean your mother's house?' – a response that she had apparently never said in rehearsal. In both Lavona's interpretation and in my own, this line had a double meaning. In role, the old woman was telling the teenager to show respect; she insinuated that he could only get away with such disrespectful behaviour if she had to answer to his mother. But the words also seemed to reverberate with significance outside the fictional scenario: Jesmory seemed to be drawing a line between the power structures of their parents' generation and the power structures of their own. By saying, 'Do *I* clean your mother's house?' we thought Jesmory was differentiating herself from her mother, acknowledging her mother's subservience to his, but defining her own relationship to his family as unrelated.

When I asked Jesmory and Werner about this interaction, however, they gave me two different accounts, which both differed markedly from Lavona's understanding of the scene. Whereas Lavona and I (the adult observers) both interpreted Jesmory's remark as hostile, they (the players) experienced it as playful and funny. Once again, they were apparently 'just playing.' Werner recounted the exchange as follows: 'At the Thursday night [performance], [...] she [Jesmory] said, "My mother doesn't clean your house." But her mother actually cleans our house [...]. We see that as a joke. So it's funny. We laughed about it.' In Werner's memory and interpretation, it didn't have the bite that Lavona and I had understood it to have; Jesmory doesn't seem to have been claiming power that her mother couldn't claim. Rather, the actors experienced it as a self-deprecating joke, and the comedy came from the irony that Jesmory's character claimed a status that Jesmory herself could not claim.

When I asked Jesmory to explain the incident, she told me a third version. According to her, the altercation started when Werner's character called Jesmory's character *miesies* [madam] – a word, as Jesmory explained to me, that coloured people who work as domestics use as a term of respect for their white employers. Jesmory's character dismisses Werner's performance of respect by saying, 'Your mother doesn't work in my kitchen.' The image that this line calls to mind is not that of a coloured woman working in a white woman's kitchen, but the opposite: an image of a white woman working in a coloured woman's kitchen. In the context of Clanwilliam, this idea seems absurd; moreover, the image of Werner's mother (a known entity) working in a coloured woman's kitchen feels particularly absurd. In this version of the story, as in Werner's, there is a degree of self-effacing humour involved for Jesmory. Telling this joke involves an acknowledgement that while her mother's subservience to his is a reality, the idea that his mother might be subservient to a coloured woman is so absurd that it sends an audience into fits of laughter.

I do not know – and perhaps I will never know – which of these three accounts was most accurate. Yet the multiplicity of remembered meanings may say even more than a definitive, objective account. Though Lavona and I both initially understood Jesmory's comment on performance as an act of hostility, I now believe, from speaking with Jesmory and Werner, that they both understood this interaction as playful. Moreover, I understand, based on their differing accounts, that the exact details of what they said were probably not significant. Whether the line explicitly referenced Werner's mother (as in Lavona's and Jesmory's memories) or Jesmory's mother (as in Werner's memory) is unimportant to them; what mattered was how their stage banter alluded to real-life relationships in Clanwilliam. Emboldened by the fact that they were 'just playing,' Jesmory and Werner marked a web of relationships that encompassed both the two of them and their families, the latter whom were seated in the audience. As audience members laughed aloud, they demonstrated that they were in on the joke, and could play along with the double meanings of the characters' lines. Together, actors and audiences playfully marked the power differential that separated Werner's and Jesmory's families, and indeed white and coloured South Africa.

In this instance, play operated differently than it did in the first and second episodes I described. In the first, play enabled Jesmory and Werner to nurture an emotional intimacy that transcended – or perhaps simply ignored – their racial/cultural differences. In the second, we playfully collaborated to obscure the very obvious cultural differences that made my body move so differently than most of theirs. Here, in this final episode, Jesmory and Werner were articulating the very power differentials that bound the actors together in real-life, multigenerational family relationships. The dynamics of play – this 'temporary sphere of activity with a disposition all of its own' (Huizinga 1949: 8) – offered the safety and comfort within which both parties could acknowledge the very real differences between them, without trying to 'transcend' or collapse those differences. They did not go so far as to acknowledge the stakes of that family relationship, or to unpack the severity of oppression that had arranged white and coloured families in these particular relationships. However, on their own accord, they took the first step towards an honest dialogue 'mediated by the world, to name the world' (Freire 2000: 88), an acknowledgement of unequal relationships rooted in many generations of interlocking family histories.

Conclusion

When Magnet Theatre makes space for intercultural theatre projects in towns like Clanwilliam, it inherently also makes space for intercultural play. During the three weeks that I worked on *Soek 'Os 'It Soe?*, I experienced several remarkable moments of play, often moments that seemed ripe with hope and that felt meaningful. At these moments, my gut told me that the work mattered. In the time that has elapsed since then, I have tried to scrutinize that initial instinctive feeling to determine what was at stake in these moments of play. What dialogic possibilities did they nurture, and what opportunities might they have elided?

The moments of play each functioned differently. In each of these moments, playful interaction made space for affective relationships across racial/cultural barriers; however, certain instances of play made space for the players to articulate the very cultural divisions that they were reaching beyond, while other instances of play enabled the players to ignore or obscure those differences. Play, it seems, can help to nurture the love, trust and humility that must undergird a Freirian dialogue, and it can occasionally make space for people to articulate some difficult truths – but it can also envelop an ensemble in such a delightful bubble that makes people reluctant to grapple with the potentially-polarizing dynamics of the world beyond that bubble.

By the time I left Clanwilliam, Jesmory had acquired Werner's cell phone number. Moreover, as she told me about the phone number, she had a twinkle in her eye that may have said more than the phone number itself. It was a twinkle that suggested that her relationship with Werner – and that relationships in general among South Africa's racial groups – might yet evolve. Over the course of these three weeks, the 'possibles' of play had nurtured her belief – or perhaps they caused her to believe again – in the fluidity of intercultural dynamics (Lev-Aladgem 2010: 55). By mid-July, the possibility of forming relationships in spite of cultural differences must have loomed slightly larger than it did in mid-June.

And yet, I'm not sure how much the project nurtured her inclination to form intercultural relationships in light of those cultural differences. Such relationships involve a recognition of the historical and material conditions that structure division and inequality; they emerge from a risky re-entry into real life from out of the protective bubble of play. This kind of relationship-building seems like it is still in its infancy in Clanwilliam, as Jesmory's ambivalent language suggests: 'We are getting closer like when we were smaller,' she said to me on my last afternoon in Clanwilliam, 'but it will take time.'

Fleishman's and Reznek's decision to build a home in Clanwilliam implicitly indicates their understanding of, and commitment to, the processes of incremental change that Jesmory alluded to on that final afternoon I spent in the town. That process – which may occupy Magnet for their next three decades and beyond – requires a commitment to suspending play in addition to nurturing it. It requires ensembles to bravely, reflexively and deliberately re-enter the real world together from the safer, playful sphere in which they nurture their camaraderie and synergy.

References

Bergson, H. (2008), *Laughter: An Essay on the Meaning of the Comic*, Rockville, MD: Arc Manor LLC.

Brown, S. with Vaughan, C. (2010), *Play: How it Shapes the Brain, Opens the Imagination, and Invigorates the Soul*, London: Penguin.

Caillois, R. (2001), *Man, Play, and Games*, Urbana and Chicago: University of Illinois Press.

Csikszentmihalyi, M. (2009), *Flow*, Australia: HarperCollins.

Fleishman, M. (1990), 'Workshop Theatre as Oppositional Form,' *South African Theatre Journal*, 4: 1, pp. 88–118.

——— (1991), 'Workshop Theatre in South Africa in the 1980s: A Critical Examination with Specific Reference to Power, Orality, and the Carnivalesque,' MA thesis, University of Cape Town.

——— (2009), 'Knowing Performance: Performance as Knowledge Paradigm for Africa,' *South African Theatre Journal*, 23, pp. 116–36.

Freire, P. (2000), *Pedagogy of the Oppressed*, New York: Continuum.

Frost, A. and Yarrow, R. (2007), *Improvisation in Drama*, Hampshire, New York: Palgrave Macmillan.

Huizinga, J. (1949), *Homo Ludens: A Study of the Play-Element in Culture*, London, Boston and Henley: Routledge and Kegan Paul.

Jesmory (2010), personal interview with E. Leffler, 13 July.

Keith (2010), personal interview with E. Leffler, 11 July.

Knowles, R. (2010), *Theatre & Interculturalism*, Basingstoke: Palgrave MacMillan.

Leffler, E. (2010), 'Ethnographic Field Notes,' Clanwilliam, South Africa: (unpublished).

Lev-Aladgem, S. (2010), *Theatre in Co-communities: Articulating Power*, Basingstoke: Palgrave MacMillan.

Reznek, J. (2012), 'Moving Ideas About Moving Bodies: Teaching Physical Theatre as a Response to Violence and the Violated Body,' MA thesis, University of Cape Town.

Schechner, R. (1993), *The Future of Ritual: Writings on Culture and Performance*, London: Routledge.

Turner, V. (1982), *From Ritual to Theatre: The Human Seriousness of Play*, New York: PAJ Publications.

Werner (2010b), personal interview with E. Leffler, 6 July.
——— (2010a), personal interview with E. Leffler, 12 July.

Notes

1. This article by Mark Fleishman is misattributed to Mark Fleischman [sic] by *South African Theatre Journal*. The author's name is spelled correctly here, but readers looking to find the original article may have to misspell it in order to find it through databases.
2. See De Bruyn ('Catalysing a Community').
3. In this chapter, when I use the words 'racial' and 'interracial,' as I do here, I am referring specifically to the cultural taxonomy of South Africa through which people are classified – and most often also identify themselves – as being white, black and coloured, in addition to several other racial classifications. More often, I use the word 'intercultural,' which I use as a broader term to refer to the relationships among people who identify with different cultural groups. For instance, while I, as a white American, do not consider my interaction with white South Africans as an interracial encounter, I do consider it to be an intercultural encounter on account of our differing national identities. In places where either 'interracial' or 'intercultural' would be appropriate, I typically opt for the term 'intercultural,' choosing to semantically gesture towards – and contribute to – a broader literature on 'intercultural theatre' (for a concise appraisal of this literature and an extensive bibliography, see Knowles [2010]).
4. Some of the ComNet participants are referred to by pseudonyms in this chapter, while others are referred to by their real names (reflecting the preferences of the participants).
5. Jesmory identifies as coloured, but here she calls herself black, employing a broad South African usage of 'black' which includes all non-whites. By invoking this stark black/white binary, and placing herself and Werner within it, she does not intend to obscure her identity as coloured, but rather, to emphasize to me that there are unwritten social rules that govern the interaction between white and non-white South Africans.
6. After Richard Schechner (1993: 43), Fleishman (2009: 124) has written about play as encouraging 'the discovery of new configuration and twists of ideas and experience,' and he has leveraged that idea to argue that performance is a way of knowing that might exist separately from dominant, text-based knowledge paradigms. Building on ideas from Frost and Yarrow (2007), as well as Lecoq (with whom she studied), Reznek (2012: 40) has described play as 'deeply empowering' and 'radically shift[ing] agency onto the individual' performer. While these particular ideas about play have not helped me to theorize ComNet's work, I cite them here to provide

the reader with a sense of how Magnet's co-founders have leveraged play theory to their own analytic ends.

7. Like some of the other names I use for participants, 'Denise' and 'Sandra' are pseudonyms.
8. To clarify: Csikszentmihalyi does not explicitly write about *communitas*. He theorizes what he calls 'optimal experiences,' or 'flow,' during which people experience an intense feeling of absorption in what they are doing, and he argues that these optimal experiences result in a sense of oneness with those around him. I am suggesting that this oneness can be compared to Turner's *communitas*. Therefore, I propose that Csikszentmihalyi's insight (that once people have these intense experiences of oneness, they seek to recreate those experiences) might be productively extended to nuance how we think about experiences of *communitas*, even though he does not explicitly use the term.

Chapter 20

Keeping Theatre Alive in the Community: A Conversation with Zwelakhe Khuse[1]

Zwelakhe Khuse was part of Magnet's original Community Groups Intervention (CGI) programme, facilitated by Mandla Mbothwe in 2003 in Khayelitsha. He was introduced to Magnet Theatre through the CGI workshops, where he performed in the plays The Tears of Our Ancestors *(2007) and* 3 Rats *(2008), as well as in Mbothwe's collaboration between UCT and the members of the CGI programme,* Isivuno Sama Phupha *[Harvest of Dreams] (2007). He has since graduated from the University of Cape Town Drama programme, and currently works as a fieldworker in Magnet's Culture Gangs Project, a current incarnation of the previous CGI.*

For Khuse, Magnet's value lies in 'going to people in their disadvantaged groups, and then trying to groom their work, and try to teach them.' He is encouraged by Magnet's mission to correct systemic imbalances through training and education. 'The students don't even pay a cent,' he marvels. 'Magnet takes them to theatres and offers them transport. Even for them to visit a theatre, and for them to be exposed to other people's work so that they can grow – that's important [...]. I don't know if there are other companies that do that [...]. It's beneficial to the people, to society.'

After learning from Mandla Mbothwe in the CGI, Khuse started working on a project initially set up by Nolovuyo Sam with small groups in Dunoon (an informal township to the east of Cape Town city centre). 'So I'm facilitating those groups and trying to help them develop their plays [...], teaching them how to raise the standard, to make these plays better.' Khuse works with youth after school, teaching them vocal and bodywork, research skills and character building: 'I try to facilitate them to learn more about theatre [and] how to work with images to help them become actors, writers, directors. I try to teach them a bit of everything. Then they have an opportunity at the end of the year to showcase their work.' But beyond theatre skills, Khuse is also making vital interventions with township youth in Cape Town. 'I'm also trying to teach them discipline,' he says, 'Some of the techniques that we use in arts can also be useful outside of arts.'

He says that empowering others as he was empowered, 'encouraging them to tell their own story [and] training them to come up with their own stories – township stories,' is one of his central goals as a theatre-maker. 'I want to help them to tell our stories, in our language as well, so that they can express their feelings and whatever they want to express in a way that they are comfortable with.'

'Giving back to his community through theatre,' he says, is vital 'so that theatre like this doesn't die, in terms of our community, you know? In our community there are people who kill, and there are no people who have knowledge about theatre. In our community they are not doing theatre. There is no money. So I want to help them without thinking what I will get from that.'

He sees professional training as an important first step towards balancing the historic inequalities in South African culture. Because of the training Magnet offers, and the work Khuse himself continues in the townships, he says '[t]here are many potential actors and potential writers that are now thinking of applying for festivals [...]. We encourage them to go to these festivals, like Zabalaza,[2] and help them improve their standard, and work out their constitution so that they are able to get funding.' He adds, 'They didn't know about this before Magnet Theatre. After being involved with Magnet, they go to these auditions and pass them. We are helping them. We are helping them to grow and they are growing.'

Reflecting on his work with Magnet, Khuse says it has been a good balance between affording him autonomy and offering guidance when needed: 'I love working with them because they gave me a programme. And then they taught me to run the programme the way I want to run it. I still have their guidance. If it's challenging, I go to Jennie and then she helps me. So I love working with them a lot.'

As a teacher and facilitator, Khuse says his approach with youth is to try to encourage them to make discoveries for themselves: 'I'm trying to get them out of the box,' he explains, 'to think, to go wide, to not contain themselves in what I'm teaching them.' Khuse is interested in making work that offers multiple interpretations: 'I don't want to do a play with one conclusion. I want to do a play that gives options to solving problems,' he claims, 'because what may be a solution for me, might not be a solution for you. That's why I want to show options, so that a person can choose which option is suitable for him or for her [...]. They can choose for themselves what will work for them.'

His work is focused around community issues and concerns, and he believes passionately in the impact of this work: 'It is helping. I don't *think*, I *know* it is helping.' In Dunoon, for example, he devised a piece with the Magnet Trainees called *Forgotten City*. He explains:

> We did research with a group in Dunoon. [We] went in there and collected all the facts about the people of Dunoon; what they think, what they need. We created a devised theatre production to encourage them to solve their problems. Then we performed that play first here at Magnet Theatre and then also in Dunoon. It was called *Forgotten City* because of the issues that are played out. The government doesn't take care of them: there are no toilets, it's dirty, there are no jobs, no hospitals. Those people need a school. There are no proper facilities.

The play offered options for community members to 'challenge the municipality and the council about the facilities. We created a script according to the things that the people were saying to show the councillor what the people feel. At the end of the play, the councillor was there, and he came to me and said that I opened the debate. He told me that he didn't know about those things we brought to his attention.'

Combining arts and advocacy, Khuse 'wanted to create something; to be a voice for those who don't have a voice, those who are scared to have a voice, for themselves.'

Inspired by Magnet's intervention model, Khuse's plan for the future is to have his own company. 'I'm also wanting to do something similar to what Magnet is doing in future,' he adds, 'to help those who are in need. The people who are most in need now are people who are poor. My plan is to teach them how to do theatre and then maybe in five years maybe we grow to other groups, something similar.'

References

Khuse, Z. (2013), personal interview with A. Krueger, 11 June.

Notes

1. Interview quotes in this chapter are taken from Khuse (2013).
2. Since 2011, the Zabalaza Theatre Festival has been hosted annually by the Baxter Theatre in Cape Town.

Chapter 21

Magnet Never Forgets its People: A Conversation with Nolovuyo Sam[1]

Nolovuyo Sam first trained with Magnet's Community Groups Intervention (CGI) programme. As a result of her experience with the training programme, she went on to enrol as a student at the University of Cape Town, where she completed her teacher's diploma. She is the first university attendee and graduate in her family, and is currently teaching drama in Western Cape schools.

'Magnet never forgets its people,' beams theatre educator Nolovuyo Sam, 'even if it is after a few years – they come back and find out how you are doing and how they can assist you getting back on stage. They are indeed a Magnet!'

'I got involved with Magnet Theatre at a very early age,' Sam continues, 'I think towards the end of my primary school, when Magnet Theatre was introducing a Community Groups Intervention programme in my township. I was part of a drama group called Masibambisane which also took part in the intervention. From that year onwards, I have been a family member of Magnet Theatre till this day.'

At the time of the interview, Sam was a resident artist at Chris Hani High (an arts and culture focused school in Khayelitsha) and was also completing her Post Graduate Certificate in Education. She says, 'Theatre is worth doing because it is educational, but mostly it's because theatre has the potential to allow us to freely express ourselves; face our personal demons, fears, anger, love and all sorts of emotional states that we find ourselves in.' Sam adds that 'society does not give us the opportunity to do that for the majority of the time, because of the ways in which we've been socialized.'

Sam claims that Magnet challenged her to push beyond what she thought were her capabilities: 'The content of the professional work is extremely challenging. The style of work they use challenges and freaks you out at first (it makes you feel like you can't), but as you work with them it gets better. Magnet is gifted when it comes to grooming and developing talent and producing thought-provoking work.'

'I have always been a bubbly person,' she says, 'however, being involved with theatre has really opened me up in terms of the way I think – my perspective, questioning things, curiosity, finding solutions, discipline, behaviour etc.' She now passes what she had learned working with Magnet on to her own students: 'After a while of working with my learners, I have noticed some changes which verify that, in some way or other, theatre plays some role in changing or transforming a person.'

'There is a lot to gain and learn in drama,' she says, 'like personal and interpersonal skills. I want to make a difference through drama (even if it is only to one person at a time) by provoking people's thoughts and feelings. I want to assist people in discovering and acknowledging that hidden spark, or a love and talent they haven't yet realized they've got. I want to challenge the way the society thinks and does things. I want to educate and push people to the extremes of their personal journey of discovery through theatre.'

During her interview, Sam related a story of her own personal growth and how Magnet changed her outlook on life:

> When I was in my matric year, I always knew that the following year I was going to work at a Pick 'n Pay[2] near my home. Whether I had passed or not, that was beside the point. I just never dreamt big. I knew that I wanted to be some social worker or something, but I just never even had an idea of how to go about making that dream come true. So I actually thought being a cashier or working on the floor of a supermarket was enough. However, through Magnet Theatre, that small-minded me got eye-opened. Mark Fleishman and Jennie Reznek saw the other talent in me (which I kind of knew I had, but never thought of nurturing). They thought I had potential and I deserved to be given an opportunity to nurture it.

Sam says Magnet helped her (and many others) apply to and get accepted at the University of Cape Town to study theatre and performance. 'Today I look back and laugh at myself for not believing I was worth it. Thank you to Magnet for recognizing the talent, nurturing it, and allowing me to own it!'

References

Sam, N. (2013), e-mail interview with A. Krueger, 23 June–16 August.

Notes

1. Interview quotes in this chapter are taken from Sam (2013).
2. Pick 'n Pay is a popular chain of supermarkets in South Africa.

Magnet Funders

Funders that have contributed to the work of Magnet Theatre over the years include: The National Lottery Distribution Trust Fund; National Arts Council of South Africa; HCI Foundation; Oppenheimer Memorial Trust; Rand Merchant Bank; National Arts Festival; Distell Foundation; Pro Helvetia (Arts Council of Switzerland); Western Cape Cultural Commission; The Arts & Culture Trust in association with Nedbank Arts Affinity; Pick'n Pay Foundation; Kathy Ackerman-Robins; Fairheads Benefit Services; The City of Cape Town; Grand West Culture and Heritage Foundation; The French Institute in South Africa; Art Moves Africa; Spier; African Centre for Cities; Donald Gordon Institute for the Performing and Creative Arts; Nussbaum Foundation; Cliffe Deckker Hofmeyer; Johannesburg Repertory Players; Milagro Foundation; Cederberg Municipality; Rooibos Limited; Artscape Theatre Centre; University of Cape Town, Western Cape Department of Cultural Affairs and Sport; BASA; Woolworths Financial Services; ATKV; Jacob Levy Trust; Zoo Biscuit; Ackerman Foundation; Grahamstown Foundation; Trade Centre Credits; Ratanga Junction; Mozal Foundation; Common Plants; Foschini Trust; Cape Town Holocaust Centre; Nussbaum; and South Africa Jewish Board of Deputies.

Index

references to images in *italics*, *c-references* to colour plates

N

O

www.ingramcontent.com/pod-product-compliance
Lightning Source LLC
LaVergne TN
LVHW060727310826
846742LV00016B/47